The Medieval Military Orders, 1120–1314

The Medieval Military Orders
1120–1314

Nicholas Morton

PEARSON

Harlow, England • London • New York • Boston • San Francisco • Toronto • Sydney
Auckland • Singapore • Hong Kong • Tokyo • Seoul • Taipei • New Delhi
Cape Town • São Paulo • Mexico City • Madrid • Amsterdam • Munich • Paris • Milan

Pearson Education Limited
Edinburgh Gate
Harlow CM20 2JE
United Kingdom
Tel: +44 (0)1279 623623
Fax: +44 (0)1279 431059
Website: www.pearson.com/uk

First edition published in Great Britain in 2013

© Pearson Education Limited 2013

The right of Nicholas Morton to be identified as author of this work has been
asserted by him in accordance with the Copyright, Designs and Patents Act 1988.

Pearson Education is not responsible for the content of third-party internet sites.

ISBN: 978-1-4082-4958-1

British Library Cataloguing in Publication Data
A CIP catalogue record for this book can be obtained from the British Library

Library of Congress Cataloging in Publication Data
A CIP catalog record for this book can be obtained from the Library of Congress

10 9 8 7 6 5 4 3 2 1
16 15 14 13 12

Set by 35 in 10/13.5pt ITC Berkeley
Printed in Malaysia (CTP-PPSB)

Introduction to the series

History is narrative constructed by historians from traces left by the past. Historical enquiry is often driven by contemporary issues and, in consequence, historical narratives are constantly reconsidered, reconstructed and reshaped. The fact that different historians have different perspectives on issues means that there is also often controversy and no universally agreed version of past events. *Seminar Studies* was designed to bridge the gap between current research and debate, and the broad, popular general surveys that often date rapidly.

The volumes in the series are written by historians who are not only familiar with the latest research and current debates concerning their topic, but who have themselves contributed to our understanding of the subject. The books are intended to provide the reader with a clear introduction to a major topic in history. They provide both a narrative of events and a critical analysis of contemporary interpretations. They include the kinds of tools generally omitted from specialist monographs: a chronology of events, a glossary of terms and brief biographies of 'who's who'. They also include bibliographic essays in order to guide students to the literature on various aspects of the subject. Students and teachers alike will find that the selection of documents will stimulate discussion and offer insight into the raw materials used by historians in their attempt to understand the past.

Clive Emsley and Gordon Martel
Series Editors

For Dina

Contents

Acknowledgements

The first person I would like to thank is Mari Shullaw from Pearson Education. It was Mari who made the original suggestion that I write this book and throughout the production process her support and advice have been absolutely invaluable. I am also deeply indebted to Bernard Hamilton and Malcolm Barber for their expert guidance and their comments on an early draft of this book. Their encouragement has been vital and is deeply appreciated. I would also like to thank the reviewers appointed by Pearson who looked through my work so carefully and provided such detailed feedback. There have been many other friends and colleagues who have offered me specific guidance on points of detail and I would particularly like to offer my thanks to Simon Barton and Jonathan Phillips. For her ongoing linguistic support, it is a pleasure to express my gratitude to Renee Shenton for all her help. I am as ever deeply grateful to my parents for their tireless support and also for contributing some of the photographs for this work. I would also particularly like to thank my wife, Dina, to whom this book is dedicated, for her ongoing love and assistance.

Publisher's acknowledgements

We are grateful to the following for permission to reproduce copyright material:

Plates 1, 2, and 4 by Nicholas Morton; Plates 3, 5, 6, 7 and 8 by Juliet Morton; Plate 9 courtesy of The Master and Fellows of Corpus Christi College, Cambridge; Plate 10 © Zen Radovan/BibleLandPictures/Alamy.

Map 1 from Phillips, J., *The Crusades, 1095–1197* (Pearson Education, 2002); Map 2 from Barber, M., *The Two Cities: Medieval Europe 1050–1320* (Routledge, 2004).

In some instances we have been unable to trace the owners of copyright material, and we would appreciate any information that would enable us to do so.

Who's who

Afonso, king of Portugal (1114–1185): The first king of Portugal, Afonso was a vigorous ruler who strove to expand his kingdom against both his Christian neighbours and Islamic al-Andalus to the south. Amongst his most significant victories was the conquest of Lisbon in 1147. This significant advance was achieved with the support of a naval force participating in the Second Crusade. He was an important patron of many military orders, including the international orders of the Temple and Hospitallers, many of the Spanish orders, and his own Portuguese order of Évora (later known as Avis). These institutions held many critical frontier castles and assisted Afonso in his campaigns of conquest.

Alfonso I, 'the battler' king of Aragon (1104–1134): Alfonso is famous as the man who attempted to leave his kingdom to the Templars, Hospitallers and the canons of the Holy Sepulchre. During his lifetime he fought wars on many fronts, including many successful campaigns against Islamic al-Andalus. Amongst his most significant victories was the capture of Zaragoza in 1118. He was a staunch advocate of the military orders and he founded the knightly confraternities of Belchite and Monreal del Campo.

Alfonso VIII, king of Castile (1158–1214): Son of Sancho III, Alfonso was the king of Castile at a crucial period in Spain's history when the fortunes of war with Islam hung in the balance. In 1195 his army suffered a catastrophic defeat at Alarcos at the hands of the caliph, al-Mansur. This led to a series of territorial losses, including much of the *Campo de Calatrava*. Nevertheless in 1212, towards the end of his reign, Alfonso raised a large army with contingents from several Spanish kingdoms and France to regain this region where he scored the significant victory of Las Navas de Tolosa. Alfonso was also an active patron of many military orders.

Amalric, king of Jerusalem (1163–1174): Father of Baldwin IV, Amalric was described by the archbishop of Tyre as tall, fat and bearded. He is well known for his many wars in Egypt, during which he unsuccessfully attempted to secure control of the country to prevent Nur ad-Din (the Turkish ruler of Syria) from doing so. During his reign the Templars and Hospitallers both continued to grow in prominence and the Templars in particular are reported, by William of Tyre, to have posed a threat to his authority.

Andrew II, king of Hungary (1205–1235): A veteran of the Fifth Crusade, Andrew was at times a patron of both the Hospitaller and Teutonic orders. In 1211 he granted the Teutonic Knights the frontier region of Burzenland, however, growing disputes between the order and his aristocracy eventually forced him to expel the brethren in 1225. He had a number of children among who was Elizabeth of Thuringia (see entry below).

Baldwin IV, king of Jerusalem (1174–1185): At an early age Baldwin was diagnosed with leprosy and this disease defined much of his later rule, preventing him from marrying and having children and incapacitating him for long periods. Even so, when able to do so, Baldwin proved himself to be a capable ruler. By this stage both the Templars and Hospitallers possessed significant military resources in the kingdom of Jerusalem, which formed a vital element of the royal army. Nevertheless, these forces also gave them political power which they used to exert their influence on the crucial questions facing the kingdom concerning the succession and the need for a regent.

Baybars I, Mamluk Sultan (1260–1277): A former slave-warrior and renowned for his ferocity, Baybars rose to become sultan of Egypt in 1260 shortly after the Egyptian victory against the Mongols at Ayn Jalut. Following this victory, Baybars rapidly expanded his territories, conquering Damascus and Aleppo. From this position he was able to launch a series of highly destructive attacks on the Latin East which led to the loss of many fortresses held by the military orders.

Bernard of Clairvaux (d.1153): Head of the Cistercian order and an outspoken advocate of crusading, Bernard of Clairvaux was amongst the most famous individuals of the twelfth century. He played an important role in bringing about the rise of the Templars, both encouraging their development as a religious order and writing the treatise *In Praise of the New Knighthood* celebrating their labours and values. Following his death the Cistercian order became closely linked to many military orders, which were either founded by their members or strengthened by their support.

Clement V, pope (1305–1314): Born in *c.*1255 and the former archbishop of Bordeaux, Clement V became pontiff at a time of strained relations between the papacy and the French Crown. In October 1307 Philip IV of France arrested the Templars across the kingdom, justifying his actions with a wide range of allegations and accusations. The ensuing trial of the Templars and the diplomatic manoeuvring that surrounded it dominated much of his pontificate. He also made strenuous attempts to raise a new crusade to the Holy Land and these resulted in a small expedition in 1308.

Elizabeth of Thuringia (d.1231): The daughter of King Andrew II of Hungary, Elizabeth married Louis of Thuringia in 1221. After her husband's death, she devoted herself to the care of the sick by founding a hospital in Marburg. She herself died in 1231 and her hospital passed to the Teutonic Order. In later years she was canonised and her memory was deeply revered by the order.

Frederick II, emperor of Germany (1220–1250): Famous as the ruler who led a crusading army to the east whilst excommunicated, Frederick's reign (and particularly his ongoing quarrels with the papacy) dominated European politics for many decades. He was an enthusiastic advocate of the Teutonic Order and was a close friend of the Teutonic Order's master Hermann von Salza. He supported the order during his crusade to the Holy Land and encouraged them to expand into Prussia. Nevertheless, his ongoing disputes with Pope Gregory IX repeatedly placed the Teutonic Knights and the other major military orders in a conflict of interests between their secular and ecclesiastical loyalties.

Gerard of Ridefort, Templar master (1185–1189): Gerard joined the Templars in 1180 and became the master of the order in 1185. At this point the Latin East was locked in an ongoing conflict with Saladin, which would come to an end in 1187 at the battle of Hattin. Gerard is often remembered as one of the men who persuaded King Guy of Jerusalem to pursue a strategy at Hattin that would eventually cause the destruction of the kingdom's army. Earlier that year, he also led a mixed Templar and Hospitaller force to defeat at Cresson when he attacked to engage a far larger Muslim force. He died at the siege of Acre in 1189.

Gilbert of Assailly, Hospitaller master (1162–1170): Hospitaller master during the reign of King Amalric, Gilbert actively bolstered his order's commitment to the defence of the kingdom of Jerusalem, rebuilding the great fortress of Belvoir in 1168 and offering significant support to Amalric's Egyptian campaigns. Nevertheless, through these schemes Gilbert brought his order to the point of bankruptcy and, when this became clear, he attempted to resign and retired to live as a hermit. This resignation provoked disputes within the order concerning its vocation and the amount of power that should be exerted by the order's master.

Gregory IX, pope (1227–1241): An active proponent of crusading on many frontiers, Gregory's pontificate was an important phase in the history of the military orders. He supported the Teutonic Knights' early expansion in Prussia and subsequently he arranged for them to be merged with the Swordbrethren in Livonia. His long struggle with the German Emperor Frederick II posed problems for many of the major orders who had long-term relationships with both the empire and papacy.

Hermann Balk, Prussian master of the Teutonic Knights (1230–1238), **Livonian master** (1237–1238): Hermann Balk was among Hermann von Salza's (master of the Teutonic Order c.1209–1239) most trusted officers. During the 1230s he assumed control of his order's ongoing conquest of Prussia and then in 1237 he was sent to Livonia to manage his order's take-over of the Swordbrethren.

Hermann von Salza, master of the Teutonic Knights (c.1209–1239): Herman is remembered as the man who transformed the Teutonic Order from a relatively small establishment into an international military order. During his time as master he developed his order's position in the Holy Land, arranging the construction of its fortress of Montfort, and he organised the extension of the order's activities to include commitments in Hungary, Prussia and Livonia. To achieve these ends he worked closely with Emperor Frederick II and the papacy, who both supported his ambitions, and he in turn helped them to raise crusading forces for the defence of Christendom during the 1220s and 1230s.

Hugh of Payns, Templar master (1119–c.1136): The first master of the Templar order, Hugh of Payns was born in Champagne (France) but subsequently settled in the Latin East. Initially, he and his fellow Templars patrolled the pilgrim roads from Jaffa to Jerusalem but, under his leadership, the order grew considerably in later years. This was achieved in part by his tour of Western Christendom in 1127–1129 during which he recruited crusaders for a new crusade to the east and won many patrons for his order. It was also during this trip that he attended the council of Troyes where his order was officially recognised as an institution of the Church.

Philip IV, king of France (1285–1314): Philip IV was famously the king who arrested the Templars in October 1307, making a range of accusations concerning their morality and way of life. This provoked the Trial of the Templars and, in time, the dissolution of the order at the council of Vienne 1312. Whether Philip actually believed his own allegations, or whether he was motivated primarily by the desire to acquire their wealth has been a source of debate amongst military orders historians. The trial and the diplomatic manoeuvring that surrounded it was also a symptom of his long-standing power struggle with the papacy.

Saladin (d.1193): Born into a Kurdish family in Takrit (Iraq), Saladin rose to prominence in the service of the Turkish ruler Nur ad-Din. In 1169 he became the governor of Egypt and then, following Nur ad-Din's death in 1174, he seized control in many of the city states bordering the Latin East. Having drawn many regions under his control he came to pose a major threat to the Franks, eventually winning the decisive battle of Hattin in 1187 which led directly to the fall of Jerusalem later that year.

William, archbishop of Tyre (d.1186): Archbishop of Tyre, chancellor of the kingdom of Jerusalem, tutor to King Baldwin IV, William of Tyre was amongst the most influential magnates in the kingdom of Jerusalem. He also wrote a detailed history of the kingdom of Jerusalem that is amongst the most important sources for historians studying the Latin East. This chronicle also reveals William's deeply felt concerns about the Templars and Hospitallers who he felt had come to exert too much power in the kingdom.

Zengi, governor of Mosul and Aleppo (d.1146): Father of Nur ad-Din and a famous warrior, Zengi was a successful Turkish warlord who drew much of Muslim Syria under his rule between 1127 and 1138. He fought many wars against the Latin East, although he is best known for his conquest of Edessa in 1144. The loss of this city was the event which provoked Pope Eugenius III's call for the Second Crusade.

Glossary

Please note that many of the entries below define the roles and responsibilities of the personnel found in the military orders. It should be remembered, however, that these roles were not necessarily common to all the orders and even where the same role could be found in a number of different institutions, there could be significant differences in the duties of the incumbent(s). The definition given here reflects their broad function.

Admiral: The official in charge of naval activities in the Hospitaller order.

Assassins: A sect of Isma'ili Shia Islam which controlled areas in Persia and northern Syria. Their leader was a mysterious figure known as the 'Old Man of the Mountains' and they became famous for their political assassinations.

Brother knights: These were fully professed members of a military order who could perform a combat role. Many orders insisted that brother knights should originate from a knightly or noble family.

Brother sergeants: Like brother knights they were fully professed members of a military order and they could perform a range of roles including combat. They generally came from a less prestigious social background than the brother knights.

Confratres: Lay affiliates of a religious order.

Draper: The official responsible for supplying brethren with clothes and equipment.

Excommunication: A punishment in which an individual is cut off from the sacraments of the Church.

Grand commander: A senior official in many of the larger military orders who was responsible for the operational management of an order.

Hauberk: A chainmail jacket.

Indulgences, plenary indulgences and penance: In the Catholic Church, when an individual confesses their sins he/she will be expected to perform a specific action – a penance – to atone to God for their sinful behaviour. An indulgence was when the Church permitted this individual to replace a penance with another defined action. A plenary indulgence (often granted to crusaders) permitted an individual to replace **all** penance on **all** confessed sins for a specified act (i.e. going on crusade).

Latin East: A collective term for the Catholic Christian territories established in the Levant, the earliest of which were founded during the First Crusade.

Mantles: A garment, also known as a habit, worn by members of religious orders. The colour of the mantle and the cross or device shown upon it designated the order to which the wearer belonged.

Marshal: In the military orders, this official was an order's main military commander.

Master: The leader of a military order.

Mendicant orders: Religious orders (i.e. the Franciscans and Dominicans) of friars who, unlike other traditional monastic institutions, did not live in a monastery but travelled from place to place. They spent their lives preaching and providing pastoral care whilst sustaining themselves by begging.

Responsions: An annual payment (typically one-third of all revenue) made to a military order's headquarters by its dependent houses across Christendom.

Rule: A document outlining the structure by which the members of a religious order should organise their community and live their lives.

Turcopolier: An official appointed in the Latin East to command local 'turcopole' cavalry and in some cases an order's sergeants.

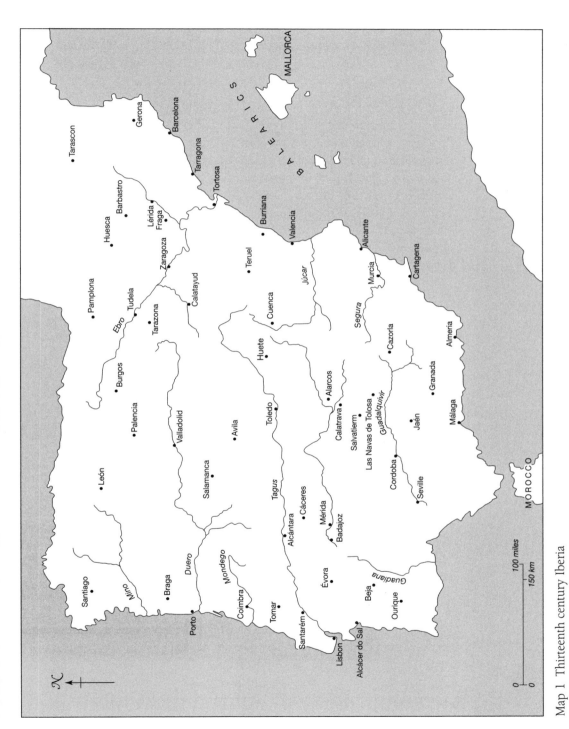

Map 1 Thirteenth century Iberia

Source: Adapted from Barber, M., *The Two Cities: Medieval Europe, 1050–1320* (Routledge, 2004)

Map 2 Prussia and Livonia

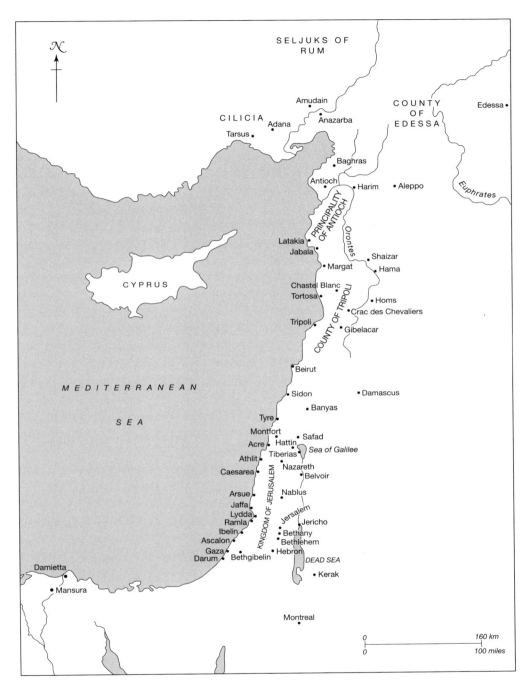

Map 3 The Latin East

Source: Adapted from Phillips, J., *The Crusades, 1095–1197* (Pearson Education, 2002)

Part 1

ANALYSIS

Introduction

At times of danger it is natural for human beings to band together for mutual protection. For those exposed on embattled frontiers, living constant danger, the need for co-operation can be particularly acute. Throughout the medieval period Western Christendom (made up of the countries which acknowledged the authority of the papacy) was engaged in prolonged wars, both of defence and expansion, against a bewildering array of foes. Its opponents varied from the Turkish horse archers of the Holy Land to the pagan raiders of the Baltic. These conflicts were fought for many reasons, but in all cases religious adherence was a crucial factor that defined the identity of all sides. Christendom's warriors were not merely fighting for land or money, but to protect their faith and for many groups of knights this quest became a lifetime's commitment. Theirs were the frontier societies in which the idea of an institution which was simultaneously an order of the Church and a fraternity of knights took root and spread until these 'military orders' became Catholicism's frontline against its enemies. This book is a history of these unique organisations.

By the mid-tenth century, Christendom had long been under assault on multiple fronts: in the north by the Vikings; in the east by the Slavs and the Magyars; and in the south by Islam. Many frontier rulers were forced to fight for their very existence in the face of overwhelming enemy attacks. Few regions were safe and one community of monks, fleeing out of fear of Viking raids from their monastery of Noirmoutier (west coast of France), was forced progressively eastwards only to be attacked by the Magyars invading from the other direction (Davis, 1958: 169). This besieged land was weakened further by internal squabbles as kings and princes vied with one another for supremacy. Some semblance of shared purpose was provided by their common adherence to the Catholic Church. Royal families were also bound to one another by marriage and in some cases by common descent from Charlemagne, the renowned emperor who had once proclaimed a revival of the now long-lost Western Roman Empire. Even so, in the ninth century,

Rome itself was under direct threat from Muslim attack and communications between all Christendom's defenders were problematic at best.

By the eleventh century, however, the tide was perceptibly changing. Europe's population began to grow; the Viking attacks slowly faded as Scandinavia embraced Christianity; Spanish lords began to push their way south against Muslim rulers preoccupied by their internal quarrels; and the German Emperors gradually established control over their eastern frontiers. In this more positive climate the papacy was able to assert its authority, seeking to improve the conduct and education of its clergy. As the frontiers began to expand through conversion and conquest, new bishoprics were created whilst newly won lands were divided into dioceses and parishes, becoming functional parts of Christendom. Europe was reviving and facing its future with growing confidence. This process did not take place without internal conflict, however, and while the papacy's reforms were broadly welcomed they met resistance when attempts were made to control the appointment of senior churchmen. Secular rulers did not care to yield their ability to choose successors to highly lucrative bishoprics and archbishoprics – money and power were at stake – and they were prepared to fight to retain this privilege.

Amidst these great upheavals, concerning news arrived from the east. During the eleventh century a confederation of Turkish tribes swept into Islamic Iran and later Iraq. Overcoming the Muslim forces sent against them, they advanced rapidly and in 1055 sacked Baghdad. As their conquests mounted, they continued to expand into Syria and Palestine, destroying the local Arab and Kurdish potentates. During this process the Turks gradually adopted Islam, although they still retained much of their original shamanistic identity. In 1071 they invaded Anatolia (modern day Turkey), part of the Christian Byzantine Empire (the continuator of the former Eastern Roman Empire), where they won a major victory at the battle of Manzikert. Following this reverse the Byzantine position in Anatolia collapsed and fears abounded that the capital, Constantinople, was threatened. Aware of their need, emissaries were sent to the papacy in Rome appealing for help.

Wars within Christendom prevented the immediate despatch of reinforcements to the east, but finally in 1095 Pope Urban II launched the long-desired expedition: the First Crusade. This campaign was not merely designed to support the Byzantines against the Turks but was intended to march deep inside Turkish-held territory and to retake the holy city of Jerusalem. Jerusalem was – and is – a city of immense importance to the Christian religion, being the site of Christ's crucifixion and resurrection. By the eleventh century it had long been lost to Christian control, having fallen to Islam in AD 638. During the intervening period many pilgrims had visited the holy city – a process fully accepted by the Arab Muslim authorities – although the recent Turkish invasions rendered the overland routes through

Anatolia increasingly dangerous. In 1095 Urban harnessed this pilgrim tradition and presented the crusade as a military pilgrimage conducted as an expression of God's will. The response to his call was overwhelming.

By launching the crusade, Urban initiated a new phase in Christian holy war. The compatibility of Christianity with lethal violence has always been a subject of intense debate. The fundamental precepts of Christ's teaching, as outlined in the New Testament, are to live in such a way that you show compassionate love to those around you, even your enemies. Even so, as Christianity took root across the Roman Empire, it became spliced with a political system that had always put its faith in its armed might. Compromises were made and thinkers, such as St Augustine, considered how war might legitimately be waged by the Christian faithful in defence of Rome.

In time the Western Roman Empire fell to tribal peoples who then intermarried and mixed with the surviving Roman populace and subsequently came to embrace both its values and religion. Their leaders' adoption of Christianity was, in most cases, both voluntary and sincere, and lessons of charity, commitment and piety were often well taken. Even so, these tribes were governed by military elites for whom pacifism would have been out of the question. Indeed, many converted precisely because they felt that God had brought them victory in battle. By the eleventh century, these groups had developed considerably, transforming themselves from migratory tribes into permanent territorial kingdoms. Ideas of warfare had also evolved with renewed attempts to differentiate legitimate bloodshed from illegitimate. Medieval writers, in search of biblical authority for their masters' battles, generally turned to the Old – rather than the New – Testament, drawing upon the stories of God-led warfare surrounding warriors like King David, Joshua and Judas Maccabaeus.

Thus, at the dawn of the Crusades, attitudes towards killing had passed through a long period of gestation in which Christian, Roman and ancient tribal practices had been fused into a philosophy that accepted that it could take place provided that certain conditions were met. Broadly speaking these were the principles laid down by Augustine: that wars must be defensive (or at least aimed at the reconquest of lost lands), launched by a legitimate authority and conducted by warriors whose motives were righteous, not acquisitive or bloodthirsty.

The First Crusade marked an important phase in Christian thinking on war. Pope Urban offered Christendom's knights – spiritually stained by a lifetime of feuds and petty wars between rival families – the opportunity to cleanse themselves of their sins through participation in an expedition that was presented as a direct extension of God's will. By 1099, after four years of war and suffering, these forces had marched hundreds of miles into Turkish-held territory and achieved their wildly improbable objective. Their victories had been enabled in part by rivalries between leading Turkish families and ongoing Arab resistance to Turkish control. The continuation of these disputes in later years created enough chaos for the remaining crusaders to establish a series of Christian territories within the Middle East (the county of Edessa in 1097, the principality of Antioch in 1098, the kingdom of Jerusalem in 1099 and the county of Tripoli in 1102). These are commonly referred to collectively as the '**Latin East**'.

Latin East: A collective term for the Catholic Christian territories established in the Levant, the earliest of which were founded during the First Crusade.

When news arrived of Jerusalem's fall, a wave of celebration broke across Christendom and for many contemporaries this fact alone was sufficient proof that the venture had received God's blessing. The challenge now was to secure and defend these distant lands. This imperative – like the crusade itself – was considered a sacred task, requiring skilled and devout warriors and in this environment a group of knights banded together to provide escorts for pilgrims travelling to Jerusalem. It so happened that they lived near to the Temple of Solomon (the Aqsa Mosque) provoking the nickname 'Templars'. In time this small confraternity decided to take the monastic vows of poverty, chastity and obedience – a symbol of their spiritual dedication – and were later endorsed in this role by the papacy. In doing so they formed the first military order: a religious order which performed a military function. Under the dynamic leadership of Master Hugh of Payns this institution came to the attention of Western Christendom and quickly proved a massive success.

In time, the Templars also inspired the establishment of new military orders and the militarisation of existing monastic institutions. Some of these were, like the Templars, dedicated to the defence of the east, including the Hospitallers, Teutonic Knights and the Order of St Lazarus, but others were created to protect other frontlines. During the twelfth and early thirteenth centuries crusading ideology spread to encompass all Catholic frontiers. The defenders of the Baltic and Iberia argued that, like the First Crusaders, their struggles were also God-led endeavours waged in the name of the cross and they demanded the extension of crusading privileges for their own wars. The ongoing dissemination of crusading ideas to such areas led many rulers likewise to consider either the establishment of their own military order or the introduction of an existing institution. New orders included those of Alcántara, Calatrava, Santiago and Avis in Iberia and the Swordbrethren and the order of Dobrin in the Baltic. The military orders then were an aspect of the crusading movement which swept across Western Christendom, reshaping the nature of Christian conflict.

Brother knights: These were fully professed members of a military order who could perform a combat role. Many orders insisted that brother knights should originate from a knightly or noble family.

The **brother knights** of the military orders were not simply fighting monks as is often claimed. As their statutes make clear, theirs was a new kind of religious observance drawing upon a range of influences in its formation. Like monks they were professed religious, taking vows of poverty, chastity and obedience and living according to a monastic **rule**. They also joined monks, hermits and other members of the Church in the struggle against the devil through prayer and moral conduct. Even so, they did not spend their days within a monastic cloister but in the field waging war, performing a role previously forbidden to either priests or monks. In this capacity their inspiration was the crusader, who took a temporary pilgrim's vow to visit and defend Jerusalem, before returning home to ordinary life. The authorisation granted to a crusader to combine bloodshed with a formal religious role – albeit temporary – was the crucial link that later allowed the Templars to splice the vocation of a monk to that of a knight. Thus, fully fledged members of the military orders represented a new form of religious life that formed its identity from all these groups.

As historians, we can learn about the deeds of these pious knights through the sources which have survived from this period. These take many forms, from the remains of mighty fortresses such as Crac des Chevaliers to the contents of ancient latrines. Seals, coins and other items can also give us an insight into their lives. Many of the most informative sources, however, are textual. These include written histories, poems, letters, administrative records and legal documents. By drawing together the available materials from all the cultures and religions with which the orders had contact, it is possible to begin to frame their history. Even so there are many challenges. Sometimes the evidence is incomplete and the sources one-sided. We know, for example, very little about the pagan enemies who opposed the military orders in the wars in the Baltic. Written evidence from these peoples has not survived and historians must rely almost entirely on Catholic accounts. In other cases documents have been: forged; written a long time after the event; or are based on second- or third-hand information. Confronted with these issues, historians have frequently disagreed over their interpretations of the sources, creating important areas of debate which will be covered in this study.

Our predicament as historians is complicated further by those who have brought other agendas to the history of the military orders. To take one example, during the World Wars, German commentators drew parallels between their own campaigns and those of the Teutonic Order (a military order established in 1190). Such comparisons have affected the way in which the order's medieval exploits are viewed by historians in many countries. More recently writers have capitalised on the many myths surrounding the Templars to create colourful – if outlandish – conspiracy theories involving the order. The best known of these is Dan Brown's *Da Vinci Code*, although he is by no means alone in this respect. Both the Templars and Hospitallers have also featured in films, television series and, more recently, computer games. The images of the military orders propagated through such media

Rule: A document outlining the structure by which the members of a religious order should organise their community and live their lives.

have done much to keep them in the public eye, but too often they have also embedded preconceptions concerning the orders' purpose and conduct that bear little resemblance to the contemporary sources.

The purpose of this work is to provide a brief history of the orders based on the information that *has* survived and to introduce them as religious-military institutions in the context of their period. To this end, this study reflects and incorporates the most recent work of historians in this area and aims to provide a starting point for research. In most cases works written in English have been suggested for further reading and discussed in the sections that deal with key historical debates, to make them more accessible to an English-speaking audience; however, it should be noted that a huge quantity of important material on the orders has been written in many languages.

This work covers, at least briefly, the history of all the major orders and their roles on a number of frontiers, between the twelfth and early fourteenth century. There are also thematic sections in each chapter covering important topics, such as: 'competition between orders' and 'women in the military orders'. For the four most important of these topics (patrons, finances, military activities and contemporary attitudes) discussion is developed in a series of sections spread over a number of chapters. These sections have been designed so that they can be read in two ways; either as part of the chapter in which they are found, or sequentially (i.e. finances 1, 2, 3), to acquire a deeper knowledge of a particular topic.

The time span covered by this work does not encompass the entire period in which the military orders operated. The Hospitaller order, for example, was to enjoy a long history which would include famous episodes such as its defence of Malta in 1565 against the armies of the Ottoman Empire. Likewise, many of the Teutonic Knights' most important battles were fought in the fifteenth century. Nevertheless, the period under discussion here marks the crucial formative phase in which the idea of the military order was created, flourished and came to maturity. At the end of our period the Templars, the original military order and the template for many imitators, was suppressed and therefore within this time span we have the opportunity to explore orders at different stages in their life cycle, from creation to dissolution.

Academic introductory works on the military orders

Barber, M. (1994) *The New Knighthood: A History of the Order of the Temple*. Cambridge: Cambridge University Press.

Forey, A.J. (1992) *The Military Orders: From the Twelfth to the Early Fourteenth Centuries*. Toronto: Toronto University Press.

Nicholson, H. (2001) *The Knights Hospitaller*. Woodbridge: Boydell and Brewer.

Nicholson, H. (2004) *The Knights Templar*. Stroud: Sutton Publishing Ltd.

Riley-Smith, J. (1967) *The Knights of St John in Jerusalem and Cyprus, 1050–1310*. London: Macmillan.

Riley-Smith, J. (2010) *Templars and Hospitallers as Professed Religious in the Holy Land*. Paris: University of Notre Dame Press.

Urban, W. (2003) *The Teutonic Knights: A Military History*. London: Greenhill Books.

Works discussing specifically the definition of the 'military orders' and their personnel (in addition to the above)

Constable, G. (2008) 'The Military Orders', in *Crusaders and Crusading in the Twelfth Century*. Aldershot: Ashgate, 165–182.

Luttrell, A. (2007) 'The Military Orders: Some Definitions', and 'The Military Orders: Further Definitions', in *Studies on the Hospitallers after 1306: Rhodes and the West*. Aldershot: Ashgate, I 77–88; II 5–10.

1

The Idea of the Military Orders and the Rise of the Templars

INTRODUCTION

On 13 January 1129, the members of a church council at Troyes (north-east France) assembled to hear an address by Hugh of Payns, the leader of a band of knights from distant Jerusalem. Hugh's request was the acknowledgement of his group as an order of the Catholic Church. His supporters had apparently been taking the monastic vows of poverty, chastity and obedience since c.1120, but they still needed the Church's formal recognition. Accepting any new religious order was a serious business, but this was an especially contentious application.

Hugh and his followers were committed to the military protection of those who had travelled by sea to the ports on the Levant and wished to visit Jerusalem and the surrounding holy sites. Attacks, even upon large pilgrim groups, were common and as recently as 1119 a party visiting the river Jordan had been ambushed by Muslim troops, who killed 300 and took 60 captive. With the circulation of such tales across Christendom at this time, the importance of Hugh's work would have been plain; even so, to make his organisation a religious order was symbolically to link the roles of monk and warrior. For many this was a deeply disturbing development. Monastic warfare was the spiritual struggle against evil through prayer, not the physical battles of mankind. Some years before, when the abbot of Cerne (Dorset, England) had attempted to take part in the First Crusade, he had received a stern rebuff from the Archbishop of Canterbury. The message was clear: campaigning was not compatible with the cloistered life. Thus, for the prelates at Troyes, led by the papal legate Cardinal Matthew of Albano, the acceptance of the Templars would represent more than a simple endorsement of their work, it would symbolise a public shift in the Church's theology.

Nevertheless, this council took place at a unique point in history where a number of specific pressures and influences converged to persuade them that it was acceptable to launch this new concept, a military order.

THE LEGACY OF THE FIRST CRUSADE

In the years before Troyes, ideas concerning Christianity's compatibility with warfare had developed rapidly. Against all the odds, the First Crusade had succeeded and now, for the first time in centuries, Jerusalem was in Christian hands. Returning pilgrims were widely feted and when the crusade commander Bohemond of Taranto travelled to France his fame was so great that he was permitted to marry the daughter of Philip I of France and contemporaries report that people named their children after him. His heroic status would have been regarded with envious eyes by knights who aspired to become just such a champion and thousands set out for the east in later years.

For many, the scale of the First Crusade's victories erased any remaining doubt concerning the validity of Church-led warfare. The crusade became, in their eyes, a re-enactment of the Old Testament wars, fought in defence of the Promised Land. The suffering endured by the participants and the trust they placed in God was presented as proof that they had followed the example of Christ, and been rewarded with victory. It is not clear whether Pope Urban II had ever expected 'crusading' to be a long-term policy. For him, under pressure both to render aid to the embattled Byzantine Empire and to find a way to prevent the warriors of Christendom from fighting among themselves, it may merely have been a temporary measure. Nevertheless, with such widespread approval, crusading was now firmly embedded in contemporary minds as a legitimate form of Christian activity.

With such a precedent many of the theological barriers, which might otherwise have prevented the authorisation of the Templars, were removed. Not only did the campaign reshape existing ideas of religious war, but it began to connect concepts of violence with the monastic vocation: a critical foundation for the subsequent idea of the military order. Monks themselves had been explicitly forbidden from taking part, but even so the army had assumed a decidedly monastic aspect. The participants (like monks) took vows, left their homes and families and voluntarily chose impoverishment and chastity until their work was complete. The expedition was punctuated by regular church services and acts of devotion. Eyewitnesses describing the campaign drew express parallels between the crusaders' search for salvation and the monastic lifestyle. In this way the expedition took the appearance of a 'nomadic fighting monastery' (Riley-Smith, 2010: 12), a model that required only a little adaptation to become a monastic military order. Moreover, it may have seemed natural that, with the conquest of the Levant by fighters serving as temporary churchmen, there would be a need for men who were prepared to make a permanent spiritual commitment to defend the newly won holy sites. In these conditions, the ordered life of a monastic community provided an ideal framework for such warriors, given that its religious character suited the spiritual character of the Holy Land, while its disciplined lifestyle was an excellent basis for a military force.

THE DEVELOPMENT OF THE LATIN EAST AND THE ORIGINS OF THE TEMPLARS

From the beginning, the Christian territories created by the First Crusade were chronically short of manpower. In 1100, after the majority of the First Crusaders had returned to the west, one of the few pilgrims to remain claimed that there were only 200 knights and 700 infantry left in Jerusalem. These pioneers needed reinforcements but could rely only on those warriors who were prepared to visit or settle in the Levant, along with any troops which could be sourced from the local population. Thus, hundreds of miles away from support, the Franks (European settlers in the Levant) were a desperately small ruling minority surrounded by established Muslim states. The Templars seem to have been formally established at a time when this need was particularly severe. In 1119 the principality of Antioch suffered a heavy defeat at the battle of the Field of Blood and for King Baldwin II of Jerusalem (king, 1118–1131), who was responsible for the principality's defence because its prince was still a child, this reverse dramatically increased his military burdens. To discuss the developing crisis, Baldwin called a council at Nablus in 1120 and it is likely that it was at this meeting that the Templars were officially formed.

Our knowledge of the Templars' earlier history is obscured by a lack of sources, but it seems that they were founded as a confraternity of knights committed to protecting pilgrims and were attached to the Church of the Holy Sepulchre (the church built over the locations where Jesus Christ was believed to have been crucified and buried). Such knightly confraternities were common at this time and during the First Crusade a number of warriors created a brotherhood whose members pooled their funds so they could purchase horses. Likewise, in 1122, a troop of knights formed the Confraternity of Belchite in Aragon to fight against the neighbouring Muslim powers. Nevertheless, when the Templars first took monastic vows in c.1120, they separated themselves from previous confraternities, beginning a journey that would end in their acknowledgement as a fully fledged religious order. Much of this process was conducted by the order's first **master**, Hugh of Payns, who is believed to have come to the east in 1114 with his lord, Count Hugh of Champagne (Nicholson, 2004: 22).

Master: The leader of a military order.

In their early years, the Templars were reliant on the support of the patriarch of Jerusalem (the highest-ranking Christian prelate in the kingdom) and the king of Jerusalem for their maintenance. These rulers were generous in their endowments, given their limited resources, and made a number of concessions including the 'Temple of Solomon' (the Aqsa mosque), but by 1127 the Templars' wealth was sufficient only to maintain a small company of knights. Like all the major religious orders, the most effective way to grow was to seek new benefactors. Fortunately for Hugh, his knights had already forged links with some secular and ecclesiastical figures from Western Christendom, who had travelled on pilgrimage to the east. In 1120, Count Fulk of Anjou had visited the Holy Land and attached himself to the Templars. On his return home, he made a series of gifts to the brotherhood. This was a start, but more assistance was needed if the Templars were to become an international institution.

Hugh's main chance to attract major patrons came in 1127. During the 1120s King Baldwin II's need for men remained constant. There were times when the Latin East acquired new territory and there were times when it suffered defeat, but in either case the demand for troops was relentless. By 1126 Baldwin had greatly expanded his kingdom but had failed to achieve a decisive victory over his major opponents. In 1124 and 1126 respectively he had attacked the key Turkish-held cities of Aleppo and Damascus but he had failed on both occasions. Faced with these reverses, Baldwin needed to maintain the momentum of his attacks and to do this he needed more manpower. Consequently, he asked Hugh to travel to Western Christendom and to raise a new crusading army that would help him to break the deadlock in the Levant.

Hugh's mission was threefold: to find the troops to support Jerusalem; to seek papal recognition for his order; and to identify benefactors. These objectives proved to be compatible because while Hugh recruited crusaders from across England and France, he simultaneously drew attention to his order's work, provoking a stream of gifts. Among the Templars' early major patrons were Count Theobald of Blois and Count William of Flanders. Both these men were the sons of First Crusaders and they may well have seen a chance to continue their fathers' work in defence of the Holy Land through their support of the Templars. In England, Hugh received silver and gold for his campaign from King Henry I, whose brother and brother-in-law had fought in the First Crusade. Likewise, King David of Scotland was deeply impressed by the order.

Thus, when Hugh addressed the Council of Troyes, seeking authorisation for his order, he was no isolated petitioner from a foreign land, but rather a crusading leader seeking to unite Christendom in a dramatic new venture. Moreover, he was speaking to a receptive audience. Many of the assembled nobles and churchmen had either been on crusade themselves or had predecessors who had done so. They were fully aware of the Latin East's need for troops and one of the most prominent prelates present, Bernard, abbot of Clairvaux, had written explicitly on this subject a few years beforehand. Even those without personal links to the Holy Land would not have been unaffected by the wave of popularity created by the First Crusade and Hugh's advocacy for Baldwin II's wars. With such an audience and at such a time, Hugh was ideally placed to seek authorisation for a military-religious order that would support Baldwin's efforts to secure and extend his kingdom. Everyone knew that Jerusalem needed trained knights.

SECULAR AND RELIGIOUS KNIGHTHOOD

Enriched with benefactions from nobles across Christendom it must have been clear at Troyes that the Templars held a strong appeal for the warrior elite in Christendom. This fact was significant because the knightly classes posed a series of problems for the Church at this time.

From the pope down to the lowliest priest, it was the Catholic Church's responsibility to guide Christendom's laity along the path that leads to salvation. To do this they: preached about correct behaviour; provided pastoral care and attempted to provide a moral example. Nevertheless, the deliverance of the warrior classes had always presented difficulties because their martial vocation so often led them into bitter family feuds that were irredeemably sinful. The Church responded to this civil strife by establishing the 'Peace' and 'Truce of God' movements. These attempted to prevent bloodshed and defined certain periods (particularly during Christian festivals) when fighting could not take place and imposed punishments on transgressors. Nevertheless, when these schemes proved inadequate, the Church began to look for alternatives, finding one eventually in the First Crusade. This campaign gave knights a 'meritorious' outlet for their violent tendencies. The promised reward was a plenary indulgence – the removal (or 'remission') of all confessed sins. According to Catholic doctrine, the spiritual stain created by sin has to be wiped clean by an act of penance, which demonstrates an individual's repentance. Much of the crusade's popularity seems to have hinged on the fact that such warriors were given a chance of salvation through an act that was in full conformity with their military vocation. The problem was that, having returned home, former crusader knights often simply resumed their infighting.

The crusade leader Thomas of Coucy had been one such rebellious lord fighting his corner in a patchwork of rivalries that spread across France. His early life was punctuated with repeated clashes with his king and other magnates. He then participated in the First Crusade – an act that transformed him into a hero – but having returned he simply resumed his old conduct and was excommunicated in 1114 for assaults upon the Church (Slack, 2001: xviii–xxiii). Clearly, in Thomas' case at least, the First Crusade had only been a temporary solution in the Church's attempts to curb lawless barons; what it needed was to steer the knightly class towards a new ideal.

This would have been a pressing issue for many of the prelates at Troyes. Notably, two of the senior clerics present, Archbishop Henry of Reims and the bishop of Laon, were both Thomas' neighbours and were themselves trapped in his vicious web of local politics. For them the arrival of Hugh of Payns gave these clerics the opportunity to present the Templars as a new ideal of knighthood. Their pious yet military behaviour could provide a role model for men like Thomas that could steer them away from disruptive and sinful behaviour and divert their energies to new goals defined by the Church. Bernard of Clairvaux certainly spotted this opportunity and later he wrote that they live 'as a model to imitate or as a cause of shame for our soldiers who are plainly fighting for the devil and not for God' (tr. Barber and Bate, 2002: 222). The Templars then had a relevance that went far beyond the defence of the Holy Land; they could also become part of the Church's wider efforts at social reform.

REACTIONS TO THE NEW KNIGHTHOOD (CONTEMPORARY ATTITUDES 1)

It is not clear which of these factors weighed most heavily with the prelates at Troyes, but cumulatively they were sufficient to persuade them to approve the formation of the Templars. As a newly founded religious order, the Templars' immediate need was for a monastic rule. Formerly they had been following the rule attributed to St Augustine, but this was adapted to their particular needs at Troyes. Given that Bernard of Clairvaux played an important part in this process, it is not surprising that elements of the Benedictine rule (which formed the foundation of the rule of the Cistercian order of which Bernard was the head) were also introduced. The Templar statutes, known as the 'primitive rule', begin with a prologue and then go on to describe the daily life, practices and functions of the brethren. Bernard also permitted the Templars to use the white **mantles** of the Cistercian order. These became key elements in the Templars' identity and were a symbol of Bernard's support. Pope Honorius II offered his approval for these decisions

Mantles: A garment, also known as a habit, worn by members of religious orders. The colour of the mantle and the cross or device shown upon it designated the order to which the wearer belonged.

soon afterwards. Through the Council of Troyes the order was transformed. What had started as a relatively humble band of knights patrolling the roads to Jerusalem was now presented as a new form of Christian knighthood, fighting evil on both earthly and spiritual plains.

The public approval shown by the legate and Church council was vital to the Templars' development. From their newly authorised position they were able to win privileges from the papacy (more about privileges in Chapters 2 and 5) and donations poured in from across Christendom. Over the next few decades they achieved a position of prominence, bolstered by the gifts of patrons who wished to show their support for the Holy Land. To fuel this rise, the Templars needed to publicise their work as widely as possible. For Hugh, the vehement and passionate Bernard of Clairvaux was the perfect advocate. Accordingly, at some point before 1136, Bernard wrote a document entitled *In Praise of the New Knighthood* to eulogise the order [**Doc. 1, p. 144**]. It is not clear how widely this treatise circulated; however, it reveals the ideas that Bernard felt would inspire his audience. He began with a straightforward call to arms, describing the struggle to hold Jerusalem as a war of good against evil. He stressed that, as churchmen and warriors, the Templars were able to fight both earthly foes and demons; expanding the traditional monastic war against evil through prayer. He then described the behaviour of contemporary knights, deriding their vanity and pride and stating that such vices would lead them to Hell. In striking and intentional contrast to this bitter condemnation he then elevated the Templars, stressing their military virtues, their workmanlike equipment and the advantages of their disciplined way of life. To emphasise his ideas he drew parallels between the Templars and the warriors of the Old Testament, such as the Maccabees and the Israelites. Given that the First Crusaders had frequently been compared to these ancient warriors, Bernard was intentionally positioning the Templars in such a way that they would profit from their reflected glory.

Even so, despite his commendations, Bernard was clearly worried about his association with the Templars at the time when he came to write this work. He opened this treatise by claiming that Hugh had asked him to write this document on three separate occasions before he had consented to his request. This may merely be a symptom of the monastic style of writing, which demanded that the author show humility. Nevertheless, it may also indicate some degree of caution on his part. Certainly, Bernard had good reason to be careful. The Templars may have offered a solution to a number of contemporary problems, but they *were* ultimately an innovation. At a council in Sens in 1121 the famous philosopher and teacher Peter Abelard had been condemned for the theological speculations made in his work *Treatise on the Unity and Trinity of God* and neither his academic status nor his reputation had saved him. If Bernard needed reminding that introducing new ideas was a hazardous business then he had only to cast his mind back to his own denunciation of Peter at this time. Even among some Cistercians, the existence of the Templars was a source of controversy and Isaac of l'Etoile, a Cistercian abbot, later denounced the order claiming that their warlike behaviour bore closer comparison to the Devil than Christ.

On the whole, however, the clerical opinions that have survived are generally positive. Some had concerns about this new form of religious life, but many were enthusiastic. The majority of chronicles written by churchmen at this time praise the order and their work. Clearly they understood the pressing need which the order had been founded to address. Others remained supportive, but were more cautious. Prior Guigo of the Carthusian order was of this persuasion and, in a letter to Hugh of Payns written in c.1129, he stressed that Hugh's knights should take care to prioritise their inward pursuit of Christian virtue before engaging with worldly enemies. His main fear seems to have been that the Templars' knightly temperament would subvert their pious calling, destroying their purpose as a religious institution. His emphatic advocacy of humility perhaps hints at a fear, which over the next century became a regular accusation, that the order was vulnerable to the temptations of pride.

These represent a handful of the comments made in the years after Troyes, but while their reservations, or even outright condemnation, explain Bernard's caution, they should not obscure the enormous and immediate popularity that the Templars enjoyed. Many saw hope in this new idea and knights flocked to commit themselves to Hugh's new crusade to the Holy Land. The Templars were in the ascendancy on a self-propitiating spiral of patronage and popularity that would suffice to see them ranked as one of the foremost orders in Christendom. Although some were alarmed, the overwhelming clamour was positive – for the present.

Further reading

Barber, M. (1970) 'The Origins of the Order of the Temple', *Studia Monastica*, 12, 219–240.

Forey, A.J. (1985) 'The Emergence of the Military Order in the Twelfth Century', *Journal of Ecclesiastical History*, 36, 175–195.

Luttrell, A. (1996) 'The Earliest Templars', in M. Balard (ed.) *Autour de la Première Croisade*. Paris: Publications de la Sorbonne, 193–202.

Morton, N. (2010) 'The Defence of the Holy Land and the Memory of the Maccabees', *Journal of Medieval History*, 30, 1–19.

Nicholson, H. (1995) *Templars, Hospitallers and Teutonic Knights: Images of the Military Orders, 1128–1291*. Leicester: Leicester University Press.

2

The Defence of the Holy Land, 1130–1187

THE ORIGINS AND MILITARISATION OF THE HOSPITALLERS

When the First Crusaders established the Latin East, the area had merely been a rebellious province in the recently conquered Turkish Empire. Initially, the Franks' main source of opposition was the Shia Muslim rulers of Egypt, whose armies crossed the Sinai Desert and then attacked the kingdom of Jerusalem from their frontier city of Ascalon. Nevertheless, their incursions did not prevent the expansion of these Christian territories both along the Levantine coast and deeper inland. As the century progressed the Turks of northern Syria and Iraq began to overcome their internal divisions and crush the resistance shown by many of their Arab subjects. Their opposition to the Franks hardened and following the above-mentioned battle of the Field of Blood 1119, Aleppo, a major city that only one year previously had contemplated voluntary capitulation to the Franks, sided decisively with the Turks.

Subsequently, with increasing calls for *Jihad*, Turkish attacks on Christian territory intensified and in 1128 Zengi, Turkish governor of Mosul, took control in Aleppo. This act created a territorial power-block, which by 1140 had expanded to include much of northern Syria. From this position, Zengi began to instigate a series of invasions into Christian lands and the Muslim writer Ibn al-Athir commented that where in 1129 the Franks in Antioch could demand a share of Aleppo's taxes (even from buildings just outside its wall); by 1136 Zengi was launching raids from this city deep inside Christian territory. The Franks worked vigorously to strengthen their position in the face of mounting resistance, but few advances were made after the mid-1120s. Even Hugh of Payns' much-vaunted crusading expedition collapsed in the face of enemy resistance and adverse weather conditions while marching on Damascus in 1129.

With heavy fighting in northern Syria in the 1130s, the extremely wealthy and popular Hospital of St John in Jerusalem must have felt increasingly obliged to offer assistance to the ongoing defence of Jerusalem. The Hospital was not founded for a military purpose. It was established in Jerusalem by the Benedictine abbey of St Mary while the city was still under Muslim control to provide a hospice to care for pilgrims. When the First Crusade arrived in 1099, legend reports that the Hospital's master threw bread down from the walls to the starving crusader army. In the wake of the campaign, the Hospital grew, benefiting from the gifts it received from the rulers of the kingdom of Jerusalem and from visiting lords and knights. With a shared interest in the care of pilgrims, the Hospitallers and Templars developed with common goals and it is likely that a strong connection developed between them in these early years. In 1113, Pope Paschal II issued a bull confirming the Hospital of St John as an independent institution. He also referred to their growing network of hospices, located in Asti, Pisa, Bari, Otranto, Taranto and Messina; testaments to their rising fame. Many of these establishments lay on the routes to the Holy Land and provided facilities for pilgrims, supporting the routes to the east.

By the 1130s the order's dedication to pilgrims and the sick had become famous, but, as we have seen, the pressing need was for military support. The ongoing struggle against Zengi frequently compelled the king of Jerusalem, Fulk of Anjou (king, 1131–1143), to lead his armies north, imperilling the kingdom's southern frontier, which was threatened by Egyptian forces based at Ascalon. Although all prior attempts to capture Ascalon had failed, the rulers of Jerusalem had built a series of fortresses to blockade the city and in 1136 one of these castles, Bethgibelin, was given to the Hospitallers. The concession of Bethgibelin to the Hospitallers gave this medical establishment responsibility for one of the most exposed outposts in the Levant. Clearly, Fulk was confident that the order already had sufficient resources to make the best use of such an important stronghold.

Exactly when the order developed a military wing is a source of much speculation among historians. As Forey pointed out (1984), several attempts have been made to identify the moment at which this change took place and conclusions have ranged from the 1120s to the 1160s. The reason for this broad spread of dates lies in the sources which contain many clues concerning this transformation, but which have been interpreted in different ways. To take one early example, in 1126 there is a reference to a Hospitaller 'constable' named Durand in a list of witnesses found in a legal document granting the Hospitallers the property of Algie in the kingdom of Jerusalem. The office of 'constable' is one that might imply some military responsibilities and for some historians, such as Delaville Le Roulx (1904) and King (1931), this has been accepted as the earliest proof that the order had adopted a military role. Others, however, such as Prutz (1908), were less sure, arguing that a 'constable's' responsibilities were not inevitably military, but could be concerned with the management of the stables. The problems involved in interpreting what his role entailed are complicated by the fact that the office of 'constable' did not survive in the Hospitaller order and so we cannot use references to the tasks performed by later 'constables' to define Durand's responsibilities. Subsequently, historians have also noted that Durand was included at the end of the list of witnesses suggesting that he was not an official of much importance (Hiestand, 1980: 65). These and other arguments tend towards the view that he was either a non-military official or, even if he was, he was probably unimportant. A different view has been taken by Riley-Smith (1997) who believed this title to be military and demonstrated that this document was drawn up by warriors participating in a campaign against Damascus; thus reviving the idea that Durand may have had military responsibilities. Burgtorf (2001) likewise has noted that Algie was located on an embattled frontier; thus the Hospitallers' acquisition of this property had strategic implications. He also argued that in the Latin East particularly the title of 'constable' automatically carried military connotations.

The above discussion serves as an example of the problems faced by historians seeking to establish when the Hospitallers assumed a military role. Given that we lack a definitive statement on this question, the debate on this subject has hinged on the interpretation of clues such as Durand's title. This is not the only piece of evidence that frames this debate. Should we see it as significant, for example, that the Hospitaller master Raymond of Puy accompanied the royal army on campaign in 1128? Does a document outlining the Hospitallers' acquisition of the fortified site Calansue in the same year suggest that they had assumed a military role? (Tibble, 1989: 37) In all these cases there are problems involved in interpreting the sources and it is not possible to be definite. A related question revolves around whether the Hospitallers acquired a military role suddenly or whether it was introduced gradually. The long-term consensus seems to be that the order acquired troops – whether guards for pilgrims, mercenaries or pilgrim knights – before its own brethren engaged in warfare. Indeed, the possibility has been raised, most recently by Riley-Smith (2010), that they may have initially allowed pilgrim knights to affiliate themselves to the order for some time before they allowed their own brethren to take up arms. This seems likely and certainly the first definite references to 'brother knights' occur long after the first references to the Hospitallers' involvement in war.

Amidst these debates one point to which several historians return is the concession of the above-mentioned castle of Bethgibelin. This was not the first castle granted to the order – they acquired the fortified site of Calansue in 1128 – however Bethgibelin was far more strategically sensitive. Reflecting upon this event, several historians including Nicholson (2001), Forey (1992) and myself have rejected the idea that the brethren would have been entrusted with such a dangerous assignment if they did not already possess significant military resources. It seems far more likely that they already had a strong military wing. Nevertheless, even if we accept that the order had involved itself in major military activities at some point before 1136, this still does not explain precisely when this commitment was first made, nor does it explain when a military role was assumed by the Hospital's commanders in other regions such as Iberia. The debate goes on . . .

TEMPLAR AND HOSPITALLER RESOURCES IN THE WEST (FINANCES 1)

In the eyes of Western Christendom, the military orders were charitable organisations publicly promoting causes that were widely considered to reflect the will of God. These included: the care of pilgrims, alms for the poor and the defence of the Holy Land. All were popular objectives and many responded by offering their support, whether financially or personally. Even so, potential patrons could choose from a range of existing monastic or charitable institutions, which were similarly deserving of aid. The challenge for a new order then was to demonstrate and broadcast the value of its work as widely as possible to generate the donations that would allow it to prosper in a competitive environment.

In the years following the establishment of the Latin East thousands of pilgrims set out for the Holy Land. They carried back stories of heroism, miraculous events and war. Even so, only those who could afford the time and costs of the journey could go in person. Others were compelled – whether by illness, poverty or the burden of their responsibilities – to remain at home. These individuals may have felt an equally strong desire to support the Holy Land, but were unable do so. The rise of the Templars and Hospitallers, however, created an opportunity for all Catholic Christians, whether they had been on crusade or not, to express their support for the Holy Land through donations. In return for their assistance, patrons believed that their benevolence would bring them spiritual rewards, helping them to win a place in heaven. To this end, representatives from the military orders travelled across Europe soliciting donations both in money and land. We can see this process in operation through the legal documents (or 'charters') which have survived and specify such endowments. In southern France in c.1133, for example, a lady named Laureta, with the consent of her husband William, gave all the property she had inherited from her father in a neighbouring town and village to the Templar agent Hugh Rigaldi. Her stated reasons for this gift were to help prepare her soul for heaven and to support the Templars in their struggle against the Muslims. The papacy encouraged such gifts and in 1144 Pope Celestine II published the bull *Milites Templi* instructing the clerics of the Church to organise collections for the Templars and allowing them to offer an indulgence of one-seventh of penance in reward. Both the Templars and Hospitallers were also exempted from paying tithes and other forms of church taxation, which helped them to maximise their income [for a papal bull issued to support a military order see **Doc. 6, p. 159**].

Having acquired this initial land and wealth, the orders then exploited these assets to build a system of landholdings across Western Europe. Permanent establishments known as commanderies were founded in many regions to manage their various properties and to act as recruitment centres. These were often built within ports or close to major roads so that goods could swiftly be despatched to the east. To take one example, in Provence the Hospitaller commandery of Trinquetaille was founded when Archbishop Atton of Arles gave the order the church of St Thomas of Trinquetaille (between 1115 and 1126) in Arles. The house then prospered through the donation or purchase of lands and property. Situated on the Rhone (a vital trading artery) and near the Mediterranean coast it became a vital link in the Hospitallers' international supply chain (Selwood, 1999: 54). With such foundations in place, a proportion of their annual revenue could be sent to the order's headquarters in the east. For both the Templars and Hospitallers every commandery was required to make annual payments, known as a **responsions**, which consisted of one-third of its income. As the Templar and Hospitaller estates grew in size and number across Western Europe, their responsions grew proportionately.

Responsions: An annual payment (typically one-third of all revenue) made to a military order's headquarters by its dependent houses across Christendom.

Over time, for administrative purposes, these commanderies began to be grouped into regional districts (known as 'priories' by the Hospitaller order and 'provinces' by the Templars). These were then placed under the care of appointed commanders (known as a priors or preceptors) to facilitate the overall management of the order. To transport donations and responsions to Jerusalem, both orders either purchased or chartered ships from ports on Europe's Mediterranean coast such as Marseilles, Bari, Venice and Brindisi. These vessels were rarely warships (during the twelfth and thirteenth centuries at least), but were transports capable of carrying large cargoes and many passengers. The chronicler Ramon Muntaner described this process in the thirteenth century:

> At that time, the ships belonging to the Temple and the Hospital would end up in Brindisi and those from Puglia came to pass the winter with the intention of transporting pilgrims and provisions from the kingdom. The orders all possessed much property, and still do, in Brindisi as well as through Puglia and across the entire kingdom. So, once spring had

arrived, the ships which had wintered in Brindisi would take on pilgrims and load their cargoes of oil, wine and fine wheat and go to Acre.

(tr. Hughes, 2006: 22)

The Templar vessel *The Falcon*, for example, purchased in the later thirteenth century, was said to be the largest ship in the Mediterranean and was capable of carrying over 1500 people. The orders also purchased or built harbour installations, warehouses and accommodation buildings to facilitate their naval supply routes.

Through these labours and acquisitions the military orders created a supply system across Western Europe, designed primarily for the collection and bulk export of materials from these 'producer' regions to frontline 'consumer' regions. This was necessary because war was – and is – expensive and the costs involved in equipping even a single knight were considerable. To give some idea of scale, each Templar knight was permitted 3 to 4 horses and in thirteenth century Aragon the price of a single warhorse was around 1300 sous (the same amount necessary to ransom the lives of 7 to 8 crossbowmen). The maintenance of the orders' castles likewise involved huge annual expense. When the Templars rebuilt their major fortress of Safad during the 1240s, the cost of the work was estimated at 1,100,000 bezants (a truly vast sum of money, given that the price of the nearby estate of Toron was assessed at 60,000 bezants in the same period). Moreover, this was only one castle among many and Forey has calculated that at various points during the twelfth and thirteenth centuries the Hospitallers controlled 56 fortresses in the Levant (Forey, 1992: 59).

The financial importance of an order's supply infrastructure in Western Christendom cannot be overstated, but it also performed a number of further valuable roles. Each commandery could act as a recruitment point, encouraging active young men either to join the order or to participate in a crusade (see Chapter 7). It may have been with such purposes in mind that King Malcolm IV of Scotland granted the Hospitallers a smallholding in every burgh in his kingdom; an act that effectively gave them the opportunity to maintain a presence in every major community across the country. The orders' international networks could also facilitate regular communications, allowing messages to be transported rapidly over great distances. This in turn was an excellent basis for a system of banking, which again could generate additional revenue. The financial services provided by the Templars soon became famous and by the thirteenth century Templars were managing and auditing the finances of the kingdom of France (De la Torre, 2008: 121–128). They also became famous for loaning money and in 1148 King Louis VII of France borrowed 32,000 *livres parisis* from the order while on crusade. This was a truly huge amount given that Louis' demesne revenues were only

60,000 *livres* p.a. (Barber, 1994: 68). Considering that only 20 years earlier the Templars had only been a small-scale operation, their ability to offer such sums in the middle of a major crusade highlights the speed at which they acquired financial power.

At the core of these vast trans-national operations was each order's head-quarters in Jerusalem. For the Templars this was the Temple of Solomon and its surrounding properties; a large site occupying a sector of south-east Jerusalem. The Hospitallers' headquarters buildings have largely been destroyed or dismantled over the years, but they formerly occupied an area south of the Church of the Holy Sepulchre. These establishments were the nerve centres of their respective orders, acting as: centres for decision-making and organisation; reception areas for overseas news and responsions; distribution points for materials intended for the orders' far-flung garrisons; workshops and armouries; treasuries; and places to entertain guests. Visitors to the holy city commented with awe at the scale of the orders' work and the German pilgrim John of Würzburg claimed that the Templars had stabling for 2000 horses or 1500 camels in their headquarters alone.

Nevertheless, however powerful the Templar and Hospitaller networks may have been – complete with their commanderies, castles, squadrons of knights, ships, etc. – both their organisational structures shared the same inherent weakness. Both orders consolidated their military resources almost exclusively on the frontline, leaving their estates in Western Christendom virtually defenceless. Inventories of the Templars' estates in France reveal that they maintained few weapon hordes or barracks in these areas. These economic heartlands were therefore both vital and highly exposed and their protection could only be guaranteed if they retained the goodwill of local potentates.

CASTLES AND FORTIFICATIONS (MILITARY ACTIVITIES 1)

In the 1130s Zengi's attacks against Christian territory increased in intensity. Among his main targets was the county of Tripoli, which he invaded in 1133 and 1137. The Tripolitarians put up a fight but proved incapable of protecting their northern frontier. Eventually, Count Raymond II turned to the Hospitallers for help and in 1144 he granted them a series of castles, including the famous Crac des Chevaliers and the towns of Rafanea and Montferrand. This was a tough assignment which demanded that the Hospitallers reverse the fortunes of a devastated region that was within striking distance of Zengi's cities of Hama and Homs and which lay directly on the principal invasion path into the county of Tripoli. Furthermore, both Rafanea and Montferrand had fallen to Zengi seven years previously and would need to be recaptured.

Nevertheless, if the Hospitallers could secure their position in this area then they stood to benefit from the fertile farmlands of the wide plain dominated by these fortresses. The Hospitallers' acceptance of this challenge must have been a calculated risk that would only have made sense if they already had the resources and determination to reverse the fortunes of such an embattled frontier. Time would prove that the gamble had been worthwhile and when Muslim forces later attacked Crac in 1163 they were badly defeated. This is an early example of a trend that was to become commonplace as the twelfth century progressed. As secular rulers proved unable or unwilling to defend key frontier castles, they began to hand them over to the military orders, who could draw upon their support networks in Western Christendom to provide the necessary cash and troops to fortify and garrison these positions. After receiving such sites the military orders generally endeavoured to strengthen their defences and both Crac in *c.*1202 and the above-mentioned Bethgibelin in the 1170s were heavily refortified to reflect changes in their usage and the political situation during this period.

The orders also constructed their own fortifications. In some cases these were great frontline castles, designed to confound the assaults of a major army. Belvoir is a good example of these. It was built by the Hospitallers on the site of an existing castle to guard the western side of the Jordan valley. Its concentric design reflected the most sophisticated techniques of the day and, although the cost of building was enormous, it later proved its worth when it was besieged in the 1180s. Fortress builders generally sought to make the best use of the topography to enhance defensibility and all the order's castles were carefully sited. Some, such as Montfort (belonging to the Teutonic Knights), were built on valley spurs and were therefore defended on three sides by sheer slopes and on the fourth by rock-cut trenches across the spur itself. The Templars' coastal castle of Athlit, built for the order in 1217–1218, was erected on a narrow outcrop projecting into the sea. The growth in the number of strongpoints held by the orders did not pass unnoticed and when in the 1160s King Thoros of Armenia visited Jerusalem he joked to King Amalric of Jerusalem that:

> When I came to your land and inquired to whom the castles belonged, I sometimes received the reply: 'This belongs to the Temple'; elsewhere I was told: 'It is the Hospital's'. I found no castle or city or town which was said to be yours, except three.
>
> (tr. Forey, 1992: 59–60)

This was a light-hearted remark and should probably not be taken literally, but it hints at the scale of the role played by the orders in the Latin East. Strategically speaking they had become its armour plating.

Frontline strongholds, however, were only one type of fortification created by the orders. Many others existed and the Templars built several small outposts, such as Destroit and Yazur, along the major pilgrim routes to Jerusalem and the holy places; thus affirming their dedication to the protection of such travellers. These forts were not large, needing only to be strong enough to fend off marauders and bandits. Many other smaller fortifications were created or purchased and these could range from small towers – designed either to defend villages or police commercial routes – to fortified mills, churches or estate centres. Surviving examples range from the Templars' fortified mill of Doc, to the Hospitallers' church at Fontenoid. In the Levant, builders had to be mindful of the dangers of invasion, local rivalries or raiding, and anyone contemplating the storage or maintenance of anything valuable – whether machinery, religious sites, hoarded wealth or crops – needed to address the issue of defending these assets given the area's exposure to risk and the constraints of available money and manpower.

In addition to their own establishments, the orders also played an important role in the defence of the major urban centres. Cities such as Acre, Tripoli and Tyre, relied on one (or sometimes two) lines of ramparts. As wealthy orders with expertise in construction, the Templars and Hospitallers often assumed responsibility for maintaining long stretches of such defences and in some cases they took control over a settlement in its entirety. Gaza, Tortosa, Arsuf and Sidon were among the towns they governed at different times. Through these roles, they shouldered a major part of the burden of defending the east, and by return they greatly enhanced their influence.

Within the Latin East's major cities, the orders constructed establishments from which they could manage their rural possessions. Again, these were often fortified, not necessarily against external enemies, but against urban unrest. Particularly in the thirteenth century, cities, such as Acre, saw a rise in vicious internal conflicts, creating a need for defensible properties within the city. A famous example of these is the Templar fortress in Acre, which was located in the south-west of the city on the seafront. It was heavily defended and held out for several days following the fall of the city in 1291. The sheer size of this citadel would have made it important, but the Templars were careful to enhance its visual impact by mounting great golden lions on each of its four corners. Strongholds of all kinds were practical buildings, performing military, economic and religious functions, but they were also statements of prestige and power, reminding all who saw them of an order's might.

Military orders in all frontline areas made extensive use of fortifications. As we shall see, they were an essential aspect of war, whether in Prussia, Livonia, Iberia or the Aegean. Strongholds in these areas varied considerably in size and purpose, ranging from a fortified oak tree to huge monastic fortresses. Castles were highly versatile buildings, acting as bases for offensive operations during periods when crusading forces were available, or as a line of defence at times when the brethren stood alone. Newly won territories could be consolidated through the construction of fortresses, while major trade routes or lines of communication could be secured by them. Nevertheless, castles across these regions were not always built in the same way. The military orders in Prussia and Livonia, for example, made use of extensive local timber resources to create their early forts. Timber castles had the advantage of being cheap and swift to construct, but were not as strong as stone equivalents. In later years, the Prussian castles tended to be built in brick, again making use of locally available materials. In the Holy Land, where good quality wood was scarce, fortifications were built in stone.

THE HOLY LAND, 1144–1170

In 1144 a Muslim scholar in Norman Sicily informed his Frankish overlord that the city of Edessa had fallen to Zengi. The Christians present laughed, believing it to be impossible. Nevertheless, later reports proved the story true. Through a strategic sleight-of-hand, Zengi had achieved the capture of the capital city of a major Christian territory. News of this defeat provoked a dramatic reaction in the west and on 1 December 1145, Pope Eugenius III launched a new crusade (now known as the Second Crusade) to retake the city. In the months that followed two of Christendom's mightiest rulers, Louis VII of France and Conrad III of Germany, raised major armies and in June 1147 they set out for the east. The campaign itself was a crushing failure; both leaders followed the route taken by the First Crusaders and suffered heavy defeats from the Turks in Asia Minor. The survivors eventually reached the Holy Land and joined the kingdom of Jerusalem's army in an attack on Damascus, which ended in retreat. For the forces of Islam this was a great triumph, which Zengi's son Nur ad-Din extended when he scored a further victory over the Antiochene forces in 1149. For Christendom, the destruction of two major crusading armies caused horror and apprehension. Over the next few years, Nur ad-Din and the rulers of Jerusalem became locked in a battle for ascendancy, which neither won. Nur ad-Din strengthened his position in April 1154 when he captured Damascus from its Muslim ruler, while the Christians secured their southern flank by finally capturing Ascalon in 1153.

In 1163 both Nur ad-Din and Amalric, the new king of Jerusalem (king, 1163–1174), saw an opportunity to break the deadlock when civil war rendered Egypt vulnerable for invasion. The capture of Egypt would have been a major victory to either side. The Nile Delta offered vast agricultural wealth, while the ports of Alexandria and Damietta enjoyed huge revenues through trade. In 1167, after three major campaigns, the kingdom of Jerusalem stood on the verge of achieving this ambition. In this year, Nur ad-Din had sent his general Shirkuh to seize the country, but Amalric, along with the military orders, had forced him to retire. Aware of their need for protection against Nur ad-Din, the Egyptians had signed a perpetual peace with Amalric and agreed to pay a vast annual tribute. These advantages were all thrown away, however, when in the following year Amalric broke the treaty and invaded for a fourth time.

By this stage the military orders were a key component in any Christian army and the Hospitallers staunchly advocated this new expedition to Egypt, promising an enormous contingent of 500 knights and 500 turcopoles (light cavalry). The resulting campaign was a fiasco and succeeded only in provoking Shirkuh to invade and stage a successful takeover in Cairo. In late 1169 Amalric made one further attempt (his fifth) to capture Egypt and dislodge Shirkuh but his hopes were again disappointed. Reflecting on Nur ad-Din's expansion of power in both Syria and Egypt, the Archbishop William of Tyre wrote: 'Wherever I turn I find only reasons for fear and uneasiness. The sea refuses to give us a peaceful passage and all the regions round about are subject to the enemy, and the neighbouring kingdoms are making preparations to destroy us.' (tr. Babcock and Krey, 1943: v.1, 358)

In this struggle for supremacy, the Templars and Hospitallers played a vital role, defending strongpoints and supplying troops for the major expeditions. Barber estimates that by the 1170s the Templars had around 600 knights and 2000 **sergeants** in the Latin East, garrisoning castles and serving in the field (Barber, 1994: 95). The Hospitallers' forces would have been slightly lower. These knights and sergeants would have been supplemented by mercenaries and infantry. To give some idea of the scale of the military burden assumed by the orders, it is instructive to note that the largest army deployed by the kingdom of Jerusalem in the twelfth century, including a large contingent of Templars and Hospitallers, consisted of 1300 knights and c.15,000 infantry.

Brother sergeants: Like brother knights they were fully professed members of a military order and they could perform a range of roles including combat. They generally came from a less prestigious social background than the brother knights.

During this period of intense fighting there was also an ongoing need to secure support from abroad and here the orders offered considerable assistance. Their huge support networks provided corridors both for the conveyance of troops, money and equipment into the Latin East and, by return, the transmission of appeals for help to every corner of Western Christendom. The king of France was the target of many letters requesting aid and in 1164 the Templar commander Geoffrey Fulcher described the defeats suffered by the Latin East in the 1160s writing: 'do not expect any other messengers from here because in the absence of the king and the master we do not dare send any fighting man in these difficult circumstances.' (tr. Barber and Bate, 2002: 99)

THE MILITARY ORDERS AT THE TIME OF WILLIAM OF TYRE (CONTEMPORARY ATTITUDES 2)

In *c.*1186 Archbishop William of Tyre died a worried man. For over two decades he had worked with the leaders of the kingdom of Jerusalem to steer the kingdom safely through Muslim invasion and infighting among the Christians, but he was well aware that the position was becoming desperate. William was born in around 1130 in Jerusalem and, upon reaching adulthood, he was sent to university in Europe to train as a churchman. Soon after his return in 1165 he was appointed as archdeacon of Tyre, later rising to become chancellor of the kingdom and archbishop of Tyre. He spoke multiple languages, possibly including Arabic and Persian. In a portfolio of works, including a history of Islam, William wrote a long and detailed history of Jerusalem, focusing primarily on the period under Latin rule.

William knew both military orders well and, given their determination to offer medical and military support to the Holy Land, it might be thought that he would have been fulsome in his praise. When describing the Templars' early years, he confirms that 'they remained faithful to their noble vows, carrying out their duties fairly satisfactorily' (tr. Barber and Bate, 2002: 26). Despite this rather grudging acknowledgement, his concerns quickly break through as he describes their growing pride and independence. William had several reasons to resent the Templars and Hospitallers. Both orders were exempt from the authority and taxation of all clerics, excluding only the pope himself. In this way, neither William nor the patriarch of Jerusalem (the leading Christian churchman in the kingdom of Jerusalem) could exercise any direct restraint upon them. The tension this caused had already provoked conflict in 1154 when, as William reports, the complaints made by the patriarch about the Hospitallers on a number of issues led to disputes of such severity that the order made a vicious attack on the Church of the Holy Sepulchre, even firing arrows into the building. Worse still from William's perspective, when a group of churchmen appealed to Rome seeking justice, the papacy sided with the Hospitallers.

As a loyal supporter of King Amalric, William's work also reflects his concern at the orders' rising military and political power. In 1168 William reports that the Templars refused to participate in Amalric's expedition into Egypt; ignoring the need to support the royal army. In 1173 the Templars disgraced themselves further in William's eyes when they ambushed an envoy travelling from Assassin territory to the kingdom of Jerusalem. The Assassins were an extreme Shia Muslim group who specialised in murder as a political tool and this attack destroyed all hope of an alliance between them and the kingdom of Jerusalem. King Amalric was furious and punished the Templars personally.

William's general attitude towards the orders then was not positive. He seems to have considered them to be something of a necessary evil; providing too much military support to be suppressed, but also causing considerable disruption. His account however poses two important questions for the historian; first, is his version of events accurate? and second, does it reflect wider opinion? These are thorny and inter-related issues for historians who have only a limited amount of information at their disposal. In this case, one test that can be applied is to look at how other contemporaries characterised the events described in William's chronicle. Describing the above attack on the Assassins, for example, Walter Map, archdeacon of Oxford, provides a second account which differs in some points of detail but still places blame on the Templars and so this might be thought to be corroborative evidence. Nevertheless, there is a good chance that Walter met William at a Church council in 1179 and may have had this story directly from him. This is not known for certain, but when comparing different accounts of an event it is vital to consider whether there is a link or relationship between the authors and, if so, whether this has an impact upon its reliability.

To take another example, in his account of the capture of Ascalon in 1153, William tells his readers that when a breach was made in the city walls the Templars charged into the city whilst preventing the other Christian forces from following them so that they could keep all the loot to themselves. The result was a massacre in which the entire Templar contingent was destroyed. William intended this whole episode to be a dramatic parable outlining the dangers of greed; but is it accurate? William was not there and he wrote some time after the event. Moreover, as Nicholson has shown (Nicholson, 2004: 74–75), another chronicle based on an eyewitness account tells a different story. This source reports that the Templars entered the city and were then abandoned by the remainder of the army, who were unwilling to follow them. Perhaps, the other Christian commanders may have claimed that the Templars prevented them from following to excuse their cowardly behaviour. This latter account, although agreeing in its fundamentals with William, puts a very different perspective on the Templars' actions.

Clearly William put the blackest complexion possible on the orders' deeds and his enmity towards the Templars in particular would presumably only have deepened when he learnt that his brother Ralph had been killed in an action led by the Templar master Odo of St Amand in 1179. Even so, despite his political and personal objections, his hostility was not necessarily unrepresentative of some clerical circles. The participants in the Third Lateran Council were sufficiently convinced that the Templars and Hospitallers had abused their privileged position to demand in the resulting canons that they curb their behaviour. This is an important piece of evidence because it purports to reflect a consensus of opinion – at least among the participants – rather than the views of an individual. Nevertheless although this evidence is significant, it should not be construed as proof that clerical opinion across Christendom had turned decisively against the orders. They were to be censured, not dissolved and there were other delegates at the council who were not convinced by all the allegations made against them. Walter Map, who was no admirer of the orders, commented: 'perhaps many lie when they tell those stories about the lords Templars: let us ask them themselves and believe what we hear. How they behave at Jerusalem I do not know: here with us they live harmlessly enough' (tr. James, 1983: 69).

Ultimately, Archbishop William, Walter Map and every commentator on the military order encountered the orders in different ways, whether through alms collectors; through political dealings; through stories carried by returning crusaders. Perhaps a bishop in one area argued with a pushy Templar alms collector and subsequently judged the whole order to be corrupt; perhaps a knight in another area heard a magnificent song about the orders' exploits and considered them to be heroes. Either way, their views would be different and would not necessarily reflect wider opinion. Perhaps the strongest conclusion that it is permissible to draw from William's evidence is that the orders were controversial and, in some circles, a source for concern, but as we saw in the first chapter, they always had been.

THE FALL OF JERUSALEM

When his forces captured Egypt in 1169, Nur ad-Din completed the virtual encirclement of the Latin East on its landward frontiers. This created an ideal platform from which to invade. By this time his lands in Egypt were governed by Shirkuh's nephew Saladin, who had taken over as Nur ad-Din's representative following his uncle's death later in the year. Thus when Saladin attacked the Christian stronghold of Montreal in 1171, Nur ad-Din ordered that together they should execute a pincer attack on the kingdom of Jerusalem. This could have been decisive, but Saladin did not comply with his master's instructions and simply withdrew to Egypt – rumour suggests that he feared Nur ad-Din might remove him from power. Hiding behind many protestations and explanations, Saladin continued to avoid any joint action until Nur ad-Din's death on 15 May 1174. At this point, Saladin's strategy immediately shifted focus and he began to take power in Nur ad-Din's former territories, forcibly disinheriting his late master's heirs. This process was finally completed on 12 June 1183 when he took control in Aleppo.

During this time severe internal disputes arose among the Franks. King Amalric also died in 1174 and shortly afterwards it was discovered that his heir, Baldwin (king, 1174–1185), had leprosy. This was a terrifying reality for the kingdom. Baldwin would not be able to produce an heir and therefore a suitable successor would need to be identified. Furthermore, his youth and later his illness rendered him incapable of ruling for long periods, creating the need for a regent. In this situation, questions over the succession and the regency drew the most powerful groups in the Latin East (the barons, the rulers of Antioch and Tripoli, the Church authorities and the military orders) far more deeply than normal into the business of governing the kingdom. These magnates formed factions and vied with one another for authority, stimulating infighting. Baldwin was no weakling, but his illness prevented him from following the firm example set by his father. The military orders as major power-brokers likewise took sides, using their influence to steer political decision-making.

Meanwhile, the orders remained deeply committed to struggle against Saladin. In 1177 Baldwin's current regent, Raynald of Châtillon, defeated an invasion staged by Saladin from Egypt at the battle of Mont Gisard, with the assistance of a group of Templars under their master Odo of St Amand. Wishing to maintain the momentum of his victories, in 1178 Baldwin led the army in person to Jacob's Ford to build a castle that would apply pressure on Damascus. The castle, like so many of the kingdom's frontier posts, was given to the Templars who stationed 80 knights there. For Saladin the threat posed by the castle could not be ignored and he first offered 60,000 dinars to encourage the Christians to retire. They refused this offer, provoking an invasion by Saladin that led to a notable victory over the kingdom's army. Shortly afterwards, Saladin captured and destroyed the castle.

In the spring of 1185, after years of war and diplomacy, Baldwin IV died aged 23. By this time, the infighting within the kingdom of Jerusalem had escalated just as the king's physical condition had deteriorated. By marrying his sister Sibylla to a foreign magnate named William Longsword, he had hoped to secure his succession; however, William died in 1177 and his infant son (Baldwin V 1185–1186) died shortly after Baldwin IV. The magnates of the kingdom were viciously divided on the subject of the succession and this threatened their ability to work together on campaign. Furthermore, increasingly the kingdom fought alone. The disillusion caused by the failure of the Second Crusade and a spate of major wars in Western Christendom dissuaded or inhibited rulers from responding to calls for a new crusade. Those contingents which did arrive were well received but never offered more than a temporary relief. The Byzantine Emperor Manuel Comnenus sent considerable support to Amalric and Baldwin during the 1160s and 1170s, but he died in 1180 and his successors were not inclined to continue his friendly policy.

On the other side of the frontier, Saladin was himself under pressure. After a two-year truce (1180–1182), he had invaded the kingdom repeatedly with large armies but despite his considerable resources he had achieved few solid advances. By seizing Aleppo, he had effectively surrounded the Latin East, but he had yet to justify his usurpation of Nur ad-Din's heirs with the long-promised blow against the Franks. In 1182, Raynald of Châtillon launched a naval raid into the Red Sea attacking Muslim pilgrims en route to Mecca and Medina. Although Saladin destroyed their ships and had the prisoners publicly executed, they had struck deeper into Islamic territory than ever before. Saladin's position was built on his claim to be a great leader of the *Jihad*; now he needed to prove it.

In 1186, following the death of Baldwin V, the kingdom of Jerusalem desperately needed a new ruler. The obvious choice was the nobleman Guy of Lusignan, who was married to Baldwin's elder sister Sibylla. Guy had a number of supporters, including the Templars, but many felt that he was unfit to rule and demanded that Sibylla divorce him. Sibylla agreed to this demand, but only on condition that she could choose her next husband and, therefore, the future king. The barons accepted Sibylla's terms, but Sibylla simply chose to remarry Guy, making him the new king. Many felt cheated and the leader of Guy's opponents, Count Raymond of Tripoli, signed a treaty with Saladin. For Saladin, now at the peak of his power, this was an ideal opportunity and, when a Muslim caravan travelling through Christian territory was attacked, he invaded. Aware of Saladin's intentions in April 1187 the masters of the Temple and Hospital were sent to make peace with Raymond in an attempt to present a united front against Saladin. Nevertheless, events overtook them on 1 May when their small force was destroyed by a force of 7000 Muslim cavalry at the battle of the Springs of Cresson. Although the Templar master, Gerard of Ridefort, survived, the master of the Hospitallers and almost all of the other knights were killed.

Soon afterwards on 2 July 1187 the Christian leaders assembled in council to discuss their response to Saladin's invasion; he had crossed the river Jordan and attacked Tiberias, on the shores of the Sea of Galilee. For the Christians encamped at the tower of Sapphorie the key decision revolved on whether their army would march out across barren territory to meet him. The assembled barons agreed that this was too dangerous to attempt, but later the master of the Templars and Reynald of Châtillon persuaded the king to change his mind. They had long served as props to Guy's authority and he could not ignore their advice lightly. The following day the field army of Jerusalem marched out from Sapphorie, in accordance with their advice, and after heavy fighting became trapped in a waterless iron-age fort named the Horns of Hattin. Exhausted and dehydrated, the Christian army was then surrounded and annihilated. In the wake of the battle Saladin had all the

Templar and Hospitaller prisoners executed, excepting only Gerard of Ridefort. During the months that followed the Latin East collapsed and Jerusalem itself fell in October. The great cross was cut down from above the Templar headquarters and was carried through the city where for two days it was beaten with sticks. The military orders, like all the other defenders of the Holy Land, had failed.

Further reading

Boas, A.J. (2006) *Archaeology of the Military Orders: A Survey of the Urban Centres, Rural Settlements and Castles of the Military Orders in the Latin East (c.1120–1291)*. London: Routledge.

Borchardt, K. (2001) 'The Templars in Central Europe', in Z. Hunyadi and J. Laszlovszky (eds) *The Crusades and the Military Orders: Expanding the Frontiers of Medieval Latin Christianity*. Budapest: Central European University Press, 233–244.

Edbury, P. and Rowe, J.G. (2008) *William of Tyre: Historian of the Latin East*. Cambridge: Cambridge University Press.

Forey, A.J. (1984) 'The Militarisation of the Hospital of St John', *Studia Monastica*, 26, 75–89.

Hamilton, B. (2000) *The Leper King and His Heirs: Baldwin IV and the Crusader Kingdom of Jerusalem*. Cambridge: Cambridge University Press.

Jacoby, D. (2007) 'Hospitaller Ships and Transportation across the Mediterranean', in K. Borchardt, N. Jaspert and H. Nicholson (eds) *The Hospitallers, the Mediterranean and Europe, Festschrift for A. Luttrell*. Aldershot: Ashgate, 57–72.

Luttrell, A. (1999) 'The Earliest Hospitallers', in B. Kedar, J. Riley-Smith and R. Hiestand (eds) *Montjoie: Studies in Crusade History in Honour of Hans Eberhard Mayer*. Aldershot: Ashgate, 37–54.

Nicholson, H. (1998) 'Before William of Tyre: European Reports on the Military Orders' Deeds in the East, 1150–1185', in H. Nicholson (ed.) *The Military Orders, Volume 2: Welfare and Warfare*. Aldershot, Ashgate, 111–117.

Phillips, J. (1996) *Defenders of the Holy Land, 1119–1187*. Oxford: Oxford University Press.

Riley-Smith, J. (2002) 'The Origins of the Commandery in the Temple and the Hospital', in A. Luttrell and L. Pressouyre (eds) *La Commanderie, institution des ordres militaires dans l'Occident médiéval*. Paris: Comité Des Travaux Historiques Et Scientifiques, 9–17.

Chronology

1099 *15 July*	Conquest of Jerusalem.
1113	Pope Paschal II confirms the Hospitallers as an independent institution.
1119 *28 June*	The principality of Antioch is defeated at the battle of the Field of Blood.
1120 *January*	Council of Nablus.
1129	Council of Troyes.
1130s	The order of St Lazarus is founded during this period.
1136	The Hospitallers receive Bethgibelin.
1144	The Hospitallers receive Crac des Chevaliers.
1144 *24 December*	Fall of Edessa to Zengi.
1147–1149	The Second Crusade.
1153	Ascalon falls to the kingdom of Jerusalem.
1154	Disputes between the patriarch of Jerusalem and the Hospitallers.
1163–1169	Amalric launches five expeditions into Egypt.
1177 *25 November*	Saladin is defeated at the battle of Mont Gisard.
1178	The Franks are defeated at Jacob's Ford.
1179 *March*	Third Lateran Council.
1182	Raynald of Châtillon launches a naval raid on the Red Sea.
1183	Saladin takes control in Aleppo.
1186	Baldwin IV dies.
1187 *1 May*	Battle of Cresson.
1187 *4 July*	Saladin defeats the kingdom of Jerusalem at the battle of Hattin.
1187 *October*	Fall of Jerusalem to Saladin.

3

Iberia

THE INTRODUCTION OF THE MILITARY ORDERS INTO THE IBERIAN PENINSULA

In 1131 Alfonso 'the battler', king of Aragon (1104–1134), made his will, while besieging the town of Bayonne in Gascony. He decreed that after his death his entire kingdom should be divided equally among the Hospitallers, Templars and the canons of the Church of the Holy Sepulchre. This extraordinary decision – even for a childless ruler – was unprecedented, voluntarily cutting his own family out of the succession. Nor was it simply an impulsive gesture because three years later he confirmed these provisions for a second time.

Alfonso was the scion of the small kingdom of Aragon, which was struggling to maintain its position against its Christian and Muslim rivals. For decades, Aragon and the other Christian kingdoms of northern Spain (Castile-León, Navarre and later Portugal) had been fighting their way south in an effort to regain the lands lost to Islam in the eighth century. This process is often referred to as the *Reconquista* (the Reconquest). Some early Christian gains had been made by serving as mercenaries for one or other of the many Muslim 'taifa' kingdoms that dominated central and southern Iberia. These wealthy, but rival rulers paid handsomely for Christian troops, creating an environment of military opportunity. The rulers of Spain also received considerable assistance from French noblemen who were prepared to march to their aid.

In 1085 the Christian cause took a leap forwards when Alfonso VI of León-Castile conquered the city of Toledo, driving deep into central Spain. From this time, the retention of this city was to be an ongoing concern for the Christian powers, while repeated Muslim expeditions were despatched against it. Towards the end of the eleventh century Islamic attacks on Christian territory increased in intensity with the advent of the Almoravids. They were a conglomeration of North-African Berber tribes, who promoted a hard-line Islamic way of life. They first defeated the Muslim rulers of Morocco and then crossed into Spain. Initially they came at the invitation of the taifa rulers, but they quickly took control for themselves. While the Almoravid threat grew in the south, Christendom was swept by a new phenomenon: the Crusade. So successful was the call to retake Jerusalem that Pope Urban II had to forbid Spanish lords from taking part; fearing that in their absence, Iberia might be left unguarded. Spanish enthusiasm for crusading persisted however and during the 1120s the papacy began authorising crusades on the Iberian frontier.

One of the principal advocates of Iberian crusading was Alfonso of Aragon. His brother, Pedro I, had taken a vow to travel on crusade to Jerusalem in 1100 and Alfonso himself had been authorised by the papacy to fight a holy war in 1118, during which he captured the city of Zaragoza. Like the warriors of the First Crusade, he considered himself to be fighting to support the Holy Land. The only difference was that while they had marched through Anatolia and Syria, he wished to reach distant Jerusalem via Spain and North Africa. He took this obligation seriously, raiding deep into Muslim territory and expanding his kingdom. He also established two religious-military establishments in frontier locations that were designed to institutionalise this drive southwards; the confraternities of Belchite (1122) and Monreal del Campo (1128). These were not military orders, but secular confraternities of knights. Even so, they, like the Templars and Hospitallers, were designed to act as a focal point for those who wished to dedicate themselves to crusading and holy war.

By this stage, Christian Spain was ripe for the introduction of the military orders. The Hospitallers were granted property in Catalonia as early as 1108 and the Templars in Portugal in 1128. From this point, both orders established themselves across Iberia and in this way Alfonso's decision to leave his kingdom to the Templars, Hospitallers and the canons of the Holy Sepulchre comes into focus. For a deeply pious crusading monarch, whose life had been spent fighting to build a road to distant Jerusalem, the decision to hand his kingdom over to institutions which embodied these goals does not seem particularly strange. In the event, however, Alfonso's will was not implemented and rule passed to his brother Ramiro and then to the counts of Barcelona (the orders were compensated for their loss by the latter). It remains, however, a remarkable demonstration of how enthusiastically the monarchs of the Iberian Peninsula adopted the idea of the military order.

THE SPANISH MILITARY ORDERS AND THE RECONQUEST, 1157–1195

According to the account by Roderigo Jiménez de Rada (archbishop of Toledo from 1209–1247), in 1157 the Templars abandoned the town of Calatrava claiming that they could not hold it against a feared Muslim invasion. For the newly crowned king Sancho III of Castile this was a dangerous moment. Situated around 65 miles south of Toledo, Calatrava was a vital frontier stronghold and if these elite warriors were not prepared to defend it then its loss would endanger the whole Christian position. The threat of invasion at this time was very real. In the early twelfth century, Almoravid power had fallen into decline. Initially this had enabled considerable Christian advances, including the conquest of Calatrava itself in 1147, but soon a greater threat emerged with the rise of the Almohads. The Almohads, like the Almoravids, were also a tribal confederacy formed in North Africa that adopted a fanatical form of Islam. They considered the Almoravids to be morally corrupt and seized power from them in much of North Africa and mainland Spain. With this growing consolidation of power, the Almohads renewed the threat to Christian territory and in the months before Sancho's coronation in 1157 they had already made considerable advances. The Templar withdrawal from Calatrava was therefore a major problem.

By January 1158 it was clear that none of Sancho's nobles were prepared to respond to this need. Lacking any other options, he finally consented to an offer made by Raymond, abbot of the Cistercian monastery of Fitero, to defend the town along with a force of volunteers. Raymond duly marched to the fortress, but the feared Almohad attack did not take place. Nevertheless many of those who had taken part in this venture decided to form a military order centred on Calatrava [see **Doc. 2, p. 153**]. As news of their exploits spread, the knights acquired landholdings from patrons who recognised the value of their work; the same principle that underpinned the growth of the Templars and Hospitallers, although in this case they acquired lands almost entirely in Iberia. In 1164 the papacy offered the order its protection and the Cistercians, who were closely linked to the order through Abbot Raymond, granted it a rule. The order was subordinated to the Cistercian house of Morimond.

In later years the rulers of all the Iberian kingdoms which had a frontier with Islam established or patronised military orders to help them protect and expand their territories. At first they generally backed the Templars or Hospitallers. These international institutions, however, were primarily devoted to the defence of Jerusalem and were expected to send a significant proportion of their wealth to the east. This was clearly a concern and when in 1169 the king of Portugal granted the Templars one-third of all future conquests, he stipulated that the money raised from such lands must be spent in Portugal, not in the Holy Land. Thus, these rulers may have considered it more expedient to encourage smaller specifically Spanish orders that would devote their full attention to local matters. Two such orders were founded in León in the late twelfth century; those of Alcántara and Santiago. Both were to have an illustrious future and within a few years of its founding the order of Santiago in particular was given responsibility for a vast swath of territory on the Leónese and Castilian frontier with Muslim Spain.

Santiago: The order of Santiago was established in 1170 by King Ferdinand II of León to protect the city of Cáceres. Like the order of Alcántara, it began as a knightly confraternity and took the name 'Santiago' (St James) after St James the apostle. Legend reported that St James had been buried in Spain and his tomb at Santiago de Compostela was (and still is) an important place of pilgrimage. Santiago was famed as the defender of Spain and therefore had immediate relevance as the patron saint of an aspiring military order. The confraternity took the name 'Santiago' in 1171 following the Archbishop of Santiago de Compostela's decision to connect himself with the order. Within a few years, the brethren established outposts across Iberia, as well as in France and Italy, receiving fortresses in Castile as early as 1171. Its rule received papal approval in 1175 and the order flourished in many Iberian kingdoms through the patronage of local rulers and elites.

Alcántara: The order of Alcántara was established as a knightly confraternity based at the convent of San Julian del Pereiro near Ciudad Rodrigo. It gained papal approval in 1176 and later became a military order in the early 1180s, following the Cistercian rule. It took the name 'Alcántara' after receiving a castle of this name on the river Tagus from the Calatravans in 1218. At some point before 1187 it accepted the authority of the Calatravan order with some key aspects of this arrangement concluded in 1218. The brethren gained considerable support from the kings of Iberia, who encouraged them to join their campaigns against the Moors.

Sancho III's elevation to the throne of Castile in 1157 was also the moment when his father's kingdom of León and Castile was divided between him and his brother Ferdinand II of León in accordance with the political customs of the time. The inevitable friction caused by this division was only exacerbated when Sancho died the following year to be succeeded by a 3-year-old heir, Alfonso VIII (king of Castile, 1158–1214). Without an active ruler, Castile soon became a battleground as various Christian factions fought to rule in Alfonso's name. The main beneficiaries of this infighting were not the Almohads, who were similarly divided, but the Portuguese. For decades Afonso I Henriques of Portugal (1114–1185) had been engaged in a struggle to expand his territories and to assert his independence from León. He enjoyed considerable success in both these ambitions and in 1140 he adopted the title of 'king'. Like the other rulers of Iberia he fully understood the value of the military orders and they made an early appearance in Portugal when on 19 March 1128 Afonso's mother Teresa granted the Templars the castle of Soure. They later helped him to capture Santarém in 1147, an act which pushed his frontier far to the south. Lisbon fell to Afonso later the same year with the support of crusading forces en route to the Holy Land. The orders were well rewarded for their support and in 1158 the Templars received the town of Tomar.

By the time of Sancho III of Castile's death in 1158, Afonso was again ready to seize more territory and infighting among the Almohads only strengthened his position. In the following years Portuguese forces attacked south and east, rolling the frontier back. During this time several further military orders acquired landholdings in Portugal and in 1176 a specifically Portuguese order was established to protect the highly strategic city of Évora, which had been captured in 1165. This order later became known as the order of Avis.

The order of Avis: This institution was founded in 1175–1176 to defend Portugal's southern frontier and to defend the crucial town of Évora. It was initially known as the order of Évora, but later assumed the name 'Avis', having been granted a fortress of the same name in 1211. In 1187 the brethren placed themselves under the authority of the Calatravan order. They owed much of their early development to the support of the kings of Portugal and were active in the reconquest of the Iberian Peninsula.

The defence of newly conquered land was an important task for Avis and all the Spanish orders. The order of Santiago had been established in 1170 to protect the city of Cáceres and the following year it received a string of strongholds protecting the Leónese border. The other orders of San Julian del Pereiro (later Alcántara) and Calatrava performed similar roles in other vulnerable regions. Although the reigning Iberian monarchs were rarely responsible for the foundation of a military order within their lands, in all cases they swiftly realised their potential and endowed them with the wealth necessary to perform their military vocation. For Afonso of Portugal, anxious to secure papal recognition for his newly formed kingdom, patronage for the military orders may also have been part of a wider effort to win favour in Rome, a campaign which came to a successful conclusion in 1178. The 1170s were generally years of Christian conquest and by 1180 both Castile and Portugal had made notable territorial gains. The young Alfonso VIII of

Castile took Cuenca in 1177 and Afonso retook Beja in 1178 and launched a series of raids towards Seville. Almohad responses, including expeditions against Huete (1172) and Santarém (1184), met with little success.

These advances, however, were not to last. By 1190 the Almohad caliph al-Mansur (1184–1199), having spent the first six years of his caliphate establishing himself in North Africa, was ready to strike into Christian Iberia. His first attack cut into Portugal causing widespread devastation. He forced the surrender of Santarém, which he then destroyed, before attacking the Templar fortress of Tomar. Here he was held and eventually compelled to withdraw. The following year he first took the stronghold of Alcácer do Sal and then besieged Tomar for a second time, which the Templars were eventually forced to surrender. His next campaign was far more decisive. In 1195 he marched on Castile, entering Calatravans' large territory, known as the *Campo de Calatrava*. The knights of Calatrava posed a serious threat in this area and only one year previously they had joined forces with the archbishop of Toledo for a raid into Moorish territory. Upon hearing news of al-Mansur's advance, Alfonso VIII travelled south to confront him and was then heavily defeated at the battle of Alarcos on 17 July. In the wake of this disaster the order of Calatrava, which had contributed a major contingent to Alfonso's force, lost most of its frontier castles in this region, including Calatrava itself. The shock caused by this battle was felt across both the Christian and Muslim worlds and the notice taken by contemporary historians as distant as Mosul in Iraq and Yorkshire in England stands as testimony to its impact. The following year was marked by heavy setbacks in which the military orders, who were on the frontline, bore the brunt of multiple losses and the Castilian position was weakened further by a Leónese invasion. Christian Iberia was on the back foot.

FRONTIER REVENUE: IBERIA AND THE HOLY LAND (FINANCES 2)

Transforming a small military order into a major international institution required the dedication of its members and patrons, but also the establishment of a viable financial structure that would cover its many costs. As we have seen, the Templars and Hospitallers developed huge estates in Western Europe, which could generate resources for the Holy Land. The Spanish orders also acquired properties away from the frontline and these were located primarily in Iberia. Commanderies situated behind the frontier had the virtue of being secure from external invasion, but there were also considerable expenses and challenges involved in the transportation of resources from these establishments to where they were needed. More accessible, but more exposed, were economic assets located in frontier regions. Most of the castles granted to the military orders came with attendant estates and in 1168, when the Calatravans were given the highly strategic castle of Chillon in Castile, it came complete with its agricultural lands, vineyards, mills, meadows, pasture land and fish farms. These properties however were vulnerable to attack and needed careful management and protection to ensure that they would not fall into enemy hands.

This was a period when pitched battles were comparatively rare and commanders, whether Christian or Muslim, conducted warfare primarily through heavy raids that were designed to destroy an enemy's crops and industries as well as killing or capturing livestock and workers. Battles were risky. We have already seen that the kingdom of Jerusalem collapsed in 1187 after a single encounter. Only a ruler with a very good reason or simply no other alternative would chance such an engagement. Through raiding, however, a commander could defeat his opponent by robbing him of the financial strength to raise a major army, without fighting a major battle. In the Holy Land in 1217, for example, the Templars and Hospitallers joined a raid from Acre towards Damascus, in which they destroyed their enemy's orchards, olive-groves and fruit trees, while seizing crops and taking captives. Medieval warfare, therefore, had a strong economic dimension and the military orders all sought to protect their frontline assets, whether mines, crops, flocks, etc., while seeking to deprive their enemies of theirs.

Spanish rulers likewise encouraged military orders to fight these border wars and offered powerful incentives. In June 1173, for example, Alfonso VIII of Castile granted the order of Calatrava a fifth of all the land taken from the Muslims, excepting cities where they would be given four urban properties (although this was later reduced). Similar deals were made on many other frontiers. The basic trade-off was that the rulers would expand their kingdoms; the military orders would increase their power/revenue; and both would contribute to the reconquest. Although this was the operative principle, deals made between ruler and order could take many forms. In 1211, for example, the order of Avis was granted property by the king of Portugal on condition that they build a castle on that site. Considerations of economic dominance could also shape decisions concerning the location of strongholds. The German crusader Oliver of Paderborn described how the Templars' fortress of Athlit in the kingdom of Jerusalem allowed the Christians to control the surrounding territory and make use of salt mines, pasture land, fields and fisheries, while forcing neighbouring Muslim rulers to abandon large areas of cultivated land.

In addition to profits from campaigning, the orders sometimes won income by compelling neighbouring enemy rulers to pay them an annual tribute. This was the case in Syria, where the Hospitallers, operating out of Crac des

Chevaliers, waged war against the neighbouring Muslim rulers of Homs and Hama for much of the thirteenth century. Again this was a conflict characterised by raiding, with victory measured in the capture of livestock and the outcome of skirmishes, rather than the conquest of territory. At times the Hospitallers claimed tribute from these cities and in the early 1260s Hama paid the order an annuity of 4000 dinars. This money would have naturally boosted the order's frontiers finances while weakening its enemies.

Within an order's territory it was naturally in its interests to make the best possible use of the available resources. Agricultural land, mines and other resources were potentially lucrative assets, but crops and infrastructure were vulnerable to destruction by enemy raids and in the autumn the gathered harvest was a lucrative target. Efforts to reduce this risk explain in part the need for castles, which contained great store-houses where such commodities could be safeguarded. Often fragile and expensive agricultural machinery was maintained within such strongholds. This was the case with Crac des Chevaliers, where archaeological evidence suggests that a windmill was mounted on one of the towers. At other castles, evidence has been found for wine-presses, ovens and forges. As we have seen, there were also a number of fortified houses and mills owned by the orders, which again were designed to provide a defensible centre for rural administration as well as the storage and processing of crops (see Chapter 2).

In all cases, frontier industry and agriculture required a workforce, but areas which had been subjected to prolonged warfare tended to be relatively depopulated and ambitious frontier lords often sought to introduce trustworthy settlers to make up the labour shortfall. The military orders were no different and they competed with nobles and churchmen to secure such workers. Very often orders were granted territory specifically so that they would transform a wilderness into productive land. This was a key factor in Alfonso I of Aragon's decision to found the confraternity of Monreal del Campo in 1128 and it explains many of the major concessions made to the military orders in later years. Naturally cultivation on a major scale requires a huge number of families and it can only be imagined how many would have been needed for some of the orders' largest estates, such as Calatrava's *Campo de Calatrava*, which by 1188 was around 340 sq. miles in size (Estow, 1982: 271). In other areas, they either rented properties to tenants and/or co-operated with their conquered Muslim subjects. An alternative source of labour was slaves. By the twelfth century, slavery in much of Europe had long been in decline to be replaced with serfdom. In the Mediterranean world, however, it continued to flourish. The Templars and Hospitallers are both known to have made use of Muslim slaves in the Latin East and when in 1263 the Egyptian sultan suggested a slave exchange with the kingdom of Jerusalem – at a ratio of 1 Christian for 2 Muslims – the orders blocked the deal, claiming that their slaves were trained craftsmen whose services were too valuable. Overall, economic management on the frontier was a multi-faceted enterprise involving a warrior's eye for depriving an opponent of his crops and herds while protecting one's own; a merchant's instinct for exploiting every possible asset; and a conqueror's capacity to locate, control and protect a workforce. With considerable experience in all these matters, the military orders were often among the most advanced practitioners of their day.

THE STRUGGLE FOR SPAIN, 1195–1232

The defeat at Alarcos in 1195 was a critical moment for Castile. The following year Muslim armies plundered the Tagus valley while Leónese forces, working in co-operation with the Caliph al-Mansur and the kingdom of Navarre, attacked from the west. In 1197 al-Mansur launched a further attack against Castile, thrusting deep inside the kingdom. Under attack on many fronts, King Alfonso VIII's initial pleas for peace were batted aside, but later that year al-Mansur agreed to a 10-year truce and the following year he crossed back to Morocco. With his departure, Alfonso VIII was free to vent his wrath on the Leónese who were themselves under immense pressure from the papacy to desist from attacking their Christian neighbours. A treaty was signed shortly afterwards.

In the following years the military orders had a chance to assess the damage they had sustained. Many had lost frontier properties. The order of Alcántara's fortress of Trujillo had fallen in 1196, while the order of Calatrava had lost a great swath of territory controlling the southern approaches to Toledo. Its master Nuño clearly felt disgraced and resigned. Unlike the Templars and Hospitallers, the Calatravans did not have a sophisticated support structure behind the frontier from which they could draw rein-forcements. They needed outside help and this they received in part from Alfonso VIII, who made concessions to the order writing that:

> Taking pity on your poverty because of the unhappy affair of Alarcos (where you were with me and where, because of our sins, it did not please divine power to grant us victory), you lost your chief house of Calatrava and almost all your possessions.
>
> (tr. O'Callaghan, 1986: 422)

Having lost Calatrava itself, the order moved its headquarters to Salvatierra. This was an aggressive gesture. Salvatierra was situated to the south of Calatrava, even deeper inside Muslim territory. It may have been intended as an act of defiance, perhaps even a rallying cry for the Iberia's Christian defenders. Time would prove, however, that the retention of Salvatierra was too ambitious. Initially, when in 1209 Alfonso VIII opened a new offensive, Salvatierra offered an effective base for raiding expeditions, but when the Muslim counter-strike began under the Caliph al-Nasir (al-Mansur's son) in 1211 it was his first target. The defenders held out for 51 days before seeking terms and they stopped the Muslim army in its tracks, but they were unable to hold the fortress.

The following year Alfonso VIII marched south leading a huge crusading army containing contingents of military orders and forces from across Iberia. He first regained the *Campo de Calatrava* and then advanced further south where on 16 July 1212 he inflicted a major defeat on the Almohad army under al-Nasir at Las Navas de Tolosa. Shortly afterwards he captured the castle of Dueñas which he gave to the Calatravans. The order renamed the stronghold 'Calatrava la nueva', and adopted it as their new headquarters. This victory spurred the king of León to invade Muslim territory and he took the castle of Alcántara, which he gave to the Calatravans in 1217. The order however chose to give the castle to the order of San Julian del Pereiro, who later took their name from this fortress (becoming the order of Alcántara). The momentum achieved by these advances was not to last, however, and several Christian kingdoms became embroiled with other concerns. The Aragonese became drawn into wars in southern France. Castile was riven by disputes following the death of Alfonso VIII in 1214. The Portuguese made some inroads regaining Alcácer do Sal in 1217 with the assistance of German crusaders and the Templars. The town was later handed over to the order of Santiago.

In 1217 a new determined king, Ferdinand III, took power in Castile and in 1230 inherited the kingdom of León. In doing so he united two of Iberia's most powerful kingdoms, swinging the balance of power decisively in favour of the Christians. Meanwhile Almohad power had fallen into decline and in 1228 they were forced to depart from the peninsula having been ejected from the major cities by a series of local Muslim factions. The remaining defenders of Muslim Spain then fought a rearguard action against the advancing Christian rulers from the north. The military orders played an important role in the repeated attacks and raids launched against Islamic territory at this time. These culminated in the conquest of the great Muslim capital of Cordoba on 29 June 1236. The military orders and magnates present all swore to provide for the defence of the city. The papacy encouraged the orders' efforts by allowing them to offer **indulgences** to the warriors who fought with them.

While the Castilians were driving south, the Aragonese were also making headway under a vigorous new king, James I (1213–1276). Shortly after he attained adulthood James began to make war on Moorish Valencia. Although

Indulgences, plenary indulgences and penance: In the Catholic Church, when an individual confesses their sins he/she will be expected to perform a specific action – a penance – to atone to God for their sinful behaviour. An indulgence was when the Church permitted this individual to replace a penance with another defined action. A plenary indulgence (often granted to crusaders) permitted an individual to replace **all** penance on **all** confessed sins for a specified act (i.e. going on crusade).

his initial efforts achieved little, he staged a successful invasion of Mallorca in 1229–1230 closely supported by the military orders, who were richly rewarded. From this point he concentrated his efforts again on Valencia, where Muslim rule had disintegrated into rival factions. By late 1233 preparations were complete and the royal army of Aragon marched south.

SECULAR RULERS AND THE MILITARY ORDERS (PATRONS 1)

In mid-summer 1233 King James I of Aragon was encamped outside the city of Burriana in Muslim-held Valencia. The siege was not going well and the ruins of a siege tower near to the walls only drew attention to his early failures. It had begun in May, but it was now July and it would not be long before the troops would need to return home to gather the harvest. At this moment two galleys arrived from Tarragona and James, aware that he needed naval support to protect his supply lines, asked the ships' masters to remain in his service. The ships' masters initially refused, but later said that they would remain if they were paid 60,000 sous. James did not have so extortionate an amount to hand and the masters said that they would only accept his pledge for the amount if the Templars and Hospitallers would act as security. James agreed and passed on the request to the orders. He had good reason to expect their support. Not only were they rich, but they had benefited considerably from his previous campaigns. Indeed the inspiration for his campaigns into Valencia had come in part from the Hospitaller commander, who along with another nobleman had raised the matter with the king while they were relaxing after a day's hunting. Nevertheless, having consulted together, the orders only agreed to James' proposal on condition that he confirm all the Hospitallers' privileges in Aragon and grant the Templars a considerable quantity of property.

This is an illuminating episode because it underscores the nature of the relationship between a military order and the crown. When a frontier prince either founded a military order or introduced one from abroad, the advantages to him would have been plain. Such orders could: supply or train high-quality warriors; garrison vital frontier forts; settle new areas; and provide strategic counsel. Conscious of these factors rulers often proved enthusiastic supporters, encouraging orders to take root along disputed borders. Even so, the orders were also institutions of the Church, accountable to the papacy, and were not simply theirs to command. Thus, in 1233, the Templars and Hospitallers were under no obligation to underwrite James' loan to the galley captains and were perfectly within their rights to demand significant endowments in exchange. Forty years beforehand, Pope Celestine III had emphasised the orders' independence of action when he had instructed them to continue to fight against the Muslims in Iberia even if this contravened royal truces. In theory, therefore, a ruler could only count on the orders' support where their objectives coincided. If a king wished to wage war against an Islamic ruler or to promote a cause endorsed by the Church then he could generally rely on the orders' enthusiastic co-operation. In other matters the orders could withhold their assistance.

Even so, in practice, rulers had many ways to bend a reluctant order to their will. To conduct their work, the orders required landed wealth and donations to raise troops and fortify castles. In most cases they acquired a large proportion of this power through donations from the local ruler. These gifts were made in the expectation that the orders would repay such benevolence with assistance. Moreover, as orders came to rely on such secular lords for their continued growth and ongoing legal protection a relationship of dependency was created. In most cases, kings proved willing defenders of their local orders. Even so, magnates were aware of the military orders' reliance on their goodwill and often attached conditions to their support. Several rulers – including those of England, Aragon and Castile at various points – demanded that military orders personnel seek permission before leaving their lands. In 1217, Alfonso IX of León inserted a common stipulation into a donation of lands to the Calatravans, requiring that in return they should observe royal truces.

In general it was in the orders' interests to remain in favour with local rulers because a strong relationship would improve their effectiveness on the battlefield, protect their interests and encourage the king to bestow further largess. In the case of James I of Aragon, the Templars worked hard to build royal goodwill and even undertook to educate him during his childhood at their fortress of Monzón. In return they received privileges and grants of property on a lavish scale. Co-operative relationships of this kind emerged across Christendom, but in Iberia particularly the orders seem to have prospered to a far greater degree than in other places from royal patronage. Relationships with royal courts could become very close and many brother knights rose to become trusted royal councillors and envoys. In 1272, for example, James sent the Templar Arnold of Castellnou as his ambassador to the king of France. Likewise, across the border in Castile, in 1188 Alfonso VIII encouraged the order of Calatrava to maintain a permanent presence at his court.

When rulers went to war with fellow Christians, however, conflict between crown and order could become unavoidable. In the Latin East, Iberia and in the Baltic, many orders established outposts in rival Christian countries. If these territories' rulers went to war then the orders could find themselves in a conflict of interests. This occurred to the order of Santiago during the war between Portugal and León in 1179. At this time the order, which held significant landholdings in both countries, found itself under pressure to take sides. In the event it offered allegiance to León and by doing so alienated the king of Portugal, who promptly withdrew his support for the order (Lomax, 1958: 3–37). Clearly taking sides in a war between patrons was a risky business. Rulers were not unaware that in such circumstances orders might have divided loyalties and many took steps to ensure that they could rely on their support. It may have been with such considerations in mind that in 1181, two years after the above crisis, the king of León offered the order of Santiago additional property in León if they would set up their headquarters in his kingdom. The order agreed, but then prevaricated for many years over fulfilling this agreement. It has even been suggested that the order attempted to create a bidding war, in which the kings of Castile and León competed with donations to win the order's loyalty (Lay, 2009: 183). Even so, in its future relations with its royal patrons the order acted with more circumspection and in 1183 it acted as a neutral party in a treaty between Castile and León, holding castles that would be given to the injured party if one side should break the peace (Lomax, 1958: 3–37). Mediation was a role taken by many orders in disputes between their benefactors. It created an opportunity to remain in favour with both parties without incurring the wrath of either.

In all negotiations of this type, an order's strongest bargaining counter was nearly always the knowledge that rulers *needed* their help. To take the above scenario, even though Santiago sided against the Portuguese in 1179, the kings of Portugal later resumed their patronage of the brethren – they were too valuable to ignore for long. Nevertheless, if this need evaporated then an order's position could suddenly weaken. This occurred in Aragon in the mid-thirteenth century when the expansion of Castile-León caused it to lose its frontier with Islam. With no border to patrol, the rulers' reliance on the Templars and Hospitallers was heavily diminished, while the orders themselves increasingly committed their energies to the Holy Land. Later Aragonese kings demanded that they should serve against Christians but this was clearly unsatisfactory to both parties [**Doc. 10, p. 164**]. As a result, the kings began to constrain and reduce the orders' rights in later years. The brethren turned to the papacy for protection, but ultimately the material argument for sustaining their estates in Aragon was critically weakened.

A further concern for secular rulers was the threat from over-mighty orders. Throughout this period, many orders acquired sufficient military and financial power to constitute a danger to royal authority. In Chapter 2 we saw how this took place in the kingdom of Jerusalem, with the development of rivalry between Amalric I and the Templars. This was also the case in Castile-León under Alfonso X (1252–1284). By this stage five military orders sat on the kingdom's general council (Calatrava, Alcántara, Santiago, the

Temple and the Hospital) and in 1282, when the sick and increasingly incapacitated Alfonso faced revolt from his son, the Templars, Hospitallers and the order of Santiago joined the rebels. Their prime concern may have been the kingdom's security, which Alfonso was increasingly incapable of providing, but ultimately they had sided against the crown; the very institution that had nurtured them.

EXPANSION AND THE APPEAL OF THE HOLY LAND, 1233–1300

In September 1269 in the seas off Menorca lookouts on James I of Aragon's flagship caught a glimpse of the rest of the Aragonese crusading fleet en route to Jerusalem. It had become separated after a rough night spent beating into the wind. The following day, having tried to catch up with the fleet, the weather deteriorated into storm-force conditions which lasted for days. At one point a Templar ship emerged through the spray and waves, floundering with its rudder (steering mechanism) irreparably damaged. The Templars hailed James' ship asking for a spare, but they were soon lost to sight. Eventually James' vessel encountered a Calatravan vessel whose master persuaded James to retire. James had long harboured a desire to lead an army to the Holy Land but this storm destroyed his ambitions.

James' crusade to the Holy Land failed before it had even begun, but the mere fact that it took place at all was a mighty achievement for a kingdom that could not formerly have contemplated such a venture. For decades, the Spanish kings had been fighting to reconquer Iberia and for many, under near-permanent threat from Islam, crusading to the Holy Land had been out of the question. During the twelfth century, a few isolated nobles had managed to make the journey and the small Aragonese order of Mountjoy (see below) became involved in its defence from 1177, but in general Iberia could not spare either the money or the troops for a major intervention. In the early thirteenth century, however, as the balance of power turned in favour of the Christians, the threat from Islam receded and both the defenders of Spain and the papacy became increasingly aware that their crusading resources could be deployed elsewhere.

Mountjoy: The order of Mountjoy was founded in *c*.1173 by Rodrigo Alvarez, a former brother of Santiago, in Aragon. He wanted to observe a more stringent monastic code and was later permitted to assume an adapted version of the Cistercian rule. It was named after the hill on the road to Jerusalem where pilgrims catch their first glimpse of the city. It acquired its first property in Aragon in 1174 from King Alfonso II, in the kingdom of Jerusalem in 1177 from King Baldwin IV and later in Italy. The order received support from Pope Alexander III, who approved its foundation and conferred a number of privileges. It was later amalgamated with the ransom hospital of the Holy Redeemer of Teruel in 1188 and finally with the Templars in 1196. Some brothers resisted Templar control and took control over the border stronghold of Montfragüe. They later joined the order of Calatrava in 1221.

Certainly, the Spanish conquests in the south were gaining momentum and the above-mentioned city of Cordoba was merely the first of a series of major cities to fall. In 1238 James I of Aragon captured Valencia and in later years he consolidated his position in the surrounding region. Forces from Aragon and Castile-León, spearheaded by the order of Santiago, then conquered the region of Murcia, later signing a treaty in 1244 which divided the area but, by giving Castile access to the Western Mediterranean, closed Aragon's frontier with Islamic territory. With no Muslim neighbour, Aragon was free to deploy its crusading resources elsewhere. By the time of James' crusade in 1269, the Iberia military orders had been considering expanding their activities to new fronts for some time. In 1180 the order of Santiago had discussed the possibility of taking a role in the defence of Antioch [see **Doc. 3, p. 154**] and in 1206 the papacy suggested the order of Calatrava should fight in the Holy Land. Similar plans were put forward in later years and proposals were made to deploy the Iberian orders against: the Muslims in the Holy Land (1234, 1245); the pagans threatening Poland (1245); and the Mongols (1258). In 1246 Emperor Baldwin II of Constantinople signed an agreement with the order of Santiago in which he offered to pay 40,000 marks for 300 knights, 200 archers and 1000 infantry and the permanent establishment of the order in Constantinople, although this was never fulfilled. In the event these initiatives achieved little and no large-scale deployment of Iberian military orders was attempted during the thirteenth century. Even so, these actions demonstrate the belief that with the increasing security of Iberia, the local orders could be deployed elsewhere. After all, while they may have been established initially for the defence of Spain, they were ultimately instruments of the papacy, which was committed to the overall defence of Christendom.

The discussions surrounding the redeployment of the orders' resources were mirrored by changes in wider crusading policy and increasingly Spanish crusaders were encouraged to set off for Jerusalem. In 1239 King Thibaut of Navarre (who was also Count of Champagne) joined the Barons' Crusade, while in 1269, as we have seen, James I of Aragon launched his expedition to the east. The international orders of the Temple and Hospital likewise began to scale down their operations in Iberia and a study on the Aragonese Templars reveals a marked fall in their expenditure in this region during the later thirteenth century. The Aragonese Templars had always been expected to pay responsions to the Latin East, albeit at a lower rate: 10 per cent of income rather than 33 per cent, but now as the Muslim threat receded they needed to pour their resources into the beleaguered Latin East [see **Doc. 9, p. 164**] (Forey, 1973: 58–62, 323). This did not find favour with many rulers and in 1250 the papacy was forced to respond to complaints that they were not performing their military duties in Iberia.

Meanwhile, the warriors of Iberia continued to forge south. With the coronation of a new king, Sancho II, the armies of Portugal worked with the military orders to seize the Algarve; a project that was completed in 1250. The order of Santiago supported him in this endeavour and was richly rewarded with many of the newly conquered towns. Upon reaching the south coast, Portugal lost its frontier with Islam (the forces of Castile-León reached the straits of Gibraltar to the east at around the same time). Castile-León had made considerable advances conquering Jaén in 1246 and, two years later, the major city of Seville in November 1248. Again this expansion was achieved with considerable support from the knights of Santiago and the decision to attack Seville had been made on the advice of the order's master. The papacy supported the order's efforts and offered indulgences to their supporters.

Muslim power in Iberia was soon confined solely to the mountainous region of Granada. The Christians hedged this area with fortifications, many of which were under the control of the military orders, who maintained military pressure on its borders, but who were unable to complete the reconquest of Iberia until 1492. With much of the mainland secure, the main challenge for King Alfonso X of Castile-León (1252–1284) was to consolidate the land that had already been taken by his father and this was the imperative behind the many grants made to the military orders in newly conquered territory. In addition to Granada, the main Muslim threats to Castile were now invasion from North Africa and rebellion. To combat the danger of attack from across the Straits of Gibraltar, Alfonso supported the development of the small military order of San Maria de España, based at Cartagena, which was intended to provide naval forces to protect southern Iberia. In 1253 he similarly encouraged the order of Santiago to provide an armed galley to protect the south coast. The expansion of the Spanish kingdoms was, however, grinding to a halt. In 1260 Alfonso's forces attacked Salé on the African mainland, but despite many proposals, this was to be his only overseas venture against Islam. His energies on the Muslim frontier were expended primarily in resisting attacks from Granada and Morocco, while suppressing a series of Muslim revolts. Attempts were made to involve him more in the affairs of the Holy Land, but unlike James I, Alfonso showed little inclination to set sail for the east, supplying only limited money and troops. After the death of James I, Aragonese interest in the Holy Land also declined. The Spanish kings became increasingly embroiled in games of diplomacy both among themselves and with other Christian rulers. A new age was dawning. The Iberian kingdoms were no longer simply the beneficiaries of military aid from across the Pyrenees, but were taking their place in the foremost rank of European politics. The border with Granada and the ongoing struggle against Morocco gave crusaders and military orders employment, but this was now only one duty among many and was only occasionally the focus; the momentum of the early thirteenth century had subsided.

Further reading

Burns, R.I. (1975) 'Immigrants from Islam: The Crusaders' Use of Muslims as Settlers in Thirteenth-Century Spain', *American Historical Review*, 80, 21–42.

Estow, C. (1982) 'The Economic Development of the Order of Calatrava, 1158–1366', *Speculum*, 57, 267–291.

Forey, A.J. (1973) *The Templars in the Corona de Aragón*. London: Oxford University Press.

Forey, A.J. (1984) 'The Military Orders and the Spanish Reconquest in the Twelfth and Thirteenth Centuries', *Traditio*, 40, 197–234.

Lay, S. (2009) *The Reconquest Kings of Portugal: Political Cultural Reorientation on the Medieval Frontier*. Basingstoke: Palgrave Macmillan.

Lomax, D. (1958) 'The Order of Santiago and the Kings of León', *Hispania: Revista epsañola de Historia*, 18, 3–37.

Morton, N. (2010) 'Institutional Dependency upon Secular and Ecclesiastical Patrons and the Foundations of the Trial of the Templars', in J. Burgtorf, P. Crawford and H. Nicholson (eds) *The Debate on the Trial of the Templars (1307–1314)*. Aldershot: Ashgate, 33–44.

O'Callaghan, J.F. (1975) *The Spanish Order of Calatrava and its Affiliates*. London: Variorum Reprints.

O'Callaghan, J.F. (1986) 'The Order of Calatrava: Years of Crisis and Survival, 1158–1212', in V. Goss and C. Verzár (eds) *The Meeting of Two Worlds: Cultural Exchange between East and West during the Period of the Crusades*. Kalamazoo, MI: Medieval Institute Publications, 419–430.

O'Callaghan, J.F. (2003) *Reconquest and Crusade in Medieval Spain*. Philadelphia, PA: University of Pennsylvania Press.

Purkis, W. (2008) *Crusading Spirituality in the Holy Land and Iberia, c.1095–c.1187*. Woodbridge: Boydell and Brewer.

Chronology

1085 *6 May*	Conquest of Toledo.
1122	Formation of the Confraternity of Belchite.
1128	Foundation of the Confraternity of Monreal del Campo.
1147 *21 October*	The armies of the Second Crusade conquer Lisbon.
1131	Alfonso I of Aragon writes his will granting his kingdom to the Templars, Hospitallers and the Canons of the Holy Sepulchre.
1158	Foundation of the order of Calatrava.
1165	The Portuguese conquer Évora.
1170	Foundation of the brethren of Cáceres (the future order of Santiago).
*c.***1173**	Foundation of the order of Mountjoy.
1176	Foundation of the order of Évora (the future order of Avis).
	The confraternity of San Julian del Pereiro (the future order of Alcántara) receives papal approval.
1177	Alfonso VIII of Castile captures Cuenca.
1195 *17 July*	The battle of Alarcos.
1201	The creation of the order of St George of Alfama in Aragon.
1211	The fortress of Salvatierra (headquarters of the order of Calatrava) falls to Caliph al-Nasir.
1212 *16 July*	Battle of Las Navas de Tolosa.
1230	Ferdinand III of Castile becomes king of León unifying the two kingdoms.
1236 *29 June*	Ferdinand III of Castile and León conquers Cordoba.
1238	James I of Aragon conquers Valencia.
1248 *November*	Ferdinand III of Castile and León conquers Seville.
1260	Alfonso X attacks Salé.
1269	James I of Aragon sets out for the Holy Land.

4

The Defence of the Holy Land, 1188–1291

1188–1228: THE STRUGGLE FOR THE EASTERN MEDITERRANEAN

By late 1188 the kingdom of Jerusalem had collapsed. Only Tyre, Tripoli, Antioch and a few castles had survived Saladin's onslaught following the catastrophe at Hattin. Jerusalem itself fell in October 1187 and news of its loss provoked outrage across Western Europe. Pope Urban III is said to have died from the shock. Nine days later his successor Gregory VIII launched a new crusade with a single goal: to retake Jerusalem.

The reaction to this call was enormous with contingents and armies being sent from across Christendom. Between 1189 and 1192 wave after wave of crusaders reached the east, slowly turning the tide against Saladin's forces. Their first major achievement was the recapture of the port of Acre in 1191. This siege lasted for two years, during which Saladin and the Christian army wrestled for supremacy outside the walls. The mortality rate on both sides was enormous and disease was rife. In response to the very obvious need for medical care and the burial of hundreds of corpses, a band of German crusaders established a hospice. The order's early legends report that this was established under the shade of a ship's sail. In time, this small establishment would rise to become a major military order on the scale of the Templars or Hospitallers: the Teutonic Knights. At the same time a group of English crusaders founded a house of canons regular dedicated to St Thomas of Canterbury to provide medical/burial services and also to ransom Christian captives. This establishment would become the military order of St Thomas of Acre. Having captured Acre, the crusading army, led by Richard I of England, scored a series of further victories against Saladin, but it was unable to restore Jerusalem. Richard's achievement was to regain control over the coastal lands running from Acre to Jaffa. He also captured Cyprus; a rich and strategically important island close to the mainland. The rebuilding of the kingdom of Jerusalem had begun.

From this point, the Teutonic hospital and the canons of St Thomas met very different fortunes. The Teutonic Knights flourished. According to one thirteenth-century account created by the order, at the siege of Acre the son of the former German emperor, Duke Frederick of Swabia, was so impressed by the hospital's work that he wrote to his brother, Emperor Henry VI of Germany, asking him to represent its interests to the papacy. Henry agreed and in doing so immediately connected the order to two major patrons: the papacy and the German emperors. German influence in the Eastern Mediterranean was rising at this time and in 1197 Henry VI launched a new crusade to the Holy Land during which the rulers of Cyprus and Armenia chose to accept Henry as their overlord. Towards the end of the expedition a group of leading German noblemen, with the support of the nobility of the Latin East, took the decision to transform the Teutonic hospital into a military order. Over the next two decades, German emperors, imperial nobles, pilgrims, Armenian kings, the rulers of the Latin East and, to a lesser extent, the papacy offered considerable support to the order. All these groups were committed to the rebuilding of the Latin East and they expressed this determination in part through patronage to the Teutonic Knights.

In c.1209 the Teutonic Knights appointed one of their most famous masters, Hermann von Salza. Hermann took control at a time when the kingdom of Jerusalem was frequently protected by long truces. Saladin had died in 1193 and his descendants were generally prepared to sign treaties with the Christians so that they could pursue their private quarrels. Hermann was highly ambitious for his order and at these times of peace, as we shall see, he began to open new fronts in Hungary and later in Prussia and Livonia. The event, however, which really brought the Teutonic Knights to Western Christendom's attention, was the Fifth Crusade. This campaign's primary objective was to conquer Egypt so that the Nile Delta's resources could then fund the recapture of Jerusalem. The crusade gathered in 1217 at Acre and, having staged a number of raiding expeditions, it attacked Egypt, capturing the city of Damietta in 1219. The army then moved south down the Nile in 1221 but was heavily defeated by the Ayyubid sultan of Egypt, al-Kāmil (Ayyubid: members of Saladin's family – Saladin's father was called Ayyub).

Although the crusade was a failure, Hermann von Salza used this operation to showcase his order's capabilities. He offered considerable support to German crusaders, many of whom affiliated themselves with the order. He also acted as an agent to both the papacy and Emperor Frederick II (Emperor Henry VI's son), carrying news and conducting negotiations, while demonstrating his own value as a counsellor. His personal qualities ensured that he was included in all the major councils. In this way, he compensated for his order's still limited military resources and was treated with the respect accorded to the powerful masters of the Temple and Hospital. In the wake of the campaign, many pilgrims and the papacy showered gifts and privileges upon the order, demonstrating how impressed they were by the order's work. Chroniclers also began to describe the Templars, Hospitallers and Teutonic Knights as the 'three houses', demonstrating their belief that Teutonic Knights had entered the ranks of the leading military orders.

The canons of St Thomas did not fare nearly so well. Militarised in 1228 by the bishop of Winchester, they were granted the Teutonic Knights' rule – an act which demonstrates how far they had fallen behind their former peer. Unlike the Teutonic Knights, they had not almost instantly gained active patrons. Reflecting on their early history in 1236, Pope Gregory IX commented that Richard I had not been able to support the order as much as he might have wished. In later years, it gained some properties, largely in England, but these were located too far from the Holy Land to offer much assistance. The canons also lacked both the energies of a master like Hermann von Salza and the opportunity to showcase their virtues in the same way that the Teutons had during the Fifth Crusade. In 1228 Pope Gregory IX reported that they had been living in a dissolute lifestyle and, if true, this would only have served as a further discouragement for potential benefactors. The contrast between these two institutions is striking and demonstrates some of the key factors behind the success or failure of a military order. While both were founded to answer a direct need during the siege of Acre, clearly the transformation of a minor hospice into a leading military order was a major process involving the support of highly important patrons, conspicuous and well-reported achievements, an obviously pious lifestyle and an active master.

By 1228, despite the limited success of the crusades launched between 1187 and 1221, the Latin East was reviving and the military orders were playing an active role in this process. The Hospitallers and Templars in particular were vital to the reconstruction. Both had lost their properties in Jerusalem, but they re-established their headquarters in Acre and were compensated in part by properties on Cyprus. The Latin East's fundamental needs were for troops, settlers, money and – with the loss of so many rural estates – food. To supply these shortfalls, both orders could draw upon their western commanderies and the Hospitallers demanded that commanders make a greater contribution than simply the responsions. They also sent out letters of appeal, seeking aid from foreign monarchs. With this money, they were able to re-fortify and re-supply their major castles across the Levant.

This was a period of rising Latin dominance in the Eastern Mediterranean. In 1204 the Fourth Crusade, an expedition originally destined for Egypt, conquered the Byzantine capital in Constantinople. Subsequently, ambitious nobles carved-up large areas of the Byzantine Empire, creating a series of kingdoms, principalities and most importantly the Latin Empire of Constantinople. Like the rulers of the Spanish Reconquest, these leaders saw the potential of the military orders as instruments of territorial conquest and sought to gain their support. The evidence for the orders' involvement is scant, but it seems that the Templars played an important role in the conquest of Greece in 1205–1210. Perhaps they hoped that they would develop large estates in this region which could then pump resources directly into the Holy Land. All three of the main orders gained land in Achaia in 1210, but none of them subsequently proved willing to commit themselves heavily in this area; their focus was on the Holy Land. In 1222 Pope Honorius III confirmed the adoption of a military role by the former Byzantine hospice of St Sampson in Constantinople; an institution sponsored by the Latin rulers of Constantinople. This marked the creation of a new military order, designed to defend Constantinople against the Greeks. Nevertheless, it did not prosper. Interest in this order, like interest in crusading in the Aegean, always took a poor second place to the Latin East. The order of St Sampson was eventually incorporated into the Hospitaller Order in 1309 (Stathakopoulos, 2006).

CONFLICTS OF INTERESTS (PATRONS 2)

When Emperor Frederick II of Germany landed at Acre on 7 September 1228 he brought with him a long-desired crusading army which was designed to retake Jerusalem. Frederick himself had sworn to go on crusade in 1215, but had prevaricated when invited to join the Fifth Crusade. In later years, Hermann von Salza and other leaders from the kingdom of Jerusalem had laboured continually to persuade Frederick to set out, even helping him to become king of Jerusalem in 1225, and his eventual arrival at Acre in 1228 marked the fulfilment of their efforts. At the sight of him the Templars and Hospitallers fell to the ground and kissed his knees in relief. Even so, this joy was tainted by the knowledge that, shortly before his departure, Frederick had been excommunicated by Pope Gregory IX. Gregory claimed that Frederick had postponed his departure for the east for too long and even the emperor's arrival in the east did not mollify him. More importantly for the military orders, he ordered the Templars, Hospitallers and Teutonic Knights not to co-operate with the imperial forces.

This demand confronted the orders with a conflict of interests – should they obey the instructions of the papacy or collaborate with the emperor? On one hand, they were duty bound to support Frederick who was present in the east and was prepared to aid in the recovery of the kingdom of Jerusalem.

Furthermore, all three orders had extensive lands across Fredrick's various kingdoms and disobedience, particularly at such a crucial moment, could result in the confiscation of these properties. On the other, the orders were religious institutions owing obedience directly to the Church. As we have seen the papacy had previously offered them protection, privileges and encouraged their patrons. It also had the ability to censure or even to dissolve an order. Defying the pope was a serious business. In the event each order tried to manage this delicate diplomatic predicament by attempting to appease both patrons and all were unsuccessful.

From Acre, Frederick travelled to Jaffa. The Hospitallers and Templars marched one day behind the imperial army seemingly in the hope that by doing so they could claim (to Frederick) that they had not abandoned the imperial army, but (to Rome) they were not supporting a papal enemy. They later jettisoned this policy and joined the army but specified that they were not under the emperor's command. The Teutonic Knights were prepared to offer Frederick greater support but then they were more closely tied to the imperial expedition. They had played a leading role in the preparations for Frederick's crusade and the bulk of their estates were in imperial territory. Thus, they could not simply abandon so important a benefactor, but neither could they ignore their obligations to the Church. In the event, Hermann assisted the crusade, where it could be of benefit to the Holy Land. He later acted as one of the emissaries to the Egyptian Sultan al-Kamil, who signed a treaty, the most important clause of which was the restoration of Jerusalem. This naturally was a momentous achievement for both the crusade and Frederick, but it caused further problems for the Teutonic Order.

When the crusade arrived in the holy city, Frederick expressed a wish both to hear Mass and to perform a crown-wearing ceremony in the Church of the Holy Sepulchre. As an excommunicate this was absolutely unacceptable in the eyes of the papacy. Moreover, Frederick demanded that Hermann both attend the event and translate a speech he planned to make which included references to his dealings with the papacy. Up to this point, Hermann had been prepared to support the crusade, but none of his actions had suggested any active partisanship against the pontiff. Agreeing to this demand, however, as he well knew, would expose him to retribution from Rome. In the event, he tried to strike a compromise, giving the speech on Fredrick's behalf, but persuading him not to hear mass. Document 5 [p. 157] is Hermann's desperate appeal to Gregory, explaining his predicament and attempting to reassure him of his continued loyalty. This appeal, however, was unsuccessful. Gregory had already received news of Hermann's actions from a more hostile source and his punishment was to strip the Teutonic Knights of their independence and to place them under the control of the Hospitallers. Hermann's attempts to balance his loyalties to emperor, papacy and crusade had failed. The Hospitallers and Templars also did not escape unscathed. The Templars particularly were angered by various clauses in Frederick's treaty, not least the agreement that the Muslims could retain control of the Temple (the Templars' former headquarters). Both orders opposed the treaty on strategic grounds. Rumours also circulated among the Templars' detractors that the order planned to assassinate the emperor [see Matthew Paris' comments in **Doc. 7, p. 161**].

Frederick was not popular in the Eastern Mediterranean. Before arriving at Acre, Frederick had landed on Cyprus where he had threatened the Ibelins, a leading baronial family. The Ibelins controlled the city of Beirut and were acting as regent for the king of Cyprus who was still a child. Frederick had demanded both this city and the regency for himself. This caused immense anger and when coupled with the Church's hostility towards him as an excommunicate, an atmosphere of resistance developed. Relations deteriorated and in May 1229 Frederick's forces besieged the Templar headquarters in Acre and upon returning to Italy he ordered the confiscation of the Templars' and Hospitallers' Sicilian estates. This act cut off an important area of support and damaged both orders' supply lines to the east.

These events underline an inherent problem for the orders. Technically, they had no business involving themselves with any matter other than the defence of Christendom's frontiers or providing charitable services. Even so, their reliance on patrons made requests for assistance difficult to refuse. In this case, caught in a struggle between two important benefactors, all three orders were trapped between competing demands from either side. Attempts to maintain a neutral position were aggravated by escalating events and by 1229 all three were perceived to have taken sides, provoking censure from the slighted party. This scenario highlights an inherent tension in these patronage-dependent institutions. With supporters across Christendom, warfare on any scale between patrons had the potential to place them in such a predicament. The division of power between the Church and Christendom's secular powers was one such area of conflict and the military orders could find their loyalties irrevocably torn.

In the event all three orders managed to rebuild their damaged relations. In the case of the Teutonic Knights, Hermann von Salza hurried to Italy immediately after Frederick's departure where he helped to negotiate a settlement between emperor and pope. The pope later issued a document supporting the construction of their fortress of Montfort in the hills of Galilee [**Doc. 6, p. 159**]. The Templars and Hospitallers were eventually able to restore their Sicilian estates. Even so, this had been an extremely dangerous episode in which the orders had each suffered censure and chastisement. Patronage was double-edged; it could either elevate an order or, if removed, cripple it.

COMPETITION BETWEEN MILITARY ORDERS

Among the Christian territories of the Near East, the kingdom of Armenia was the least affected by the defeat at Hattin in 1187. The Armenians had suffered from raiding by Saladin's troops but, unlike the Frankish territories to the south, their lands were left fundamentally intact. For the Armenian ruler Leon II, this created an opportunity to expand his territories at the expense of the devastated principality of Antioch. Armenia and Antioch were divided for a long stretch by the Amanus Mountains; a range with only a few passes. One of these was controlled by the Templars' castle of Baghras, which was located in the principality of Antioch. This castle had fallen to Saladin in 1188, but in 1191 Armenian troops recaptured it from its Muslim garrison. Shortly afterwards it became clear that Leon had no intention of returning it to the Templars; an act that both infuriated the order and threatened the prince of Antioch. This marked the beginning of a confrontation between these two Christian states and the military orders found themselves on opposing sides. The Templars naturally backed Antioch. Initially the Hospitallers followed suit, but in 1204 they transferred their support to Armenia after receiving significant landholdings. The Teutonic Knights also favoured the Armenians. There was a growing bond between the German emperors and Armenia and in 1211 Hermann von Salza accompanied an imperial emissary to offer a new crown to Leon II. In 1212, in gratitude, Leon gave the order the castle of Amudain. This episode underlines a crucial problem for the orders. Although disputes among Christians were technically not their concern they could hardly remain neutral if their own lands were seized in a war between rival rulers. Furthermore, financial or political incentives could compel orders to interest themselves in such conflicts, provoking divisions in their own ranks.

Disputes between military orders occurred on a variety of issues, not least where one order attempted to control or influence another. Very few military orders were entirely unique establishments. As Figure 1 shows, the Templars had close institutional ties to many other orders, including those which adopted their rule and those which they took over. The Templars also allowed smaller orders to assume aspects of their identity; for example they permitted the Order of St Thomas of Acre and the Teutonic Knights to wear their white mantles. These connections were often advantageous to all parties, but they could be a source of conflict and in 1210 the Templars wrote to the papacy, complaining that the Teutonic Knights no longer had a right to wear these mantles but were still doing so. The cause of the Templars' wrath is unclear. A likely explanation, however, is that relations deteriorated

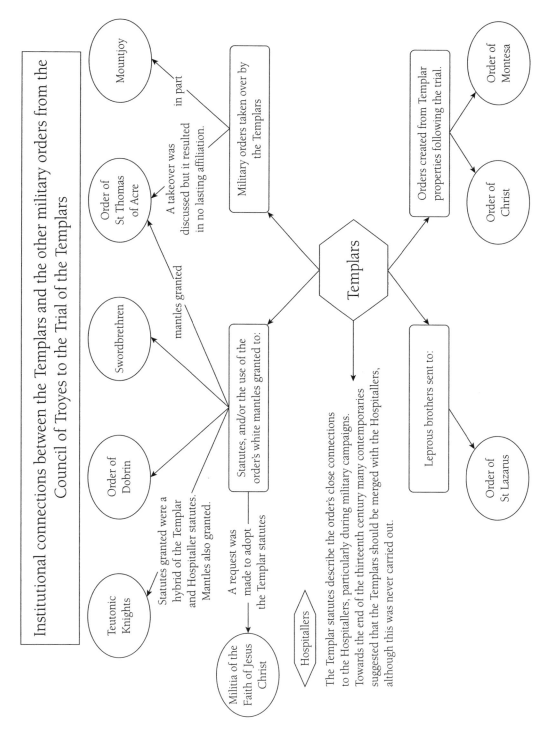

Figure 1 The Templars' institutional affiliations

when the two orders backed different parties in the above-mentioned Armenia/Antioch war. In later years Templar demands on this issue continued and letters of protest survive from 1222 and 1230. Seemingly political differences had broken their earlier accord.

Disagreements did not always hamper the orders' work or prevent them from maintaining generally cordial relations. In 1258 the Teutonic Knights, Templars and Hospitallers signed a treaty of co-operation which contained detailed systems for the resolution of disputes and the provision of mutual support. It reflects an attempt to identify potentially controversial issues in advance to maintain stable relations. The orders of Calatrava and Santiago likewise signed a number of *Hermanndades* (pacts of brotherhood), dating from 1182. The first of these settled existing points of concern and both parties swore to maintain amity. Later agreements established a framework for dispute settlement and mutual co-operation on campaign in Iberia. In 1224 Templars and Hospitallers became included in these pacts (O'Callaghan, 1969). In this way, the orders in Castile and León were generally able to manage their relations effectively, even though these two kingdoms were frequently at war with both the Almohads and each other. Generally speaking, it was not in the orders' interests to fight among themselves; lengthy court cases and appeals could be both expensive and damaging.

Despite the desirability of concord between orders, in 1306–1307 the Templar master James of Molay cast an entirely different perspective on the well-known rivalry between his order and the Hospitallers in a letter to the papacy. He reminded the pope that competition can be a useful thing and that his order and the Hospitallers prospered precisely because they wanted to exceed the achievements of the other order. He cited examples ranging from their conduct in battle through to their supply of foodstuffs to the Holy Land demonstrating that without such rivalry, part of the motivation to succeed might be lost.

1230–1260

Frederick II departed for Italy under a hail of offal thrown by the butchers of Acre, leaving behind him a troubled legacy. Jerusalem, Nazareth and Bethlehem had been restored, but they were poorly protected. More importantly, civil war broke out almost immediately between his officials and the local barons both on the mainland and on Cyprus. This was a conflict that the Latin East could ill afford if it was to recover its former strength. Fortunately for them, the Ayyubid rulers of Syria were too occupied with their own rivalries to take advantage of this disunity, while Frederick's treaty with Egypt in 1229 gave the kingdom of Jerusalem 10 years of peace.

Civil war among the Christians in the Levant was hardly in the military orders' interests and their commanders generally avoided taking too partisan a role on either side. As we have seen, they were accustomed to acting as mediators and Hermann von Salza's services were again in demand to broker an agreement. In the event, negotiations eventually failed in 1236 but by this time the imperial forces were already on the back foot. They were forced from Cyprus by 1233 and finally from the Levantine mainland in 1243. Despite these hostilities, the Latin East was regaining its former strength. After the expiration of the truce with the Egyptians in 1239 a new crusading army arrived (the Barons' Crusade) in the kingdom of Jerusalem. Militarily it achieved little, but the crusade's leaders established treaties with neighbouring Muslim rulers that restored much of the former kingdom. The military orders were also enhancing their position. They acquired lands both on Cyprus and on the mainland and the Hospitallers in particular established a great territorial block to the north of the Lebanese mountains that centred on their fortresses of Crac des Chevaliers and Margat. By the 1260s the order dominated the surrounding region and received tribute from most of their Muslim neighbours. The Teutonic Knights likewise built up their lands in the hills of Galilee and in Armenia. Commercially the kingdom of Jerusalem's great port cities of Acre and Tyre were conducting a brisk trade in goods brought from across Asia for exchange with products from Europe. The revenue derived from this commerce was so great that when Richard of Cornwall visited the Latin East between 1240–1241 he was told by the military orders that revenues from Acre alone amounted to 50,000 pounds of silver, which if true was a greater sum than the annual income of the king of England (Riley-Smith, 1973: 64). By 1243, the kingdom was smaller than it had been pre-Hattin, but it was extremely rich and was fortified by a dense network of highly sophisticated fortresses.

The Latin East may have recovered its status as a first-rate power, but in the following years the Middle East as a whole was challenged by the new world superpower. Rumours had abounded for many years about the rise of the Mongols in Central Asia and the Muslim writer Ibn al-Athir began to record tales of their attacks from the early thirteenth century. Under Chinggis Khan (d. 1227), Mongol armies launched repeated campaigns on their neighbours and between 1219 and 1223 destroyed the empire of Khwārazm (modern-day Iran and Turkmenistan). Their relentless advance caused widespread alarm and provoked a wave of refugees fleeing west towards the Levant. In this unsettled atmosphere, the Egyptian Sultan al-Salih Ayyub sought an alliance with a large group of refugee Khwārazmians. They agreed to his proposals and travelled south from the Jazira to meet the Egyptian forces at Gaza. On their way in July 1244 they attacked Jerusalem, massacring its Latin inhabitants. Facing these combined forces, the kingdom of Jerusalem and its ally, the Sultan of Damascus, marched out to meet them. The Christian army was roughly of the same size as that which had been deployed at Hattin in 1187, with perhaps half the total knights provided by the military orders. The resulting encounter, known as the battle of La Forbie (October 1244), was a catastrophe for the Christians and Damascenes. They suffered a heavy defeat and there were few survivors from the military orders' squadrons. In the years that followed the Latin East was closely assailed and its predicament was further imperilled by the disruption caused by the Mongols to the great Asiatic trade routes – commercial arteries that were vital for its prosperity. Furthermore, large bands of Turkic tribesmen began to enter the Levant, fleeing Mongol advances and raiding Muslim and Christian lands.

One such band attacked Antioch in 1248, but by this time help was at hand. In December 1244 Louis IX of France had taken the cross and by 1248 his army was assembling on Cyprus. He sent 600 crossbowmen to Antioch, but his primary objective, like that of many crusaders, was Egypt. In this endeavour, he was joined by Levantine Christian forces and all the major military orders. In June 1249 he attacked Damietta, capturing the city almost immediately. As with Christian conquests across the Mediterranean, the military orders were immediately granted properties within the city, presumably to secure their long-term interest in its defence. In November the army set out south to attack Cairo, following a branch of the Nile. The army's progress, however, was blocked by the Egyptian army which had stationed itself outside Mansura, a town on the far bank of a Nile tributary. Heavy fighting ensued which culminated on 8 February 1250 in a highly successful cavalry assault on the Muslim camp. The Christian knights however overplayed their hand and charged directly into the town of Mansura where they became trapped in narrow alleyways and were destroyed. Shortly afterwards, with the outbreak of illness and the arrival of Muslim reinforcements, the crusaders were forced into a retreat which quickly became a rout. Louis and many of his soldiers were captured or slain; the campaign had failed.

After his release, Louis remained in the Holy Land until 1254. He was concerned that if he left immediately then the entire Christian position might crumble. During this time he worked to improve the fortifications of many Christian cities and to protect the Muslim frontier. Meanwhile, affairs in the Muslim world were in flux. In 1250 the Ayyubid dynasty in Egypt was usurped by leaders from among its slave-soldiers (known as mamluks). Their brutal assumption of power enraged the other Ayyubid rulers of Syria, provoking war. Louis was not in a position to take military advantage of the turmoil, but in 1254 he was able to secure a 10-year truce with Damascus.

While the Christian and Muslim rulers of the Near East struggled with one another, the Mongol advance continued. In 1258 Baghdad fell to their forces and in 1260 they seized both Aleppo and Damascus. With an army numbering over 100,000 troops, the Mongols could outfight any of the Levantine powers and their entry into Syria threatened Christian and Muslim alike. In this climate of fear, Ayyubid resistance in Syria collapsed in the face of a Mongol invasion and in 1260 the Christians in Acre took the advice of the master of the Teutonic Knights and decided if possible to avoid any confrontation. Only the Egyptian Mamluks marched out to face the invader. In the event the confrontation between the Mongol and Mamluk forces proved to be something of an anticlimax. The vast majority of the Mongol force had withdrawn from the region shortly beforehand on receiving news of the death of the Great Khan in Mongolia. The force encountered by the Mamluks was merely a Mongol rearguard, which was defeated at the battle of Ayn Jalut in September 1260. In the following months, Mamluk forces took control in Damascus and Aleppo filling the political vacuum left by the retreating Mongols. At the conclusion of these advances the Mamluks virtually encircled the Latin East on its landward borders.

THE ECONOMICS OF DEFEAT (FINANCES 3)

In the wake of Ayn Jalut 1260, a Christian army including a large contingent of Templars, marched out to confront a group of Turcoman tribes. The expedition was a fiasco resulting in heavy casualties. For the order as a whole this was simply one further setback to add to a catalogue of defeats including Darbsak in 1237 (100 brother knights lost), La Forbie in 1244 (c. 300 brother knights lost) and Mansura 1250 (280 cavalry lost). In each case the number of casualties among the knightly brethren would only have been a fraction of the total losses sustained, which would have included infantry, crossbowmen, light cavalry along with their equipment and horses. Financially, the cost of equipping, training and then transporting the requisite number of replacement personnel to the east, while ransoming those in captivity, would have been enormous; far beyond the resources of even an important Levantine nobleman. The Templars, like the Hospitallers and Teutonic Knights, however, had the financial muscle both to absorb these costs and to rebuild their strength even when faced with repeated defeats. Their great advantage was their international network of estates and diplomatic contacts in the west which they could call upon to rebuild their armed might. Contemplating the defeats of Louis IX's crusade the **marshal** of the Teutonic Order wrote:

Marshal: In the military orders, this official was an order's main military commander.

> It is not only we who have fallen into such straits; the Templars and Hospitallers, both rich and powerful, cannot furnish a third or even a

quarter of the service they did previously, and if they did not have large incomes in various parts of the world they would hardly be able to get out of the pit of their debts.

(tr. Barber and Bate, 2010: 152–153)

In addition to the annual revenues they received from the west the orders could draw further resources from these estates in a number of ways. Property could be used as collateral for loans. This was a relatively common practice and in 1260, fearing a Mongol invasion, Thomas Bérard, master of the Templars, attempted to raise funds by offering his order's crosses, chalices and other gold and silver ornaments as security. An order might also liquidate its assets. This was an extreme reaction because orders relied on their agricultural and urban properties for their regular income. It did occur at times however and, following a defeat in the principality of Antioch in 1149, the Templar master, then in Western Europe, received a letter from his brethren in the east stating: 'sell everything you can and bring the proceeds to us yourself so that we may live on' (tr. Barber and Bate, 2010: 49). Following Hattin and later in the thirteenth century the orders frequently resorted to this expedient to maintain their readiness in the east.

Commanders in Western Europe could also approach their benefactors at times of trouble to request additional support. Many people across Christendom wanted to help the Holy Land, particularly following a crisis, and in such cases donating money or land to a local military order was one of the safest ways of ensuring that such endowments were used for this purpose. Indeed, the rise of the Hospitallers' English estates has been explained in part by the outcry following the fall of Edessa in 1144 and the failure of the Second Crusade (Gervers, 1994: 3). The military orders encouraged this process, promoting the image of themselves as international representatives of the Latin East, even designing many of their church buildings across Europe to resemble the rotunda of the Church of the Holy Sepulchre; a visible reminder that a gift to them was a gift to Jerusalem. The papacy supported the orders in these efforts and in 1188, following Hattin, Pope Clement III wrote to churchmen across Europe encouraging them to make donations to the Hospitallers and Templars, citing their recent losses.

In cases where a defeat was largely specific to one order, other orders might offer aid. After the Templar defeat at Darbsak, the Hospitallers organised the despatch of new forces for the east seemingly in an effort to offer their assistance. Thirty knights were assembled at the order's English headquarters at Clerkenwell (then just outside London). Strikingly, this squadron first processed through the city surrounded by cheering crowds. For an order that was built on patronage and public goodwill, such a display would have done no harm for their cause.

DECLINE AND FALL, 1260–1291

The Mamluk victory at Ayn Jalut redrew the political map of the Near East. The primary confrontation now would not be between Ayyubid princes and the Latin East, but between the Mamluks and the Mongols. The frontline in this conflict became the river Euphrates and for the Mamluk Sultan, Baybars (d. 1277), what was left of the Latin East was – strategically – a secondary concern. The greatest threat to him was a second full-scale Mongol invasion into Syria, but while an intense frontier war was conducted by both sides, the next major Mongol invasion would not take place until 1281. This gave the increasingly powerful Mamluk army many opportunities to stage campaigns against the Latin East.

Between 1261 and 1271 Baybars launched multiple attacks on Christian territory and losses among the military orders were high. The Christian forces were in no position to chance a battle with the Mamluks, whose armed might was now far greater than their own. In a major raid on the kingdom of Armenia in 1266 the Mamluks took the Teutonic Knights' castle of Amudain and in 1271 they took the brethren's fortress of Montfort. The Templars and Hospitallers also lost many major fortresses including Arsur in 1265, Safad and Beaufort in 1266 and Chastel-Blanc, Crac des Chevaliers and Gibelacar in 1271. Baybars took Antioch in 1268 and massacred the population, prompting the evacuation of fortresses across northern Syria. Some attempts were made to take the offensive but these were raiding operations rather than serious attempts to blunt Mamluk advances. In April 1272 news of a Mongol attack provoked Baybars to agree a truce with the kingdom of Jerusalem for 10 years and 10 months, bringing this catalogue of defeats to an end.

By 1272 most of the military orders' great fortresses had fallen. The Latin East was confined to only a few coastal settlements. In 1267 Baybars had surprised and massacred agricultural labourers working just outside the walls of Acre and advanced to the gates of the city; nowhere was safe. The ongoing Mamluk raids had shattered the military orders' agricultural lands on the frontier and their revenue plummeted. They could still draw upon their overseas estates, but these were not sufficient to bear so heavy a load. Writing to King Edward I of England, the Templar master commented:

> We have found the state of the House of the Temple weaker and more fragile than it ever was in the past; food is lacking, there are many expenses, revenues are almost non-existent.
>
> (tr. Barber and Bate, 2010: 163)

Food stocks – particularly grain – were a major concern. This had always been a critical issue throughout the thirteenth century, but with the frequent

Mamluk invasions of the 1260s, there was no certainty that any crops would survive until harvest and so it was necessary to import on a large scale. Surviving export licences from Iberia, Sicily and Italy demonstrate that the military orders were among the leading importers of food [**Doc. 9, p. 164**]. Grain became immensely precious and failure to receive and store it carefully could result in hefty punishments. According to a Templar account, on one occasion a Templar vessel arrived in Acre carrying wheat. The brother in charge of the granary inspected the cargo and found that it had become damp in the ship's hold and suggested that it should be spread on a terrace to be dried by the sun. Even so, the brother responsible did not follow this instruction immediately and sent the grain straight to the granary. When he later ordered the grain to be dried, much of it was found to be ruined and he was placed in irons; clearly this matter was taken very seriously.

As costs spiralled, the Templars' and Hospitallers' finances descended into crisis. Studies on the purchases made by the orders across Christendom demonstrate that from the mid-thirteenth century acquisitions of property declined steeply, while other documents speak of defaults on loans and the sale of estates (Bronstein, 2005). Donations also decreased in many areas, a trend common to many monastic institutions in the thirteenth century. As we shall see in Chapter 7, many families with long crusading traditions proved less inclined to take the long road to the Holy Land. These difficulties were only exacerbated by the ongoing political infighting in the kingdom of Jerusalem. Between 1225 and 1268 the throne of Jerusalem was occupied by Frederick II and his heirs, but they were deeply unpopular absentee monarchs. In practice power fell into the hands of the patriarch of Jerusalem, the *bailli* (representative of the king), the leaders of the Italian trading cities and the military orders. Between them, these magnates could dispose of the vast majority of the kingdom's military, commercial and spiritual power. After the papacy's formal deposition of Frederick's remaining descendants in 1267 the throne was claimed by King Hugh III of Cyprus. He found, however, that his claim was not uncontested. Another candidate, Maria of Antioch, emerged and received the backing of the Templars.

Following years of disputes, Hugh left the kingdom in 1276 raging that interference from the Templars made it impossible to rule. This statement – albeit spoken in anger – underlines the level of authority that the military orders had acquired. We saw in the previous chapter (looking at the rebellion against Alfonso X of Castile) that over-mighty military orders could endanger to the crown and here again we see the same danger in operation. Like Solomon's legendary watchdogs, they could pose a threat to the very institutions they were created to defend. By the 1270s they had been weakened by the Mamluk wars but clearly they retained enough power to assert their own policies. By 1277 Maria's Templar-backed claim to the throne had been purchased by Count Charles of Anjou, who was in the process of building a Mediterranean empire for himself. His officials arrived in Acre the same year and ruled in his name until 1286.

Ruled by royal absentees and competing claimants, the kingdom's fragile stability was jeopardised further by the rivalries between the Italian cities of Genoa, Pisa and Venice, for whom the ports of Acre, Tyre and Tripoli were important trading posts. The military orders were implicated in these and many other disputes in the fractured political world of the declining Latin East. They were aware, however, of the need to establish stability and although their interests often forced them to take sides, they also worked hard where possible to mediate and negotiate settlements between embittered parties. In 1286, for example, following the death of Charles of Anjou, the King of Cyprus landed at Acre with a strong force asserting a right to rule. Aware that conflict between the Cypriots and Charles' representatives was a distinct possibility, the Templars, Hospitallers and Teutonic Knights intervened and arranged a peaceful handover. The military orders – the Teutonic Knights and Hospitallers particularly – also helped to arbitrate between the Italian cities, attempting to bring an end to their maritime battles and brawling street wars. In the diplomatic sphere, the orders' commanders often represented the Christian powers in their dealings with Muslim leaders and brethren were among the ambassadors sent to arrange truces in the twelfth and thirteenth centuries, including the above-mentioned 1272 treaty with Baybars.

In late May 1291 John of Villiers, master of the Hospital, wrote to his subordinate in southern France to inform him that Acre, the capital of the kingdom of Jerusalem, had fallen. He composed this letter in a great deal of physical pain, having been wounded during the final defence of the city on 18 May 1291. He only escaped himself because his servants had dragged him bodily into one of the last ships to leave. The Templar master had not been so lucky and John reports that he saw him fall, mortally injured, from a spear wound. By 1291 this end had long been inevitable. The Latin East was divided internally and was considerably weaker than its Mamluk adversary. Moreover, it had been decades since a major crusade had arrived from the west. After a heavy defeat in 1281 the Mongols no longer posed the threat they had to the Mamluks and, although the 1272 treaty with the Mamluks had been renewed for a further 10 years in June 1283, the Muslim forces had only required a strategically propitious moment to suppress the Christian territories entirely.

Ultimately, the Templars, Hospitallers and the military orders of the Middle East had failed in their primary role: to defend the Holy Land. Even so the task they faced, involving the maintenance of a Christian position deep within enemy territory and hundreds of miles from the nearest Catholic outpost, was always highly ambitious. The military orders' achievement (if so it can be called) was to adapt and employ existing monastic structures to rally and organise international support for the Latin East while drawing upon the discipline and rigour of the monastic life to create a cadre of highly trained, economically rational and ideologically committed administrators and warriors. Although the Latin East was destroyed in 1291, the fact that this distant frontier region survived for so long can be explained in part by their labours.

Further reading

Barber, M. (1992) 'Supplying the Crusader States: The Role of the Templars', in B.Z. Kedar (ed.) *The Horns of Hattin*, Jerusalem: Israel Exploration Society, 314–326.

Bronstein, J. (2005) *The Hospitallers and the Holy Land: Financing the Latin East, 1187–1274*. Woodbridge: Boydell and Brewer.

Bronstein, J. (2008) 'The Decree of 1262: A Glimpse into the Economic Decision-Making of the Hospitallers', in V. Mallia-Milanes (ed.) *The Military Orders, Volume 3: History and Heritage*. Ashgate: Aldershot, 197–202.

Forey, A.J. (1977) 'The Military Order of St Thomas of Acre', *English Historical Review*, 92, 481–503.

Morton, N. (2009) *The Teutonic Knights in the Holy Land, 1190–1291*. Woodbridge: Boydell and Brewer.

O'Callaghan, J.F. (1969) '*Hermanndades* between the Military Orders of Calatrava and Santiago during the Castilian Reconquest, 1158–1252', *Speculum*, 44, 609–618.

Riley-Smith, J. (1978) 'The Templars and Teutonic Knights in Cilician Armenia', in T.S.R. Boase (ed.) *The Cilician Kingdom of Armenia*. Edinburgh: Scottish Academic Press, 92–117.

Stathakopoulos, D. (2006) 'Discovering a Military Order of the Crusades: The Hospital of St Sampson of Constantinople', *Viator*, 37, 255–273.

Tyerman, C. (2006) *God's War: A New History of the Crusades*. London: Allen Lane, 715–822.

Chronology

1187	The battle of Hattin and the fall of Jerusalem.
1189–1192	Third Crusade.
1190	Foundation of the Teutonic Hospital at Acre.
1191 *12 July*	Conquest of Acre by the armies of the Third Crusade.
1198 *March*	The decision is taken at Acre for the Teutonic Knights to assume a military role.
1217–1221	Fifth Crusade.
1227–1229	Emperor Frederick II's crusade to the Holy Land.
1228	The decision is taken for the order of St Thomas of Acre to assume a military role.
1229 *18 February*	Emperor Frederick II secures the return of Jerusalem by treaty.
1239–1241	Barons' Crusade.
1244 *July*	Jerusalem falls to the Khwārazmians.
1244 *17 October*	The forces of Damascus and the kingdom of Jerusalem are defeated at La Forbie.
1245 *June–July*	First Council of Lyons.
1248–1254	Louis IX's crusade to the Holy Land.
1250 *8 February*	Battle of Mansura.
1258 *8 October*	The Teutonic Knights, Hospitallers and Templars sign a treaty of mutual co-operation in Acre.
1260 *3 September*	Battle of Ayn Jalut between the Mongols and Mamluks.
1266	Safad falls to the Mamluks.
1271 *March*	Crac des Chevaliers falls to the Mamluks.
1274 *May–July*	Second Council of Lyons.
1285 *17 April*	Margat falls to the Mamluks.
1291 *May*	Acre falls to the Mamluks.

5

Eastern Europe and the Baltic

BACKGROUND

From the shores of the Baltic to the wastes of Eastern Europe three forces vied with one another for supremacy: Paganism, Christianity and the encroaching forest. Crossing the ancient battlefields of Schleswig (Danish/German border) in the 1160s, Helmold, priest of Lübeck, passed through the remains of whole settlements devastated by pagan marauders but now virtually lost under dense undergrowth. These were brutal parts.

As with so many Catholic Christian frontiers the story of the Baltic and Eastern Europe between the late tenth century and the twelfth is one of changing tides. At the start of this period, Christendom, which had for so long been the object of violent pagan raids, began to turn the tables on its erstwhile foes, driving outwards. This movement was led by merchants, warriors, missionaries and settlers, who could all see opportunities in these long border zones. Slowly – whether by conversion, armed force or cultural exchange – the traditional pagan civilisations neighbouring Christian lands became drawn into the European world, adopting its practices, social structures and religion. In time, regional pagan warlords became Christian kings; tribal warriors became mail-clad knights; and pagan shrines were replaced with Catholic churches. The fabric of frontier society was changing. During the late tenth and eleventh century, the rulers and chieftains of Norway, Sweden and Denmark converted to Christianity, aligning themselves increasingly with the Catholic world. The pagan tribes of Central Europe were being driven back, while the Poles and Magyars also became Christian, forming their own kingdoms. Christendom was advancing and, as the twelfth century progressed, was doing so with increasing aggression. Soon after the conquest of Jerusalem in 1099 crusading ideas began to seep into these border realms, remoulding local campaigns into holy war.

The great religious orders established houses on these fronts, including the Cistercians and Premonstratensians. They encouraged: the colonisation of wilderness areas; supported missionary work; and bound these regions more closely into the international networks of the Church. Indeed, it was the famous Bernard of Clairvaux who persuaded the pope formally to extend crusading to the Baltic region during the preparations for the Second Crusade in 1147. It was their shared hope that this campaign would extend Christianity into pagan territory. Crusades were authorised and amidst the cut-and-thrust of frontier life some churchmen found it necessary to take up arms. In other areas castles and monasteries were established side-by-side deep inside pagan territory, performing separately the religious and military functions of conquest; tasks of course that could be conducted jointly by a military order. The Templars and Hospitallers were first introduced into these regions through donations made by local princes and barons, who had often returned from visiting Jerusalem. These properties were not generally intended to be military bases, but to form part of their international supply structures for the Holy Land. Even so, the military orders' popularity and obvious applicability to the colonisation and defence of embattled frontlines ensured that it would not be long before they took a more assertive role in this area.

EASTERN FRONTLINES

Livonia

In 1198, Bishop Berthold of Livonia (a former Cistercian) fled in fury from his see in Livonia (modern-day Latvia) having narrowly avoided being killed by the local people. For around 18 years, attempts had been made to bring Christianity to Livonia, but they had not met with success. Berthold's answer was to demand that a crusading army should be raised to impose a Christian presence in the area. Although he was killed in the ensuing campaign, the army succeeded both in establishing itself in the castle of Holm and forcing the Livonians to accept a truce and the admittance of preachers into their hill-forts. The Christian position was precarious, however, and after the withdrawal of the crusading army the Livonians broke the truce and began to attack any clerics they found. Over the next few years German crusaders were recruited for the Livonian wars, but their support was only seasonal; a more permanent solution was needed. In 1202, shortly after a group of merchants, crusaders and priests established the city of Riga, Theodoric, a Cistercian abbot, founded a new military order known as the Swordbrethren to help secure the Christian position. This new institution received official recognition from the papacy in 1204 and was granted the Templar rule to regulate its conduct. From this time, the Swordbrethren came to play an active role in the defence of Catholic interests in Livonia, helping to hold a perimeter behind which settlers could farm the land and preachers could seek converts. The Swordbrethren's early military successes were enabled, at least in part, by their technical superiority. The construction of stone castles, the crossbow and heavy cavalry proved to be decisive factors in military encounters.

Within the settler community, the main authority was the bishop, but as the Swordbrethren grew disputes broke out between the two over the division of land and power. The order's demand was for one-third of all territory along with one-third of all future conquests [**Doc. 4, p. 156**]. As we have seen with the Iberian orders, it was not uncommon for military orders to be given such incentives to help expand the frontier and, having deferred the case to Rome in 1210, the bishop accepted. As the conquests in Livonia mounted, bishop and order operated in an uneasy alliance. Having subdued and converted much of the land, cementing their conquests with castles, their attention turned to neighbouring Estonia. Led by the Swordbrethren, multiple raiding parties were sent out into pagan territory, gathering plunder and weakening resistance. The Estonians resisted fiercely but were heavily defeated in 1217 at the battle of Fellin. Estonia was seriously weakened and the Swordbrethren and the bishop of Riga had already agreed how they would divide the territory.

The prosperity of the mission to the Baltic had not passed unnoticed. The Orthodox-Christian Russians to the north-east were deeply concerned by these developments and there had already been a series of armed clashes between Russian forces and the settlers. The Danes in the west were also showing an interest in the area and in 1206 they attacked the island of Ösel at the mouth of the Gulf of Riga. Albert, bishop of Riga (1198–1229), was aware of both these developments, but his main concern was evidently that the full conquest of Estonia would give the Swordbrethren too much power. His answer was in 1218 to appeal to the Danes to invade Estonia. The Danish forces arrived in 1219 establishing themselves at Reval and then, having defeated a local force, Estonian resistance collapsed and the Danes took over. Master Volquin of the Swordbrethren was furious when he learnt that the Danes had conquered Estonia, but it was too late, he had been outmanoeuvred. Estonia was eventually divided between the Danes and the order. By this stage, the Swordbrethren had become one Christian faction vying with the local bishop and the Danes for control of the Estonian and Livonian territories, but even so, whoever might take control in the future, their efforts had ensured that for the foreseeable future Christian bells would continue to sound across the Gulf of Riga.

Hungary

The introduction of a military order onto any frontline was almost always provoked by the existence of a problem that contemporary churchmen or secular leaders could not solve adequately by existing means. The specific threat facing King Andrew II of Hungary was the nomadic Cuman tribes which beleaguered his kingdom's eastern borders. A permanent garrison of able troops was needed and the military orders were the ideal solution. The Templars and Hospitallers had long maintained properties in Hungary, but these were intended to supply the Holy Land, not to guard the frontier. The Teutonic Knights under Hermann von Salza, however, were eager to accept just such an appointment and consequently in 1211 Andrew granted them the region of Burzenland. Andrew's attention may well have been drawn to the order by the Landgrave of Thuringia, with whom he was negotiating a marriage alliance (between his daughter and the Landgrave's son). Certainly, the Teutonic Knights were well positioned to accept this offer. The Landgrave was a close ally and the order could call upon support from their German commanderies.

The order swiftly established itself in Burzenland. Having served in the Holy Land for many years, where many massive strongholds had recently been constructed or strengthened, the brethren were able to apply advanced building techniques to the creation of at least five castles. They could also call upon German settlers to secure their position. In time, they expanded their position, driving east into pagan territory. In some ways this was exactly what the Hungarian nobility wanted – it is certainly what Andrew had asked for – but the order started to exceed its mandate. Enjoying growing power and located in a distant frontier region, the brethren began to assert their independence and to infringe their rights. This angered the aristocracy, who bitterly resented the influence of foreigners in their affairs. Andrew himself was clearly aware of the importance of the Knights' work but even he later described them as: 'a fire in the breast, a mouse in the purse, and a snake in the bosom, who reward their hosts badly'. Tensions rose and, despite an attempt to settle their differences in 1222, Andrew was eventually forced to expel the order from Hungary in 1225. Pope Honorius III had attempted to protect the order, but his appeals had fallen on deaf ears; the Teutonic Knights were no longer welcome.

The relationship between the Hungarians and the Teutonic Order follows a by now well-worn cycle that was repeated across so many frontiers. An order is initially welcomed by a beleaguered magnate – it prospers – it becomes too powerful – it is viewed as a threat – quarrels break out – finally either the order or ruler (or elements of his nobility) are either diminished in power or ejected. In this case the Hungarian campaigns proved an expensive failure for the order, but it may have taught them useful lessons that they could apply to their future campaigns in Prussia and Livonia.

In later years, the kings of Hungary looked to the Hospitallers for support when they needed assistance. The Hospitallers had developed a significant network of landholdings in the country since 1150. Many of these properties were royal gifts and in return the order had rendered the rulers many diplomatic services, not least by helping King Andrew II organise his crusade to the Holy Land in 1217. Before the 1240s, however, the order had not been expected to offer military support. This changed with the advent of the Mongols and in 1247 plans were even drawn up for them to take control of a major border area, much as the Teutonic Knights had before them. The papacy encouraged this scheme and offered indulgences for those who offered support to the order. Even so little came of the proposal.

Prussia and Poland

When the papacy described Christendom it was often as a great vineyard in which the vines (the people of God) were supported, cherished and 'watered' by the clergy. Following the biblical injunction to spread the teaching of Jesus Christ, missionaries were sent out to establish new plantations so that God's vineyard could expand to all the corners of the earth. The papacy recognised that there were many obstacles to this mission and internal threats (i.e. heretic groups), like foxes and weeds, were to be rooted out to prevent them from contaminating the crop. Similarly, foreign invaders, like wild beasts, were to be destroyed to make way for the cultivation of new vines. Prussia, like Livonia, was a vineyard in the making.

In the early thirteenth century new efforts were made to convert the Prussians, spearheaded by the Cistercian abbey of Leckno. This house was dependent upon the abbey of Morimond (the same institution that supervised the Calatravan military order). Many attempts had been made to proselytise in this area previously but missionaries often met a tragic end. On this occasion, however, their preaching was more effective and letters sent to the papacy reported the conversion of many pagans. This success, however, only created a further problem. Prussian converts required military protection if the mission were to prosper and consequently in 1217, under the leadership of Bishop Christian of Prussia (a Cistercian), a crusade was authorised to safeguard these communities. Crusading, however, could only be a temporary solution because these areas required permanent defence. The military orders could offer this kind of protection, but despite a possible attempt to involve the Hospitallers in 1198, none maintained a military base nearby. Consequently in 1226, after a series of failed campaigns, the Teutonic Knights were invited to take control of the border region of Kulm. This offer was made by Prince Conrad of Masovia and was formally confirmed by Emperor Frederick II at Rimini. This was a huge opportunity for the Teutonic Knights, who had only just been expelled from Hungary. It gave them the ability to build a semi-independent state with the full support of neighbouring princes.

Nevertheless, in 1226 they were fully engaged in preparing Frederick II's crusade to the Holy Land and so an expedition on this front had to be postponed. Faced with this vacuum, attempts were made to introduce other military orders. In 1228 the order of Calatrava was given lands in this region and in the same year Conrad of Masovia and Bishop Christian arranged the foundation of a new military order which was given the town of Dobrin on the banks of the Vistula River. This 'order of Dobrin' later received confirmation from the pope, who instructed them to model their activities on the Swordbrethren. The Dobriners then began to make inroads into Prussia, acquiring troops and seeking settlers. Nevertheless, their efforts proved insufficient to hold off the pagans; a more powerful order was needed.

The order of Dobrin: The order of Dobrin was established in 1228 by Bishop Christian of Prussia and Prince Conrad of Masovia to provide protection against the Prussians. Its master, Bruno, initially led a small force of brethren who followed the Templar rule. They wore white mantles adorned with a star and a red sword. They were given the town of Dobrin (from which they took their name) on the frontier and it was agreed that they could retain half of any territory they captured. The order was later taken over by the Teutonic Order in 1235. Some brethren resisted this union with the Teutons and served with Conrad defending Masovia; but they were defeated in battle in 1238 and then disbanded.

The Teutonic Knights were bigger, wealthier, better connected and, after the creation of a 10-year treaty with the Muslims in the Holy Land in 1229, better able to focus their attention on Prussia. They arrived the following year and immediately began to settle the area to the north-west of Dobrin, further up the Vistula. The knights made rapid progress, securing their advances with small forts and it was not to be long before the entire Prussian crusade was in their hands.

Considering these frontiers as a whole, it is striking that military orders were introduced into all areas during a relatively short period of time: 1202 (Swordbrethren in Livonia), 1211 (Teutonic Knights in Hungary), 1226 (Teutonic Knights in Prussia), 1228 (the orders of Dobrin and Calatrava in Prussia). This pattern is repeated in Iberia, where the Spanish orders – Alcántara, Calatrava, Avis, Mountjoy and Santiago – were similarly established during a narrow 19-year period. Given that the stimulus to found a military order came generally from leading nobles or churchmen, it is likely that such magnates watched their local Christian neighbours' actions closely, ever ready to make use of an innovation that could be of service. Thus, when a nearby ruler founded a military order and proved its worth, there was a strong likelihood that adjoining magnates would follow suit soon afterwards.

RELATIONS WITH THE PAPACY (PATRONS 3)

In 1232 the papal vice-legate Baldwin of Alna arrived at the papal court in Rieti complaining loudly about the conduct of the Swordbrethren in Livonia. He had formerly been sent to the region to manage the election of a new bishop of Riga, but his visit had been marked by many disputes with the various Christian factions – the bishop of Riga, the citizens of Riga and the Swordbrethren. A major point of contention had been the former Danish territory in Estonia. This region had largely been lost to Danish control following a rebellion in 1223. The Swordbrethren had then stepped in to take control for themselves and in 1225 a papal legate had arrived to mediate. He had decided that the former Danish territories should be held directly from the papacy, but this arrangement soon proved inoperable and Estonia was then returned to the Swordbrethren. Baldwin himself had arrived in 1229 and later demanded that the brethren place these territories under his jurisdiction. Their refusal enraged Baldwin, provoking his subsequent appearance at the papal court. Baldwin was not a tactful man, but Gregory IX believed his version of events and despatched him back to the Baltic with powers to curb the order. The papacy and the Swordbrethren were on a collision course.

Angering the pontiff was a hazardous business. As institutions of the Church the military orders were morally, spiritually and legally subject to the papacy and, however tactless its legates might be, an order defied their instructions at its peril. Should a rift occur then an unruly religious order could face stinging denunciations or even the threat of excommunication. The papacy was perfectly prepared to issue such reprimands and only three years before Baldwin's complaints, Gregory IX had censured the Teutonic Knights for their conduct during Frederick's crusade. This papal rebuke alone had been damaging enough, but it had also encouraged the order's other detractors to air their grievances. Clearly papal fury could open a flood-gate of criticism with an order's opponents released from all restraint.

The Swordbrethren in 1232, however, had an advantage that the Teutonic Knights in 1229 had lacked. They were powerful, semi-independent rulers located in a far-flung region of Christendom. If they were to be reprimanded then it would have to be done by force. Baldwin was aware of this and on his journey north he raised an army with which to impose his will. His troops, however, proved unequal to the challenge and he was heavily defeated in

1233. Again Baldwin returned to the papal court, but he received an icier welcome than before. He was stripped of his legatine powers and the mission to Livonia was placed in more experienced hands. Nevertheless, he managed to convince the papal curia that the Swordbrethren had charges to answer and their representatives were summoned. The trial eventually took place in 1236 and many of Baldwin's claims were found to be groundless. Even so the Swordbrethren suffered a major reverse soon afterwards at the battle of Saule and it was decided that existing proposals to merge them with the Teutonic Knights should be implemented. This took place in 1237; the Swordbrethren had been dissolved.

The events of 1232–1237 highlight the importance attached by the papacy to the conduct of the military orders even on distant frontiers. Its interventions reveal a determination to ensure that the Swordbrethren should both remain responsive to papal direction and operate within agreed parameters. These were ongoing concerns in many regions where papal representatives feared that over-mighty military orders might begin to shake free from central control and assert a wilful independence. This threat would have been apparent in the 1260s when the Templars defied the papacy's express instructions to dismiss their marshal, Stephen of Cissey. In some ways this was an issue of the papacy's own making. The major orders had all been exempted from the authority of all churchmen except the pope himself; an act which effectively stripped local clerics, such as the patriarch of Jerusalem, of all formal powers of restraint. Nevertheless, towards the end of the thirteenth century, Rome was determined to tighten its grip. In the Holy Land, the patriarchs of Jerusalem were routinely given the status of papal legates. This gave them full papal powers and circumvented the order's exemptions. In 1274 the patriarch was permitted to strip rogue orders of their privileges and later in 1288 the authority to excommunicate military orders. Clearly the papacy was not prepared to take any chances; the defiance of a major order would be deeply embarrassing and would set a perilous precedent for the rest of Christendom.

Defying the papacy could result in serious consequences, but it could also inhibit opportunities for collaboration. The papacy could offer a great deal of practical support to the military orders, from their initial endorsement as orders of the Catholic Church through to their development into international institutions. Such assistance often took the form of privileges, which might include the ability to appoint their own masters; the right to build chapels, churches or cemeteries; the opportunity to offer indulgences to supporters; and exemption from Church taxation. For some orders these rights were built up slowly, but the Teutonic Order acquired a vast haul of privileges in the space of a few weeks. In 1220–1221 during the latter stages of the Fifth Crusade, a deeply impressed Honorius III issued 57 documents for the Teutonic Order including the concession of the same rights as those enjoyed by the Templars and Hospitallers. On other occasions the papacy was prepared to defend an order's legal rights and interests against predatory churchmen and secular rulers. In 1237, for example, Pope Gregory IX supported the Calatravan order when he wrote to King Ferdinand III of Castile-León ordering him not to interfere in the appointment of their new master. It was also within the pontiff's gift to raise crusading forces to assist the orders' military campaigns or to offer indulgences to the order's supporters [**Doc. 6, p. 159**].

The papacy's primary objective through these lavish endowments was to provide for Christendom's perimeter defence. Within the many papal letters and legal documents written to the orders they are frequently described as 'walls for the house of the Lord'; a quotation from the Old Testament book of Ezekiel that captures their vital importance in the defence of the faith. In other cases the military orders could act as papal mediators or diplomats, supporting the Church's interests across Christendom. During the 1220s and 1230s the Teutonic Knights' master Hermann von Salza was repeatedly called upon to act as the papacy's representative, particularly in its dealings with the emperor, and in 1236 he was charged with the establishment of a general peace as a prelude to a major crusade. At other times the papacy recruited a number of its key officials from the military orders. Seen from the pope's perspective, the orders could provide a pool of highly capable administrators and warriors, who were ideally suited to act as papal marshals and chamberlains.

In the final analysis, co-operation was in the interests of both the papacy and the military orders and each had aspirations that could be better realised with the support of the other. To this end, disputes rarely lasted long and there was generally a willingness to make peace. Indeed, the larger orders often maintained permanent representatives at the papal court specifically to represent their interests and to defend this relationship. Nevertheless, this should not obscure the fact that in almost all cases a military order needed the papacy far more than the papacy needed the order. As the Swordbrethren's merger with the Teutonic Knights proves, military orders could be replaced.

THE TEUTONIC KNIGHTS AND THE EASTERN FRONTIER

In 1230 a force of Teutonic Knights, led by Herman Balk set out to conquer Prussia. Some brethren had been despatched to this area previously, but now, with the conclusion of a treaty with the Muslims in the Holy Land, the order could embark upon this endeavour in earnest. His was not a large force and he needed to establish a position from which he could begin to rally forces for a wider conquest. Consequently in 1231 he started to construct a base on the banks of the Vistula to which he gave the name Toron. This was dangerous work conducted under constant threat of Prussian attack. Indeed, the order's chronicler Peter of Duisburg reports that Hermann and his knights were frequently forced to take refuge in the branches of a huge oak tree until their settlement became defensible.

The establishment of Toron provided the vital starting point for the ensuing conquest and from this position the order continued to expand into Prussian territory founding a series of further settlements including Kulm, Marienwerder and Elbing over the next few years. The papacy offered its assistance from the start and in 1230 issued the first of many crusade bulls for the order, encouraging knights to take the cross against the Prussians. Meanwhile, attractive concessions were offered to those who were prepared to settle in Prussia and thereby provide the manpower to consolidate the order's advances. With this support, the brethren pushed their way north along the line of the Vistula towards the shores of the Baltic, cementing their advances with timber forts. In time the order was able to supplement its forces further with levies drawn from the subjected Prussian people, who proved numerous if rather unreliable allies. The combined effect of these initiatives was a rapid evolution of the Christian position from a vulnerable border into an established bridgehead for expansion.

With the Prussian conquest well under way, the Teutonic Knights began to broaden the scope of their activities, taking over neighbouring military orders. In 1235 they absorbed the order of Dobrin and two years later Pope Gregory IX put the remnants of the discredited Swordbrethren under their authority. The latter of these two mergers was particularly significant. It gave them the Swordbrethren's entire stake in Livonia, complete with castles, estates and their attendant infrastructure, but it also challenged them to reverse the fortunes of a fragile frontier territory still reeling from defeat at the hands of the pagans. For the order's master, Hermann von Salza, this was a bold move. His still relatively undeveloped order was now responsible for the protection of two highly active frontline regions while it remained deeply committed to the Holy Land where the truce with the Muslims would expire in only two years. In these circumstances there was a strong probability that the order would become overstretched.

The dangers of the order's position were exacerbated by growing resistance among its former Catholic supporters, who came to view the brethren as rivals rather than allies. Their claims were that the order had exceeded its original mandate and now posed a threat to their authority. A particularly outspoken critic was Bishop Christian of Prussia who returned from five years in captivity with the Prussians in 1238 to find that leadership of his mission into Prussia had been eclipsed by the rising power of the Teutonic Order. Originally he had arranged with the order in 1231 that they would retain only one-third of all land taken from the Prussians, but his prolonged absence gave them the opportunity to undercut both this agreement and his authority. Conrad of Masovia – the man who had originally granted the order land in this area – was similarly sidelined as the order bulldozed its way north.

Bishop Christian's imprisonment also persuaded the papacy to transfer responsibility for the recruitment of crusaders and the conversation of the pagans to the Dominican friars. They and the Franciscans proved to be energetic advocates of the Teutonic Order's work and, during the thirteenth century, incited many nobles to lead forces to assist its work in Prussia and Livonia. Crusading in Prussia and Livonia held many attractions for German lords. Although neither region could boast the spiritual significance of Jerusalem, the crusading indulgences offered by the papacy were the same and an expedition to the Baltic could be completed in a far shorter time and at far less expense than the journey to the east. The Teutonic Order and the advocates of these crusades also worked hard to draw connections between their labours in the north and those of the Holy Land. They named several of their outposts, including Toron and Montfort, after sites in the kingdom of Jerusalem, while their pagan enemies were often referred to as 'Saracens'. Biblical heroes and passages that were used repeatedly to eulogise crusading to the Eastern Mediterranean were re-employed to promote the Baltic crusades, creating the impression that their wars were a natural extension of the struggle for Jerusalem.

Despite their early advances, in the early 1240s the Teutonic Knights suffered a series of reverses. In 1243 they faced a major rebellion in Prussia led by Duke Swantopelk of Pomerelia. This posed a serious threat to their early advances. An expert in warfare, Swantopelk inflicted a string of defeats on the brethren, seizing many of their strongholds. The pope responded by launching a crusade in the same year, but it was not until 7 February 1249 that the uprising finally was ended by treaty at Christburg. The situation was little better in Livonia. In 1237, a strong force of 60 Teutonic knights under Hermann Balk had been sent to take charge of the Swordbrethren's former lands. One of Hermann's first objectives had been to settle the long-standing disputes which had existed between the Swordbrethren and the king of Denmark over Estonia. His negotiations were successfully concluded shortly afterwards, resulting in the Treaty of Stensby 1238, which divided the contested lands.

Meanwhile, the acquisitive gaze of many Baltic rulers was turning towards Russia, which was on the verge of collapse. Emerging from the great steppe country in 1237, Mongol hordes had swept the Russian principalities' armies from the battlefield, bringing their princes to their knees. The Danes, Swedes and Teutonic Knights were well aware of their plight and were all determined to profit from it. Multiple expeditions were launched soon afterwards, driving east into Russian territory, and in 1241 an army of Danes and Teutonic Knights captured the important city of Pskov. These advances, however, were not to last and in 1242 a Russian force retook Pskov and then inflicted a defeat on the order in a battle fought on the frozen Lake Peipus on 5 April 1242. This reverse did not place the order's position in Livonia in serious jeopardy – the continued Mongol threat ensured that the Russians were in no position to follow up their victory – but an opportunity had been lost and reports of their humiliation may have helped to encourage the revolt in Prussia.

For the papacy, the news from these fronts was bleak enough but it had further problems. Not only was it locked in a ruinous struggle with the German emperor, but in 1241 the Mongol armies reached Christendom's borders, invading Poland and Hungary, massacring the inhabitants and slaughtering all who stood in their way. Their incursion was brief and they withdrew to the steppe the following year, but by this time Christendom's eastern frontier lay in tatters. Fully aware of the possibility of a second incursion the pope's immediate priority was to rebuild these shattered defences. In this climate, it was imperative for the papacy that the Teutonic Knights – by now one of Eastern Europe's foremost defenders – remain as strong as possible and consequently it issued some of its most significant concessions to the order at this time. In 1245, after petitions from the brethren, the archbishop of Mainz was granted the *permanent* right to raise crusading forces to support the order; an unprecedented concession. Likewise, in the same year Pope Innocent IV insisted that the recruitment for crusades to Prussia and Livonia should continue even though he was launching simultaneously a new campaign led by the king of France to the Holy Land.

With close support from the papacy and its circle of noble supporters, the Teutonic Knights prospered in both Prussia and Livonia in the years following the Treaty of Christburg 1249. Frequent campaigns were launched and many leading nobles from across the empire were induced to lend their support. Pagan tribes were repeatedly crushed on the battlefield, while territorial gains were consolidated with the construction of new strongholds, often paid for by visiting lords. Increasingly these were being built in brick, replacing the earlier wooden structures. One of the most famous of the fortifications established at this time was the castle of Königsberg, built to secure conquests made in 1255 and named after King Ottokar II of Bohemia, who had participated in the campaign. Recognising Ottokar in this way was a sensible move. The order was fully aware that it depended on external support to extend its position and such an acknowledgement was an astute way of cultivating this important relationship while encouraging others to imitate their example. Acknowledgements of this kind also gave leading magnates an extra reason to provide ongoing assistance and when the margrave of Brandenburg learnt of the destruction of a castle he had built for the order in 1265 (to which he had likewise given his own name) he felt sufficiently concerned to raise a new army to reconstruct it. A similar imperative can be found in the chronicle of Peter von Duisburg (the official chronicler of the order writing in the early fourteenth century) who describes the conquest of Prussia. In his narrative he was always careful to remember and praise the many families who had marched to the order's aid, including Ottokar and the margrave; reminding readers of the glory that could be won by crusading with the order.

As the Teutonic Knights' territories expanded in both Prussia and Livonia they began to seek the unification of these realms by conquering the relatively narrow strip of pagan territory that separated them. Possession of this area would dramatically enhance their power and would draw both areas under a single administration. During the 1250s this objective seemed within their grasp and the order sent armies repeatedly from both Prussia and Livonia to secure the route. Mindaugas, the ruler of neighbouring Lithuania, could have posed a major obstacle to this scheme, but after many years of war with the order he had been persuaded to seek the order's friendship and in 1251 he converted to Christianity. He would not intervene. The local Samogitian people, however, proved tenacious and in 1260 inflicted a massive defeat upon the order at Durben on 13 July. One hundred and fifty knights were killed along with the Livonian master and thousands of local troops. The pagan tribes were not slow to exploit the order's sudden weakness and a new wave of rebellion broke across Prussia. Mindaugas also seized this opportunity and, renouncing Christianity, he attacked the order. The Second Prussian Rebellion again placed the order's retention of Prussia in jeopardy and it was only in 1283 – over two decades later – that the risings were finally subdued. The order turned the tide gradually, with the consistent support of the papacy and numerous groups of crusaders. It did so, however, at a heavy cost. In 1257 the papacy estimated the total number of brethren killed in the wars of Prussia and Livonia to be 500. Four years later, in 1261, this figure was revised to 1000. The number of knightly brethren lost was of course only a fraction of the order's total casualties which would have included thousands of crusaders, mercenaries, settler knights and infantry, tribal levies and other allies.

Despite the human and financial losses involved, with the final suppression of the rebellion, the order's position had become – for the time being at least – unassailable. Later efforts to rise in rebellion were swiftly put down while a growing number of fortresses and an increasingly sophisticated organisational network kept the Teutonic Knights firmly in place.

In a sense they had achieved their objective. The frontiers they patrolled were now effectively defended while both Prussia and Livonia were steadily becoming integrated into Europe's religious, social and commercial networks. Even so, the mission to Prussia and Livonia had always been conducted at least in part to win converts and certainly the Christianisation of this region would help to embed the order's authority (Favreau-Lilie, 2000: 147–154). Through their wars of conquest the Teutonic Knights and their Dominican allies had created an environment in which Christianity could be imposed and the infrastructure of the Church established – complete with churches, four bishoprics, parishes, etc. Concerns were raised however that the order and its Dominican allies had replaced the former Cistercian policy of winning voluntary converts with more coercive measures. Certainly the Teutonic Knights were prepared to promote forced conversion and the order's chronicler Nicolaus von Jeroschin described the conduct of one crusader affiliated with the order writing: 'He caused them (the Prussians) such misery and harried them, night and day, so ferociously that he reduced them to the point where they had to submit themselves to God and the brothers and receive Christianity.' (tr. Fischer, 2010: 84) Predictably, such brutal approaches often generated resentment among 'converts' rather than sincere faith and the Franciscan friar Roger Bacon, writing during the Second Prussian Rebellion, argued that the Prussians would have freely converted long before had the Teutonic Knights not attempted to impose Christianity by force. This was a contentious matter and voices were raised both for and against the order's actions. Ultimately, the moral question at the heart of these issues could be defined as follows: is it justifiable to use force when attempts at voluntary conversion have failed? To this challenge, some contemporaries answered 'no', the Teutonic Knights 'yes'.

DIVIDING RESOURCES (FINANCES 4)

In May 1254 Peter of Coblenz, marshal of the Teutonic Order in the Holy Land, wrote a bitter letter to King Alfonso X of Castile requesting aid and outlining the fragility of his position at Acre. He complained that it had been years since he had received reinforcements from the order's German commanderies and that those resources which were available were scarcely sufficient to maintain the order's commitments in Prussia and Livonia. Moreover, ongoing wars in northern Italy rendered the roads too dangerous for the transport of goods to the Mediterranean ports. Certainly he had good reason to be concerned. The crusade led by King Louis IX of France to the Eastern Mediterranean – to which Christendom had pinned such hopes – had suffered heavy defeats in which his order had sustained major casualties and only two months previously Louis had returned home taking the bulk of his remaining knights with him. In his estimation the total destruction of the Teutonic Order in the kingdom of Jerusalem was now a distinct possibility.

Peter's letter underlines a crucial question facing any military order with commitments on multiple frontiers: how should the available resources be divided? The Templars and Hospitallers, for example, had ongoing military commands in areas including Armenia, the Holy Land, the Iberian Kingdoms and the Aegean. In these orders, however, their priorities were always clear: the Eastern Mediterranean came first. Their great pan-European supply networks all channelled materials in this direction while commanders leading brethren in other theatres of war were generally confined to using only their immediate resources. Moreover, in areas like Aragon in the mid-thirteenth century, where the border with Islam gradually disappeared and the military orders could no longer wage war against Christendom's foes, they immediately sought to recommit their local available manpower and revenues to the east [see Chapter 3 / **Doc. 9, p. 164**].

The Teutonic Knights were not the same. They began as an institution focused exclusively on the defence of the Holy Land, but this was a time at which the Latin East was frequently covered by lengthy truces. As shown above, rather than stand idle during these periods, their ambitious master Hermann von Salza took on a series of responsibilities in Eastern Europe. This was not an unprecedented move. Military orders generally saw themselves as a form of international Christian militia, ready to offer their services where they were needed. To this end, in 1205 Pope Innocent III instructed the knights of Calatrava to offer aid to Aragon while Castile was covered by a truce; in 1232 Pope Gregory IX requested that the Swordbrethren assist the Swedes in Finland and in 1258 the Templars, Hospitallers and Teutonic Knights set out a framework for the effective co-ordination and movement of their forces across the Christian territories in the east. By the 1240s however the Teutonic Knights were in a unique predicament. Committed to the defence of the Holy Land, Prussia and Livonia they were suddenly confronted with virtually simultaneous reverses on all three fronts: La Forbie 1244 (Holy Land), Lake Peipus 1242 (Livonia) and the Prussian rebellion (from 1243). This situation naturally required the order to decide how it would respond. Unlike the Templars and Hospitallers, they could not simply prioritise the Holy Land. Their knights were not merely auxiliary forces in Prussia and Livonia – as the Templars were in Iberia – but had a central responsibility to provide for their defence. Moreover the continued Mongol threat created yet another argument against abandoning or curtailing these commitments in Eastern Europe. On the other hand the quest for Jerusalem was their founding purpose and could not be ignored.

Torn between these two imperatives the Teutonic Order split into two factions each emphasising the needs of its own region – the Baltic or the Holy Land. These divisions were only exacerbated by the ongoing struggle between the papacy and empire; two benefactors who both demanded the order's loyalties. Document 8 [**p. 161**] is a record of the decrees established in 1251 following the arrival of Eberhard of Sayn, representative of the order's Levantine brethren, in Germany and reflects an attempt by the chapter in the Holy Land to restate its authority over the order's commanders in the Baltic. Its stipulations repeatedly stress the need to seek consultation with the brethren in the Holy Land.

Within these disputes the appointment and character of the master were vital considerations. Indeed, the pitiful condition of the order's forces in the east, described so vividly by Peter of Coblenz, may have been part of a deliberate policy led by pro-Baltic master Poppo von Osterna to weaken the Levantine faction. In the event, it took the election of a new master in 1256 for significant aid to reach the east. In later years this controversy rumbled on and although many of the masters made strenuous attempts to support all fronts – even in the face of crises such as the fall of Montfort in 1271 and the Second Prussian Rebellion – the tension between these groups continued. Eventually, as the brethren continued to prove incapable of resolving this matter internally, this question was taken out of their hands. The fall of Acre in 1291 undermined arguments for the retention of a major presence in the east and although the order continued to maintain positions on Cyprus and in Armenia and Frankish Greece, its role in these areas now became decidedly secondary. Its headquarters moved first to Venice in 1291 and then to Marienburg in Prussia in 1309. The change in focus this movement implies was not immediate, but it did prove irrevocable.

The issues posed by commitments to different frontiers could be serious, but for an order that also pursued multiple vocations, there were equally pressing questions surrounding the division of its energies between its military and charitable functions. It was relatively rare for military orders to confine their activities solely to warfare. Even the Templar regulations made a number of provisions for the support of the poor and commanders were required to give a tenth of their bread to the needy. The order of Santiago likewise devoted a portion of its efforts to the ransoming of captives. Many military orders had a medical wing and this was the founding purpose of the orders of St Thomas of Acre, St Lazarus, the Teutonic Knights and the Hospitallers. Deciding how resources should be divided between these functions was therefore an important issue and in many cases, medical care became subordinated to the conduct of war. This was the case in the Teutonic Knights. After its foundation in 1190 the order created a hospital in Acre and continued to build or acquire such institutions across Christendom. By 1230 it possessed around 26 separate establishments (Militzer, 1998: 54). Nevertheless, this arm declined and the 1264 statutes specified that special permission was required before the creation of any new hospital. Hospitals were expensive and this was a time when the order had many costly military obligations.

The Hospitallers faced similar questions. As we have seen, they began as a hospice providing care for pilgrims visiting Jerusalem, but during the twelfth century they began to assume military responsibilities which increased as the century progressed. This shift in vocation, did not take place without friction. By 1170 the order's extravagant castle building and unsuccessful campaigning under Master Gilbert of Assailly had brought the order to the point of financial collapse. Shamed and broken, Gilbert attempted to resign and remove himself from these cares by assuming a hermit's life. Pope Alexander III was also concerned and wrote to the order emphasising that their primary responsibility was the support of the poor. Even so, any serious questioning of the order's military vocation was relatively short-lived. Quite possibly the immediate defensive needs of the Holy Land were simply too real to ignore. In the end, a compromise seems to have been struck which stressed the shared values inherent within both tasks: the desire to serve and protect those visiting or living in the Holy Land (Riley-Smith, 2010: 18). This episode, however, demonstrates the tensions that could occur between an order's different wings, particularly at times of military crisis.

Despite these examples, there are relatively few documented cases of serious internal controversies within the military orders. Where contemporaries occasionally complained of the rivalries between military orders, few suggested that the individual orders were prone to internal dissent.

Further reading

For a current bibliography of works in English see:
A. Murray (2009) 'The Eastern Baltic Lands in the Age of the Crusades: A Select Bibliography of Publications in English', in *The Clash of Cultures on the Medieval Baltic Frontier*. Aldershot: Ashgate, 341–355.

Bombi, B. (2008) 'Innocent III and the Origins of the Order of Sword Brothers', in V. Mallia-Milanes (ed.) *The Military Orders, Volume 3: History and Heritage*. Aldershot: Ashgate, 147–153.
Christiansen, E. (1997) *The Northern Crusades* (2nd edn). London: Penguin.
Favreau-Lilie, M-L. (2000) 'Mission to the Heathen in Prussia and Livonia: The Attitudes of the Religious Military Orders toward Christianization', in G. Armstrong and I. Wood (eds) *Christianizing Peoples and Converting Individuals*, International Medieval Research VII. Turnhout: Brepols, 147–154.
Fonnesberg-Schmidt, I. (2007) *The Popes and the Baltic Crusades, 1147–1254*. Brill: Leiden.
Hunyadi, Z. (2010) *The Hospitallers in the Medieval Kingdom of Hungary, c.1150–1387*. Budapest: CEU Press.
Laszlovszky, J. and Z. Soós (2001) 'Historical Monuments of the Teutonic Order in Transylvania', in Z. Hunyadi and J. Laszlovszky (eds) *The Crusades and the Military Orders: Expanding the Frontiers of Medieval Latin Christianity*. Budapest: Central European University Press, 319–336.
Militzer, K. (1998) 'The Role of Hospitals in the Teutonic Order', in H. Nicholson (ed.) *The Military Orders, Volume 2: Welfare and Warfare*. Aldershot: Ashgate, 51–59.

Pósán, L. (2001) 'Prussian Missions and the Invitation of the Teutonic Order into Kulmerland', in Z. Hunyadi and J. Laszlovszky (eds) *The Crusades and the Military Orders: Expanding the Frontiers of Medieval Latin Christianity.* Budapest: Central European University Press, 429–447.

Urban, W. (1973) 'The Organisation and Defense of the Livonian Frontier in the Thirteenth Century', *Speculum*, 48, 525–532.

Urban, W. (1978) 'The Diplomacy of the Teutonic Knights at the Curia', *Journal of Baltic Studies*, 9, 116–128.

Urban, W. (1994) *The Baltic Crusade* (2nd edn). Chicago, IL: Lithuanian Research and Studies Centre.

Chronology

1190	Foundation of the Teutonic Hospital at Acre.
1191 *12 July*	Conquest of Acre by the armies of the Third Crusade.
1198 *March*	The decision is taken at Acre for the Teutonic Knights to assume a military role.
1202	Foundation of the Swordbrethren.
1211	King Andrew II of Hungary invites the Teutonic Knights to defend Burzenland.
1225	The Teutonic Knights are expelled from Hungary.
1226	The Teutonic Knights are invited to defend Poland against the Prussians.
1228	Foundation of the order of Dobrin.
1230	The Teutonic Knights begin their wars against the Prussians in earnest.
1235	The order of Dobrin is merged with the Teutonic Knights.
1236 *22 September*	The Swordbrethren are defeated at the battle of Saule.
1237 *May*	The Swordbrethren are merged with the Teutonic Knights, who take control in Livonia.
1241	The Mongols invade Hungary and Poland.
1242 *5 April*	The Teutonic Knights are defeated by the Russians at the battle of Lake Peipus.
1243–1249	First Prussian Rebellion.
1260 *13 July*	The Teutonic Knights are defeated at Durben.
1260–1283	Second Prussian Rebellion.

6

Internal Structure and Identity

THE MILITARY ORDERS AS A FORM OF MONASTICISM

During the tenth and eleventh centuries, monasticism emerged as a highly dynamic force in Western Europe. This evolution began in part as a reaction against the condition of contemporary monastic houses, many of which had strayed from a true observance of the Benedictine rule (a document which defined the lifestyle of a community dedicated to following Christ). Critics complained that their commitment to austerity had been undermined by acquiring huge wealth, while the interference of secular rulers in their management had encouraged corruption. Accordingly in 909 a monastic house was set up at Cluny by the Duke of Aquitaine that self-consciously rejected these qualities, emphasising the austerity of its regime and its independence from lay control. The general desire for just such a reform was apparent soon afterwards when hundreds of houses either connected themselves to Cluny or were established on its model. This created the first monastic empire; an international organisation which was widely considered to provide an exemplar of moral behaviour to a populace, who were deeply aware of God's presence and their need for forgiveness and salvation. Benefactors flocked to show their piety by endowing such houses, some becoming permanent affiliates or **confratres**. Within this revival, monastic organisations often endeavoured to engage with specific social needs in the world around them. These could include the provision of schooling, health-care, hospitality and the support of pilgrims. In some cases houses specialised in one particular task and, as we have seen, several military orders originated as specifically medical organisations. Performing such roles and basking in secular approbation, establishments often became powerful economic units, building up networks of dependent estates which furnished them with the resources to conduct their activities and to build great monasteries.

Confratres: Lay affiliates of a religious order.

Plate 1 Marienburg

Source: Photo by Nicholas Morton

Plate 2 Cordoba

Source: Photo by Nicholas Morton

Plate 3 The Church of the Holy Sepulchre

Source: Photo by Juliet Morton

Plate 4 The Horns of Hattin

Source: Photo by Nicholas Morton

Plate 5 Crac des Chevaliers

Source: Photo by Juliet Morton

Plate 6 Jerusalem

Source: Photo by Juliet Morton

Plate 7 The Templars' Commandery at Temple Bruer (Lincolnshire)

Source: Photo by Juliet Morton

Plate 8 The Templar Hall at Strood (Kent)

Source: Photo by Juliet Morton

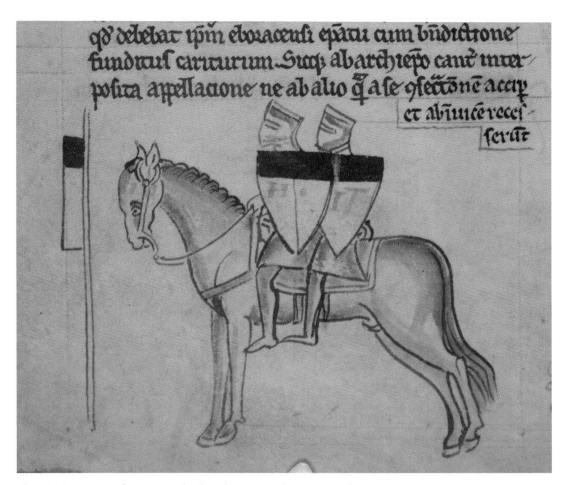

qd debebat ipm eboracenfi epatu cum bndictione
findtruf canturium. Sicep ab archiepo cane interposita appellacione ne ab alio q̃ a se confectõe accip
et ab inice recefferit

Plate 9 An image of two Templar knights in Matthew Paris' *Chronica Majora*

Source: courtesy of The Master and Fellows of Corpus Christi College, Cambridge

Plate 10 Map of Jerusalem in the twelfth century

Source: Zen Radovan/BibleLandPictures/Alamy

It was in this environment that, at the end of the eleventh century, the Cistercian order developed. They offered a new wave of monastic reform, restating the need for rigorous adherence to the Benedictine rule. Like the Cluniacs the order grew rapidly, acquiring hundreds of houses across Europe. They reflected the growing confidence and assertiveness of the Church as a whole at that time, describing themselves as a spiritual militia waging war through prayer against sin and the devil. Meanwhile Catholic attitudes towards warfare were evolving. The First Crusade had both been presented and received as an endeavour in which participants took a quasi-monastic vow and temporarily assumed aspects of the monastic lifestyle. In this environment, the Cistercians – who so embraced the spirit of the age – under leaders such as Bernard of Clairvaux, became deeply involved in crusading and the policies of Christian expansion. As shown above, Cistercian monks played a vital role in crusade propaganda, preaching and recruitment. On the frontier they also operated as missionaries and colonisers, establishing communities and settlements in newly conquered territory. In later years Cistercian monks involved themselves in the suppression of heresy, joining or even leading armies licensed by the papacy. Through such roles they encapsulated and drove the changing identity of monasticism and Catholic Christianity in the twelfth century.

Nevertheless, while the Cistercian order proved extremely flexible in its activities, the act of fighting was never accepted; monks were not permitted to shed blood. Indeed, in Bernard's eyes, there was no place for his own order in the Holy Land, where the demand was for trained soldiers not monks. Even so, defenders were needed and the Cistercians' frontline activities likewise required safeguarding. In this predicament – aware of their own vocational boundaries, but unable to supply an obvious need – the military orders offered the Cistercians an obvious solution. Reviewing the military orders described in preceding chapters it is striking how many were founded or authorised by Cistercians. These include: the order of Dobrin, established to defend Cistercian missions in Prussia; the Calatravans, founded by a Cistercian abbot in Castile and later introduced into Prussia to protect their interests; the Swordbrethren, created to protect the Cistercian mission in Livonia; and of course the Templars, legitimised by Bernard of Clairvaux to perform the deeds that his own order could not. Mountjoy, Alcántara, Avis and San Maria de España among others were also linked to the Cistercians. In this way many orders seem to have been founded as accessories to Cistercian missions. Strikingly, the orders they founded were also those which had no other major vocation beyond warfare, perhaps suggesting that the Cistercians envisaged themselves working alongside these orders and performing any other required roles.

After their establishment, the Templars, Hospitallers and Teutonic Knights developed into international institutions, just as the Cluniacs and

Cistercians had before them. With these earlier role models in place, the principle that orders could span Christendom was already well-established and the early patrons who founded the first Templar commanderies in Western Christendom clearly understood that while these lands might be hundreds of miles from any frontier they could still form a useful part of a wider international system. Likewise, the time-honoured traditions of benefaction to orders, confraternity and monastic estate management underpinned the later military order's financial successes. Their rules and statutes drew directly upon earlier regulations while their organisational structures and great offices were inspired in part by older orders. Perhaps the greatest advantages conferred by existing monastic models, which the military orders exploited to the full, were their inherent qualities of discipline, hard work, training and austerity. These proved an excellent basis from which to build a fighting force. In these and other ways the military orders were the beneficiaries and continuators of an existing tradition. Nevertheless some changes were needed. Unlike the Cluniac and Cistercian orders, the military orders' pan-European networks needed to make far greater provision for the regular transport of troops and resources. Moreover, they needed to be prepared for strategic eventualities including the formation of a major crusade, a decisive defeat or the need to build a new fortress. The idea of the brother knight, as we saw in the introduction, was also an innovation blending the vocation of the crusader, monk and knight.

This chapter explores the internal life and structure of the military orders, considering these institutions in the context of wider developments in monasticism. Although in some ways the idea of military orders was an innovation, in many respects the form taken by these organisations reflects significant continuations of existing monastic models, while their proliferation and success were often achieved thanks to the support of monastic reformers from other non-military orders.

CENTRAL CONTROL

As with modern business 'start-ups', when the military orders were founded they were small enough to be run by a single individual, but as they grew in size they required a progressively larger body of leaders and administrators to co-ordinate their various activities. This was certainly the case in the Teutonic Order. In the years following its founding in 1190, the only official reported by the sources was the order's leader (later known as the master). In 1208 there is the first reference to additional officers including the marshal (the order's military commander) and the overseer of the hospital. By this year the order had evidently become too large and complex for the master to manage all the order's functions alone and so new positions were created to manage its primary roles. Another important position to emerge around this time was that of the **grand commander**. He was primarily responsible for the administrative and organisational aspects of the order including: shipping, grain supply, workshops, the treasury, etc. In later years, as the order continued to grow, further appointments were made as the responsibilities associated with these roles increased. A 'deputy marshal' was created to support the marshal while a 'deputy commander' supported the grand commander. Other positions to be introduced included the treasurer (in charge of accounts), the **draper** (in charge of clothing and armour), and the **turcopolier** (in charge of locally raised troops and sergeants). The Teutonic Order was typical in the sense that its command structures evolved organically over time as the order's expansion required the establishment of new positions to prevent existing officials from becoming overburdened.

Major decision-making in this and other orders was generally based on consensus. At the top level, the Teutonic Order's master had considerable authority, but this was counter-balanced by regular assemblies of brethren known as 'chapters'. Of these the most important was the central chapter which generally met at the order's headquarters. It was a gathering of an order's most senior and experienced brothers and was summoned to discuss the direction of the order's policy and to pronounce judgement on key decisions. Many orders' statutes specify that the master was obliged to seek approval from the chapter before new initiatives could be launched. For example, the master could only sell/buy property, admit new brothers or appoint new officials with the chapter's express permission. This was typical and the Templar master was subject to similar restraints. He could not, for example, make war or peace without chapter approval. These central chapters could take different forms in different orders. The order of Santiago had a council of 13 known as the *Trece*. Towards the end of the thirteenth century, the Hospitaller chapter was divided into seven branches made up of brethren from different European regions, known as 'tongues' (a word which reflects the different languages spoken by each group).

In addition to these central chapters, further assemblies were held annually, known as general chapters, which involved officials drawn from far flung districts [**Doc. 8, p. 161**]. At these events, news was shared from across an order's international holdings and appointments and resignations were discussed. Provincial commanders in the larger orders were also permitted to hold regional general chapters, so that affairs of that area could be conducted effectively. A special chapter was also convened to elect a new master.

In orders such as the Teutonic Knights, roles such as 'hospitaller', 'marshal' or 'commander' were inherited from earlier military orders, particularly

Grand commander: A senior official in many of the larger military orders who was responsible for the operational management of an order.

Draper: The official responsible for supplying brethren with clothes and equipment.

Turcopolier: An official appointed in the Latin East to command local 'turcopole' cavalry and in some cases an order's sergeants.

the Templars and Hospitallers. These older institutions had themselves drawn upon existing organisational frameworks employed by existing orders, such as the Benedictines and Augustinians. The system of chapters and general chapters is one example of such borrowing, while the division of a major order's western properties into separate organisational districts followed Cluniac and Premonstratensian practices. Nevertheless, the administrations of secular monarchs were also influential because they could provide templates for resource management and military organisation that were lacking from earlier monastic organisations. It was from them that titles such as 'marshal' were taken (Burgtorf, 2008: 57).

Naturally, the military orders varied enormously in size and many smaller institutions, such as Mountjoy and St Thomas of Acre, did not require such extensive central administrations; for them the appointment of a single master was sufficient. The Hospitallers, Templars and Teutonic Knights, on the other hand, developed huge organisational networks designed to manage their enormous portfolios. The co-ordination of their extensive holdings in each case can be broken roughly into two halves. The marshals, grand commanders, turcopoliers, etc. discussed above were all expected to spend, manage or utilise the order's frontline resources as effectively as possible and, stationed primarily at the order's headquarters, they were ideally placed to conduct this work. Nevertheless, these orders all relied on materials transported from estates located far behind the frontier, which were controlled by provincial commanders/masters. Providing direction for these far-flung estates from the order's headquarters, given the technologies of communication available at this time, naturally posed problems. This obstacle was overcome in a number of ways. Written communication was extremely important and the international networks created by these orders could operate as an efficient postal system. Many letters have survived, particularly those relaying news from the Holy Land to commanderies in the west. In addition, the Templar and Hospitaller Orders both created a general master to oversee all their western territories in the thirteenth century, but the Templars later divided this role between officers known as 'visitors'. The Teutonic Order's master also appointed visitors of this kind and Document 8 is an agreement forged through one such visitation. The general chapters mentioned above were also important events to which distant provincial commanders could be summoned, while leading Levantine officials occasionally travelled back to the west.

A clear example of the above hierarchy in operation can be seen in a judicial case cited in a Catalan version of the Templar rule. According to this, there was a brother who fraudulently forged a papal document and seal for his own purposes. This crime was known to several other Templar brethren but – crucially – they did not report it to the regional commander.

Subsequently, at a provincial general chapter, the matter came to the attention of the commander who was furious and ordered all the brothers involved to be brought before him. Upon hearing their story he evidently felt that this was too weighty a matter for him alone so he appealed for advice from the master and central chapter in the Holy Land. The central chapter duly met in Acre under Master Thomas Berard, but opinion was divided. Eventually it was decided that all those concerned should be expelled from the order and given a penance. Only one brother was allowed to remain within the order because, although he had known of the forged document and not reported it, he had objected strenuously to it at the time. This episode reveals much about the Templar decision-making process. Both the crime and punishment reveal the strong emphasis placed on consultation and transparency as well as clear co-ordination between headquarters and province. It also underlines the importance of the central chapter and how it could liaise with the provincial general chapters.

CAREERS AND LIFE-CYCLE

The military orders recruited an enormous range of staff. These could include shipwrights, farm hands, ordained clerics, millers, stone-workers, lawyers, clerks, mercenaries, wagon masters and blacksmiths; each performing a vital function in an order's infrastructure. Some were not Catholic and in the Levant both Eastern Christians and Muslims occupied important positions, often working as scribes or light cavalry. The centre of every order, however, was made up of its professed brethren. These supplied its core force in battle and leading officials were recruited from their ranks. This section will look at their careers.

Recruitment

In 1234 Conrad, uncle and regent to the young landgrave of Thuringia, joined the Teutonic Order along with several fellow nobles. His family had long patronised the order and his father, Landgrave Hermann, had been present at the order's militarisation in Acre in 1198. Since then a strong accord had grown between family and order. This bond of association may have been enough to convince Conrad to become a brother, but he also had a particularly pressing reason. Two years previously he had attacked the town of Fritzlar, massacring the inhabitants and burning down the church. Given time, he clearly regretted his actions and to show his repentance he offered himself to be flogged by Fritzlar's surviving citizens; his decision to join the order may have been likewise a sign of his contrition.

People had many reasons for becoming brothers of a military order and could be admitted at different stages in their life. Often a career in the military orders was an attractive option for young noblemen who had no expectation of inheriting sufficient wealth to maintain themselves. It seems likely however that many joined the orders because they admired their qualities of piety, adventure and chivalry for which they were renowned. For others this decision was taken on the point of death and the Latin Eastern nobleman John of Ibelin entered the Templar order having been mortally wounded so that he might die as a brother. Often orders focused their recruitment efforts on certain regions. Many of the smaller regional or specifically national orders, such as the English order of St Thomas of Acre, drew primarily upon their own countrymen and the order of Mountjoy was permitted only to recruit Brabanzons, Aragonese and Basques. The larger international orders could be more diverse, although some areas were better represented than others; the Templars and Hospitallers relied heavily on France, for example.

There were limitations on who could become brothers in a military order. In the Templars, applicants had to swear that they were: in good health, unmarried (in some cases married men were accepted if their wives joined a nunnery), without debts, of free birth (i.e. not a slave) and not sworn into any other order. They also had to promise that they had not offered bribes to enter the order. Further entry requirements varied between orders and in some legitimate birth (born within wedlock) was a prerequisite. This was the case in the Hospitaller Order, although the bastard sons of the upper nobility were admitted. Many orders stipulated that recruits needed to be healthy and old enough to fight. In practice, statistical analyses have shown that, on average, recruits wishing to become brother knights in the Templars were in their twenties (Forey, 1986: 150). Many orders also demanded that those wishing to become brother knights should swear that they were of knightly descent, a stipulation common in the larger orders whose wide renown allowed them to become more discriminating. In the larger orders those from more humble origins were permitted to join as sergeants. Sergeants could serve as fighters and in this capacity they were well armed (although not as heavily as the knights); they could also work as craftsmen, professionals and labourers, often applying skills acquired in their earlier life to the smooth running of their adopted institutions.

Reception

Some orders insisted that new recruits should first complete a time of probation before entering the order. For the order of Calatrava and many others this lasted for one year, but requirements varied between orders and practices changed over time. In the case of the Templars, the continued defeats of the Latin East seem to have led them to abandon this practice so that new brethren could be deployed on the frontline with greater rapidity. The Teutonic Knights also allowed new brethren to avoid this probationary period in some cases [**Doc. 8, p. 161**]. The next stage was 'profession' where the candidates took their monastic vow, received their habit and entered the order. In the Hospitaller Order, according to statutes made in 1262, when this ceremony took place in the Holy Land, the event would take place on a Sunday and in the presence of the chapter, who would then judge whether to grant admittance. Reception ceremonies were often complex affairs in which a set formula of promises and symbolic gestures was performed. It was also at this moment when applicants would receive their mantles and take the monastic vows of poverty, chastity and obedience. Mantles – the garb worn by monks – were the uniform of the military orders and each order had their own design. Templars, for example, had white mantles with a red cross; Teutonic Knights, white mantles with a black cross; and the order of Santiago, white mantles with a red cross in the shape of a sword. Sergeants' mantles often differed slightly; in the Templars, for example, they wore the red cross, but with a black mantle. Profession was also the occasion when the order's rule might be read out to remind newcomers of the regulations that would shape the rest of their lives.

Career development

After their reception, there was considerable scope for advancement both for knights and sergeants. The orders' senior officials were drawn from the ranks of the knightly brethren while sergeants could rise to become ships' captains or even, in the Templar Order, treasurer to the Temple in Paris (and by extension to the French crown). Preferment to high office could be achieved by a number of means. Social rank was often a contributory factor. The above-mentioned Conrad of Thuringia became the order's master without having held any former post within the order. Seemingly his status as the order's most illustrious recruit to date was decisive. Towards the end of the thirteenth century, the Hospitallers insisted that their leading officials ought to be the sons of the higher nobility and of legitimate birth. Nevertheless, there was scope for social mobility particularly at an early stage in an order's development and the famous Hermann of Salza, who led the Teutonic Order from relative obscurity to international glory, came from humble origins. By the end of his career, he probably exerted the same political influence as a major prince.

Merit was also important and it is striking that entrants with proven abilities in a certain area could be drafted swiftly into senior positions. Anselm of Lucca, for example, a man of lowly birth but with considerable experience in financial and legal matters, was quickly appointed Hospitaller treasurer (Burgtorf, 2008: 377–438). The Crusader knight, Jean of Joinville, recognised the high calibre of the military orders' masters when he explained why they were never murdered by the Assassins. He believed that the Assassins would consider such an act to be futile because the order in question would immediately appoint a new man of equal ability. There was no particular age requirement for any post, although experience was naturally important. In some cases, perhaps following the loss of many brethren in battle, it may have been necessary to search for future leaders among a younger generation. Furthermore, an order's chapter was normally made up of some of its longest serving personnel who could be expected to have an excellent grasp of the order's traditions and development. As with any institution, some leading officials are thought to have advanced the interests of family members of favourites. William of Villaret, master of the Hospital 1296–1305, certainly promoted the career of his nephew and successor, Fulk of Villaret. An individual's preferment could also be affected by external factors. As shown in Chapters 3 and 5, there were times when secular rulers and churchmen influenced the appointment or dismissal of certain officers. As exempt orders, answerable only to the pope, many of these individuals had no lawful right to intervene in an order's internal business, but changing diplomatic, military or financial circumstances could make it difficult to ignore their wishes.

For the major orders holding lands across Christendom, travel was an important element in many brethren's lives. With commitments in Prussia, Livonia and the Holy Land, for example, the Teutonic Order's masters were constantly on the move. During his tenure as master, Anno of Sangerhausen (master, 1256–1273) was appointed in Rome and later visited the order's houses in the kingdom of Jerusalem, Italy, Germany, Prussia and Armenia. Templar and Hospitaller masters tended to spend most of their time in the east, but even in these orders aspiring Templars were warned at their reception that 'if you wish to be in Acre, you will be sent to the land of Tripoli or Antioch, or Armenia; or you will be sent to Apulia, or Sicily, or Lombardy, or France, or Burgundy, or England' (tr. Upton-Ward, 1992: 169). Although brethren could be sent anywhere, there was a steady movement of troops from Christendom's heartlands to the frontier.

Old age and death

For most military orders' brethren, their careers came to an end only with their death. In the vast majority of cases, masters died in office and those who retired generally did so under troubled circumstances. This was anticipated and for many orders the formal transition of power to a new master began at the point when the current incumbent realised that he was close to death. Even so, for rank-and-file brethren who were too old or too sick to continue to serve, provision was often made. In both the Hospitaller and Templar statutes, brethren no longer capable of bearing arms were permitted to hand in their equipment with the permission of the master. According to Templar regulations – and it should be remembered that many orders organised themselves according to their statutes – the marshal was then expected to give the brother a gentle horse, which he could use for his leisure. Such elderly brothers still had a role to play. They were expected to set an example for younger members and to help guide their behaviour. Other brothers could be sent back to an estate in Christendom's heartlands. The Templar house of Denney in Cambridgeshire was reserved for elderly or sick brethren (Forey, 2002: 177).

The death of a brother, like his reception, was surrounded by ceremony. In the Hospitaller Order, the dead brothers were buried in their mantles and 30 Masses were to be said for each. During the first of these services, the rule required each member of the order present to make a donation of one candle and one *denier* (a penny). This collection, along with the clothes of the deceased, was then to be given to the poor. Further psalms and repetitions of the Lord's Prayer were also to be said.

DAILY LIFE

In the prison of Aleppo, a remarkable trial once took place. Three Templars were incarcerated in a Muslim dungeon along with many other Christian captives, who had been imprisoned there for many years but who knew about the order's business. During this time, each of the three brothers confessed that he had previously stolen an item of equipment. One had taken a dead brother's **hauberk**, another had covertly exchanged his *chapel de fere* (helmet) for one belonging to a brother who was about to journey overseas, and a third had borrowed a piece of saddlery for his horse because his own was broken and he needed to take part in a raid. Having described these crimes the imprisoned captives then consulted with one another and reached the conclusion that while each act was probably sufficient to cause the expulsion of the perpetrator from the order they were all suffering quite enough at the moment without taking further action. Eventually, after their release, the matter was allowed to pass and, although it must have come to the attention of the authorities at some point, an awareness of the brothers' ordeals and their general character saved them. This fascinating story was recorded by the Templars for the edification of future brothers and it advocated an approach that was both strict in its adherence to the rules, but not so bound

Hauberk: A chainmail jacket.

by the letter of the law that extenuating circumstances and appeals of mercy could not be considered.

By joining a military order, applicants entered a highly structured monastic life in which the routine was tightly governed. In times of peace, the day was divided into regular periods – announced by the ringing of a bell – set aside for: regular religious celebrations, work and training, exercise for the horses, meal times and sleep. During services the brother knights were to remain silent but they were also expected to be active in prayer and the Templar Order required each brother to repeat 60 *paternosters* every morning for brothers and benefactors, both living and dead. Templar churches were highly ornate with walls covered in frescos and equipped with a vivid array of clerical vestments and expensive reliquaries (ornamented containers holding relics), crosses, chalices and other objects. Recently, Salvadó has shown how many of the objects found in Aragonese Templar chapels specifically recalled their commitment to Jerusalem. These included items such as icons and relics from the Holy Land which contemporaries would immediately have associated with the east (Salvadó, 2010: 190). One witness in the Templar trial considered them to be the most beautiful churches in the world. Chaplains were a vital component in any monastic community including the military orders. The Teutonic Order explains their role as follows:

> In time of peace they shine in the midst of the lay brethren, urge them to observe strictly the rules, celebrate for them divine service, and administer to them the sacraments. But when hostilities break out, they are to strengthen the brethren for battle and admonish them to remember how God also suffered death for them on the Cross.
>
> (tr. Sterns, 1969: 205)

Brother priests clearly played an important role in the preparations for warfare, but like other ordained clergy they could not shed blood themselves. In the major military orders, they were explicitly barred from reaching leadership positions, which were reserved for brother knights.

Priestly brethren were also required to bless the food provided for a community at mealtimes. In the Teutonic Order meals began with the recitation of a grace by a priest and a *paternoster* and *Ave Maria* by the brethren. Their meals consisted of meat on Sundays, Tuesdays and Thursdays; fish on Fridays; and cheese and eggs on other days. Special dispensations were made for special occasions such as Christmas. In larger houses containing 13 or more brethren lessons were read out 'so that not only the mouth is fed, but also the ears which hunger after the word of God' (tr. Sterns, 1969: 221). Conversation at meal times was not encouraged but brothers were allowed to exchange a few words with those serving them. After the meal the brethren departed together following a recitation of prayers and any half-finished loaves of bread were given to the poor. The specific regulations affecting meal-time customs and indeed all elements of the military orders' routine varied considerably between institutions, but in all cases it was carefully planned and regulated.

Our knowledge of the military orders' diet and health has advanced considerably in recent years with bioarcheological analyses of medieval latrines. Investigations into the Hospitaller latrines in Acre, used by the brethren from 1190–1291, have uncovered pieces of animal and fish bone as well as grains from cereal crops, such as wheat, rye, barley and oats, and stones from cherries and seeds from figs. Samples taken have also identified certain parasites such as roundworm, whipworm and tapeworm (Mitchell, Huntley and Stern, 2008: 213–224). These indicate that food was prepared in unhygienic conditions. Further archaeological examinations have unearthed examples of crockery in the Hospitaller compound, which give some idea of the ceramic vessels used by the order. Most of them are of Levantine or Syrian manufacture, suggesting that they were created locally, although a few are Italian or French. Most strikingly, some bowls are Chinese in origin and serve as a reminder that Acre sat astride the great international routes connecting Europe, Asia and Africa (Stern, 2008: 207).

One of the purposes of the strict routine followed by the orders was to prevent idleness and the Templar rule specifies that any unoccupied brother should set about making tent pegs to prevent sloth. Nevertheless, there were some moments of recreation. Templar brethren were allowed to compete with one another in archery and horse riding, although they were not permitted to gamble with objects of any value. Pieces of candle seem to have been the only accepted currency for wagers! They were also allowed to play a few board games although some, including chess and backgammon, were forbidden.

Breaches of the order's statutes were taken very seriously and punishments could be severe. The Templar regulations contain a list of punishments of differing severity and the offences for which they should be awarded. The most serious, including simony (purchasing a place in the order), killing a Christian, cowardice in battle and theft would result in the permanent expulsion of the perpetrator. Brothers committing relatively minor infractions could be given either extra chores or corporal punishment. These rules shaped the lives of those living within a community, but they also provided guidance for the many brethren whose occupations required them to travel either between an order's houses or as envoys to royal or ecclesiastical courts. Statutes introduced into the Hospitaller Order in 1268, for example, give specific instructions to cover the conduct of brethren travelling by ship between the Holy Land and Western Christendom. These cover the diet of the brethren, the conduct of the brother in charge of the ship, and the action to be taken in the event of a death while on shipboard. Several orders stressed the importance of good conduct for brethren visiting towns. The Teutonic Order particularly demanded that brethren's behaviour should reflect their religious vocation and that they should avoid lodging in disreputable places to avoid criticism. Teutonic Knights were also discouraged from attending weddings and other festivities and they were also prevented from becoming godfathers except in a crisis (presumably if a child's life was in imminent danger). Templars likewise had to receive permission from a superior before visiting towns, villages or castles. In all cases, these instructions reflect an awareness of the temptations found outside the order's walls and they demonstrate a strong desire to safeguard the brethren from such vices while preserving the reputation of the order.

Although the statutes governing behaviour in the military orders are often highly detailed it is not clear how well known they were to the individual brethren or how uniformly they were applied. During the Trial of the Templars several of the accused brethren stated that they had never seen the rule while others said that the order's leading officers actively discouraged ordinary members from reading it. Certainly the order's rule forbade brethren from possessing copies of the rule; a decree apparently introduced following the disclosure of the statutes by a group of squires to laymen. Other orders went to greater lengths to circulate their rules and the Teutonic Order demanded both that a copy be kept in each house belonging to the order and that they be read out to the brethren on a regular basis [**Doc. 8, p. 161**]. Reading the rule aloud would have helped to compensate in part for the widespread inability among knightly brethren to read Latin. In other cases orders' rules were translated into the vernacular, which would have broadened the audience. Even so, despite the fact that many roles within the orders required literacy as a prerequisite, illiteracy was common at this time and only a fraction of knightly brethren would have been able to read in any language.

PIETY AND IDENTITY

On 4 May 1310 Lord Percival of Mar gave evidence before the bishop of Limassol concerning the Templars, who stood accused of an array of crimes including heresy, sodomy and blasphemy. Percival had little to contribute concerning most of the 87 charges cited, but spoke out against Articles 16–19 which claimed that the Templars rejected the sacraments. As part of his evidence, he reported an account he had received from a former Genoese prisoner of war during his incarceration in Cairo. This man described how, upon hearing news of the Trial of the Templars, the Mamluk Sultan ordered 40 Templar captives to be brought before him. The Sultan then told them of the allegations made against the order and attempted to convince them to renounce the Christian faith, offering money as an inducement. The Templars all refused his offer and were then starved to death. For Percival this was irrefutable proof of the Templars' piety because, as he pointed out, if their faith had not been sincere then they would not have held out against the Sultan's offer.

Dedication to Christ, and the imitation of His work, lay at the core of the military orders' identity. Previous sections of this book have detailed their financial dealings or their actions as landowners or warriors – for which we are well provided with documents – but these functions were all performed in pursuit of specific spiritually defined objectives. The Teutonic Order's rule, for example, begins by describing its intention to transform brethren into a likeness of Jesus. The Hospitaller Order stressed that their work emulated Jesus' care for the poor and needy. Their vocation was shaped by biblical injunctions, such as the passage from the Gospel of Matthew where Jesus said 'If you want to be perfect, go, sell your possessions and give to the poor, and you will have treasure in heaven.' (Matthew 19: 21) Among the Hospitallers' ranks were some who were later canonised (declared a saint) for their devotion to God and the poor. Brother Hugh, a brother based in Genoa (d. 1233), was among these. He was famed for his charitable work in the city's hospital and the miracles he performed therein.

Other orders likewise demonstrated how their actions imitated other aspects of Christ's life. When Bernard of Clairvaux wrote in praise of the Templars, he drew comparisons between their hardships and those of Jesus on the cross. He portrayed them as martyrs fighting a war of good against evil on behalf of God [**Doc. 1, p. 144**]. The papacy similarly described them as members of Christ's army ready to prove Christ's words that, 'Greater love hath no man than this, that a man lay down his life for his friends' (John 15:13). Alongside their deep reverence for Christ, the Templars came to hold Mary, mother of Jesus, in great veneration. This was a time in which devotion for Mary was growing and her designation as the 'Queen of Heaven' dates from the twelfth century. The Templars reflected this enthusiasm and claimed that their order had been established in Mary's honour. They were not the only military order to reflect such trends. The Teutonic Knights adopted Mary as their patron saint, dedicating many churches to her and even naming their Prussian headquarters Marienburg in her honour. In 1237, when they took control in Livonia, they assumed responsibility for a land which was known as the 'dowry of Mary'. According to its defenders, Livonia was under her specific protection and she was styled as the

Christians' leader in battle. The Teutonic Knights fully endorsed this conviction and according to one poet the Livonian master once rallied his troops for battle with the cry: 'God sent us here into this land of His beloved mother that we should constantly seek means of expanding our dominion' (tr. Smith and Urban, 2001: 39).

Other orders venerated saints which had specific significance for their order. In Iberia, the apostle St James was particularly important and his shrine at Santiago de Compostela was visited by pilgrims from across Christendom. He was regarded as the defender of Christian Spain and was presented as the embodiment of the struggle against Islam. His cult was vigorously promoted during the twelfth century and his legend became closely linked to the crusading movement. Shortly after their foundation in 1170 the confraternity of Cáceres adopted him as their patron saint, becoming the order of Santiago (St James), with the support of the archbishop of Santiago de Compostela. The decision to connect the order to St James was a manifestation of the saint's intense popularity, but it also placed the order conceptually at the heart of the struggle with Islam, helping them to present themselves as a rallying point for all those who advocated this cause.

Alongside such exemplars, as we have seen, the military orders drew parallels between their warlike activities and the battles of the Old Testament. These books provided a supply of stories of holy warfare that was lacking in the teaching of the New Testament. In many cases they considered their endeavours to be a direct continuation of these ancient wars. As Bernard of Clairvaux argued, 'Do you not see how this new knighthood is frequently sanctioned by the testimony of the ancients?' (tr. Barber and Bate, 2002: 221) [Doc. 1, p. 144]. After their establishment many orders sought to establish venerable histories for themselves in which they located Old Testament roots. The Hospitallers' claimed to have been founded in the second century BC by King Antiochus or later by the Apostles. Some proposed likewise that the order of St Lazarus had been established by Judas Maccabeus. These were powerful images that connected these still youthful orders to respected biblical traditions. In a similar way, as we saw in Chapter 5, the Teutonic Order attempted to position its Prussian wars as an extension of the biblical struggle for Jerusalem. The identity projected by the military orders then was one which spliced Christ's virtues of compassion, charity and self-sacrifice with the older tales of holy war.

Viewed from another perspective, the harder heads within an order would have known both that these values were idealised in contemporary society and that if they could be presented effectively to a wide audience then the order would benefit from the resulting acclaim. Judging whether the membership of any institution truly embodies the values it espouses is difficult and here we are hampered by the scarcity of our source material.

Nevertheless, some accounts of the orders' actions contain clues about their character. To take the Holy Land as an example, the orders' commitment to the defence of the east in its last decades and their readiness to stretch their institutions to breaking point hint at a passionate commitment to objectives, which were defined principally by faith.

Nevertheless, their resolute character did not prevent them from forming close bonds with neighbouring Muslim or non-Catholic Christian leaders. Usama ibn-Munqidh, the son of a leading Arab dynasty from Shaizar, for example, numbered the Templars among his friends and described their courtesy and consideration. The Melkite Christian Archbishop Meletos stated a desire to be buried as a Hospitaller *confrater*. Likewise, the orders were prepared to employ Muslims and Levantine Christians, while the Hospitallers provided medical care for them and all the major orders helped negotiate truces and agreements with neighbouring Muslim rulers. The orders' fully understood that their survival in the Middle East required co-operation with all groups and did not consider their religious convictions to be a barrier to forming such relationships. Moreover, in their letters requesting aid from the west, the brethren rarely used violent or abusive language even when describing their enemies (Riley-Smith, 2007: 137–149). The tone is almost always one of practical assessment and measured judgement. The Levantine military orders were not staffed by rabid fanatics. Their character blended the introspection and commitment of the monastery, the pragmatic realism of the landowner and the courage and ambition of the knight.

THE MILITARY ORDERS IN THE FIELD (MILITARY ACTIVITIES 2)

At Cresson near Nazareth on 1 May 1187, the Templar master Gerard of Ridefort incited 130 knights and 300 sergeants, including many Hospitallers and Templars, to charge a Muslim force of 7000 cavalry. Grossly outnumbered, the Christian warriors were slaughtered almost to a man. According to the tale told by a later crusader, after the bulk of the knights had been killed, a single Templar named Jakelin de Mailly fought on alone; one man against an army. So intense was his defiance that the stubble around him was trodden into dust. Mounted on a white horse and dressed in white armour, he defied all comers, winning his enemy's admiration. Refusing demands to surrender he was eventually crushed by weight of numbers and was said to have finally fallen to his knees safe in the knowledge that he had received the martyr's crown.

This tale is apocryphal, but both the legend of Jakelin and the military orders' conduct during the battle of Cresson reveal a great deal about their actions in war. The decision to attack a far superior Muslim force was an astonishingly reckless act, but there was a vein of logic behind it. Man-for-man the military orders were among the most powerful warriors of their age. The backbone of their force was formed from contingents of brother knights operating as heavy cavalryman. This was a time where Christian tactics revolved on the massed charge of heavily armoured horsemen, all mounted on superbly trained warhorses and working in squadrons. Timed correctly, these charges could overwhelm a numerically superior enemy and only 10 years previously at Mont Gisard a small force of Templars and secular knights had routed a major Muslim invasion army.

The orders refined the cavalryman's role into a fine art. The combination of a disciplined monastic life with the proficiency of an experienced knight was a potent mix and while formations of secular knights tended to disperse in the search of booty or glory, the military orders held their ranks. For this reason they were often stationed as the vanguard and rearguard of a Christian force; positions requiring the steadiest troops. Muslim commentators were fully aware of their abilities and Saladin's decision to execute all military orders prisoners taken after Hattin serves as a grim compliment to their prowess.

The orders also fought in the belief that they had God's active support. Throughout this period writers drew frequent parallels between their knights and Old Testament warriors, such as the Maccabees or the Israelites [**Doc. 1, p. 144** and **Doc. 6, p. 159**]. According to one account, before the battle of Cresson, Gerard of Ridefort reminded his brothers of their Maccabean forebears. Perhaps he too felt that divine aid would counter-balance his numerical inferiority. Even so, although God's will was considered to be decisive in war, most medieval commanders understood that the anticipation of God's support should not be construed as a licence for folly. Judged by this logic, Gerard clearly got the balance wrong and, although he escaped, there were only two other survivors.

Gerard's behaviour is indicative in many respects, but it is also extreme; on most other occasions the orders were far more cautious. They were fully aware of the limits of their own resources and they generally sought to conserve their strength rather than risk dangerous ventures. To take one case, when King James I of Aragon's sons arrived in Acre in 1269, they demanded that the Christian army march out against the Mamluks who were threatening the city. The Templars and Hospitallers, however, refused to co-operate in so impetuous a venture and remained adamant even when the Aragonese princes attempted to force their compliance. They knew full well that a military debacle at this stage could precipitate the complete collapse of the kingdom of Jerusalem.

The field forces assembled by the military orders were generally composite in nature with only a core of brother knights. When in 1260 the Teutonic Knights from Prussia and Livonia marched out with a large army to meet an invading pagan force, which it later engaged at Durben, only a fraction of the total force was brother knights. The vast majority of the host was made up of crusaders, local levies and the orders' vassals. The same was true across many regions and in the Holy Land the orders relied heavily upon local horsemen, known as turcopoles, to provide light cavalry along with mercenaries. During sieges, the orders could also supply engineers to build and man the machines needed to assail the enemy ramparts. Many accounts describe their trebuchets or stone-throwers of other kinds, which were a staple weapon of siege warfare.

In all cases, the military orders' behaviour in war was highly regulated and the Templars' rule contains many stipulations concerning military operations. It outlines a clear hierarchy for battlefield command with specific brethren assigned to perform certain roles. In overall command was the master but he was supported in this capacity by the marshal. Further formations were under the control of officers including the standard bearer (squires), the turcopolier (turcopoles and sergeants) and the commander of knights (brother knights). On the march, the brethren's movements were governed by strict instructions and they could neither mount nor water their horses without authorisation. When the decision was taken to make camp, the order constructed its tents around the chapel tent. If the alarm was raised then those brethren who were nearby were required to rush to the scene to support their fellows, while the remainder were to assemble at the chapel so that they could be deployed as the situation demanded. Regulations and structures were not precisely the same in all orders and on all frontiers, but the emphasis on discipline was consistent.

MEDICAL ROLES

According to a story told by a minstrel in Reims in the thirteenth century, news was once brought to Saladin, sultan of Egypt, that no patient was ever refused care in the Hospital in Jerusalem and that after being admitted the sick might ask for anything which might speed their recovery. Saladin was intrigued and travelled in disguise to the Hospitallers' house where he pretended to be deeply unwell. Encouraged by the order's doctors to eat he steadfastly refused for three days until eventually he suggested that he could be persuaded to eat a hoof belonging to the Hospitaller master's famous warhorse. This was an unbelievably bold request, but the master consented, true to the principles of his order. The horse was brought and an axeman summoned to remove the beast's leg, but just before the blow could land Saladin relented. He then showed his admiration by showering the order with gifts and declared that he would eat mutton instead! This story is a work of fiction and this incident almost certainly never occurred. Nevertheless it reflects the near-legendary status achieved by the Hospitallers' charitable and medical work.

Theoderic, a German pilgrim visiting Jerusalem in 1169, was clearly staggered by the sheer scale of their operation and commented that 'no king or tyrant would be powerful enough to feed daily the great number fed in this house' (tr. Wilkinson, Hill and Ryan, 1988: 287). At its height the Jerusalem hospital had beds for 1000 people. These included many travellers, male and female, from Western Europe. This would have been a vital service for those whose immune systems were unprepared for the parasites and environment of the Middle East. The hospital also admitted those who had been injured in battle and, following the battle of Mont Gisard in 1177, 750 wounded were transported there for care; the order also supplied a field hospital that would accompany an army on campaign. Non-Christians including Muslims and Jews were also accepted, while considerable support was also offered to the poor and needy.

Those in Hospitaller care received the best support available. The brethren and their staff treated the poor as their lords, offering them every possible attention as an act of Christian charity and humility. Upon reception, patients first confessed their sins to a chaplain and were then handed over to sergeants, who fed them and then stored their personal property safely. They were given clean bedding along with a cup, spoon and barrel for wine. The quality of food was extremely high with the poor and sick plied with meat, white bread, wine, fruit, sugar and vegetables according to their needs. Significantly, when pork or mutton was prepared, those who could not eat such meats were given chicken instead, a reflection presumably of the sensitivity shown to the dietary customs of other faiths (Edgington, 2004: 29). Many of the above foodstuffs were very expensive, but the cost involved described an intentional commitment to offering the best service available. A dedicated staff of sergeants served each ward within the Hospitaller compound while a team of doctors checked on each patient twice daily. The hospital as a whole was managed by the 'hospitaller' who was one of the order's leading officials. Those who died in Hospitaller care received a funeral Mass with further Masses said for their souls over the next 30 days. Following the fall of Jerusalem in 1187, the Hospitallers established their headquarters in the city of Acre in 1191 where they already possessed a hospital (although Saladin permitted 10 Hospitallers to remain in the holy city for one year to look after any remaining sick). This medical facility expanded considerably in later years (Mitchell, 2004: 61–85).

The above-mentioned pilgrim Theoderic was absolutely correct; the cost of maintaining these services was indeed enormous. In addition to its main hospital the order also protected orphans, offered alms in many forms to the poor and assisted impoverished couples to get married. All this required an elaborate supply chain. Some materials were sourced locally and the Hospitallers assigned many of their nearby villages the task of providing meat and fruit. Other resources, particularly cloth and sugar were despatched from further afield. The statutes required several regional commanders to send certain commodities annually to Jerusalem as part of their responsions; the commander of France, for example, was expected to provide 100 cotton sheets. The order also ran further hospitals, both in the Latin East and Western Christendom. Many of these were located on the pilgrim routes to the east. Such establishments would have helped ease communications between the Levant and Western Europe, but would also have required funding and staffing. Cumulatively, the Hospitallers' medical and charitable work was a major expense, but these costs would have been offset to a degree by the vast quantity of donations and bequests made by admirers who wished to support their work.

Although the Hospitallers were particularly well known for their care of the poor and sick, other orders performed similar functions albeit on a smaller scale. The Teutonic Order, the order of St Thomas of Acre and the order of St Lazarus all originated as medical organisations. Of these the order of St Lazarus was remarkable for its dedication to the support of lepers. This was one of several hospitals in the Latin East designed to care for specific maladies, another being the hospital of St Anthony which cared for those with ergotism. Certainly leprosy was a serious problem in the Levant that affected all levels of society (including famously King Baldwin IV) and admission to the order would have provided sanctuary and a new sense of purpose for those who contracted the malady. They were not the only military order to provide facilities to lepers and the order of Santiago is also known to have run a hospital at Villamartín which it received in 1196.

The order of St Lazarus: This institution was established in the 1130s outside the walls of Jerusalem. It received support from the kings of Jerusalem and the nobility of the east, growing into a large establishment providing care for lepers and admitting both the leprous and the healthy into their ranks. The order of St Lazarus was also closely affiliated with the Templars, who may have helped them to shape their statutes and who transferred to the order brothers contracting leprosy. The order established a series of commanderies in the west and after the fall of Jerusalem in 1187 relocated its headquarters to Acre. Exactly when the order first assumed a military role is unclear and the first evidence dates from the mid-thirteenth century. They were later involved in several major battles including La Forbie 1244 and Mansura 1250 where they suffered heavy casualties.

WOMEN AND THE MILITARY ORDERS

In 1188, after many legal and financial trials and tribulations, Queen Sancha of Aragon in co-operation with the Hospitaller Order, established a house at Sigena intended for both monks and nuns. This was a unique institution that was intended both to form part of the Hospitaller network and to be under the influence of the queen. This arrangement was set out in a new rule authorised by all the parties involved. These regulations detailed the obligation to pay responsions to the Holy Land, like other Hospitaller houses, but also specified that the queen would have to be consulted about the appointment of any new prioress. King Alfonso II shared his wife's enthusiasm for this project and on 23 April their youngest daughter Dulce was among the first 13 sisters to join the order. He later endowed the monastery with lands, hoping – like so many patrons of monastic orders – that they would cultivate the surrounding wasteland, bringing security and productivity to this little-regarded region. In later years Sancha frequently intervened, with benevolent intent, in the house's life and, following her husband's death, became a sister. This created a tradition of royal patronage that continued long after her death. The specific constitution of the house at Sigena was exceptional in many ways, but this institution also reflects the important roles that female monasteries could play in the military orders (García-Guijarro Ramos, 2006: 113–152). Positive co-operation with secular powers, settlement activities and the maintenance of long-distance supply networks were important roles which could be played by monastic houses populated by either gender.

In time, the number of Hospitaller convents grew considerably with houses in many places including: the British Isles, Frisia, France and the Holy Land. These institutions created opportunities, as with convents in other orders, for women to pursue lives of contemplation and prayer. Women were not permitted to fight, but as in the house at Sigena, they could contribute in other ways. Several further military orders, including those of Calatrava and Santiago permitted women to become professed members and to form their own houses. Among these the order of Santiago was exceptional because it permitted the admission of married couples. Nevertheless, in all these orders the number of female convents was always very small in comparison to the male houses and at times attempts were made to limit their number.

Other military orders, such as the Teutonic Knights, prohibited the admission of sisters, but still relied heavily on women working within their organisation and forged strong relationships with female neighbours and political allies. Their estates were farmed by workers of both genders; their mercenaries and soldiers would have had wives and children, while hospitality and medical care were granted to all. Even in exclusively male orders there was room for flexibility. The Templar rule explicitly forbade the admission of women – ostensibly out of fear that their presence would cause temptation – but even so in 1248 one group of Aragonese women was granted permission to form a female house where they pursued a religious life (Forey, 2006: 45). The Teutonic Knights likewise forbade the admission of sisters deeming them too much of a softening influence, but permitted female lay affiliates (*consorores*) to live communally and pursue a monastic way of life.

Female saints could play an important role in the spiritual life of the orders. The Virgin Mary was naturally a figure of immense reverence, but there were others. In 1235, for example, Pope Gregory IX acceded to representations by the Teutonic Knights to canonise Elizabeth, wife of the former Landgrave of Thuringia. During her lengthy widowhood Elizabeth had been famed for her work in the hospital in Marburg. She was also the sister-in-law to the order's next master Conrad of Thuringia and the order acquired her hospital – despite the fact that it had been promised to the Hospitallers – following her death. The order's affiliation with Elizabeth may well have been rooted in piety, but it was also politic. The Landgraves of Thuringia were close allies and Elizabeth's canonisation ceremony was attended by noblemen from across Germany, including the emperor and the order's master. This event would have reinforced both the political importance and spiritual significance of the order at a time when it was seeking aid in its Prussian wars. These events serve as a reminder that this was an age in which religion and diplomacy worked hand-in-hand.

There were also many female benefactors who forged strong bonds with a military order. In the early thirteenth century, the Hospitallers received support from Margaret de Lacy, a particularly forceful lady and a marcher lord's daughter. In 1216 she granted them her recently founded convent at Aconbury in Herefordshire. Even so, the relationship turned sour. In 1233 she travelled to the papal court to have the house removed from Hospitaller jurisdiction. There were a number of disputed issues in this case, but the underlying problem seems to have been the Hospitallers' need to draw heavily on Aconbury's revenues to finance their actions in the Holy Land. This provoked resentment from Margaret as her cherished institution's immediate needs were subordinated to those of the east. Like so many relationships between patrons and a military order, tensions could arise when their objectives diverged. Ultimately, after much wrangling, Margaret won her case in 1237 and Aconbury assumed the Augustinian rule (Nicholson, 2006: 153–177).

Further reading

Barber, M. (1994) 'The Order of Saint Lazarus and the Crusades', *The Catholic Historical Review*, 80, 439–56.

Bennet, M. (1992) '*La Règle du Temple* as a Military Manual *or* How to Deliver a Cavalry Charge', in J. Upton-Ward (ed. and tr.) *The Rule of the Templars*. Woodbridge: Boydell Press, 175–188.

Burgtorf, J. (2008) *The Central Convent of Hospitallers and Templars: History, Organization and Personnel (1099–1310)*. Leiden: Brill.

Edgington, S. (2004) 'Administrative Regulations for the Hospital of St John in Jerusalem Dating from the 1180s', *Crusades*, 4, 21–37.

Forey, A.J. (1986) 'Recruitment to the Military Orders (Twelfth to Mid-Fourteenth Centuries)', *Viator*, 17, 139–171.

Forey, A.J. (1986) 'Novitiate and Instruction in the Military Orders during the Twelfth and Thirteenth Centuries', *Speculum*, 61, 1–17.

Forey, A.J. (2002) 'Provision for the Aged in Templar Commanderies', in A. Luttrell and L. Pressouyre (eds) *La Commanderie, institution des ordres militaires dans l'Occident médiéval*. Paris: Comité Des Travaux Historiques Et Scientifiques, 175–185.

Forey, A.J. (2003) 'The Charitable Activities of the Templars', *Viator*, 34, 109–141.

Licence, T. (2005) 'The Templars and the Hospitallers, Christ and the Saints', *Crusades*, 4, 39–57.

Mitchell, P. (2004) *Medicine in the Crusades: Warfare, Wounds and the Medieval Surgeon*. Cambridge: Cambridge University Press.

Nicholson, H. (2001), 'The Military Orders and their Relations with Women', in Z. Hunyadi and J. Laszlovszky (eds) *The Crusades and the Military Orders: Expanding the Frontiers of Medieval Latin Christianity*. Budapest: Central European University Press, 233–244.

Nicholson, H. (2004) *Love, War and the Grail: Templars, Hospitallers and Teutonic Knights in Medieval Epic and Romance, 1150–1500*. Leiden: Brill.

Nicholson, H. and Luttrell, A. (eds) (2006) *Hospitaller Women in the Middle Ages*. Aldershot: Ashgate.

Riley-Smith, J. (2004) 'The Structures of the Orders of the Temple and the Hospital', in S. Ridyard (ed.) *The Medieval Crusade*. Woodbridge: Boydell and Brewer, 125–143.

Riley-Smith, J. (2007) 'The Military Orders and the East, 1149–1291', in N. Housley (ed.) *Knighthoods of Christ, Essays on the History of the Crusades and the Knights Templar presented to Malcolm Barber*. Aldershot: Ashgate, 137–149.

Riley-Smith, J. (2008) 'The Death and Burial of Latin Christian Pilgrims to Jerusalem and Acre, 1099–1291', *Crusades*, 7, 165–180.

Weiss, D. (2002) 'Spiritual Life in the Teutonic Order: A Comparison between the Commanderies of Franconia and Prussia', in A. Luttrell and L. Pressouyre (eds) *La Commanderie, institution des ordres militaires dans l'Occident médiéval*. Paris: Comité Des Travaux Historiques Et Scientifiques, 159–173.

7

Away from the Frontier, the Military Orders in Western Christendom

THE MILITARY ORDERS IN A CHANGING WORLD

While the military orders fought to defend Christendom, the world behind the frontier was changing. A rising population led to sustained efforts to transform wooded and marginal land into farmland, while more adventurous families departed for newly conquered territory looking for new opportunities and a better life. As wasteland came under the plough and marshes were drained, food surpluses increased, supporting a larger urban population. The growing sale of produce caused in turn the clusters of buildings surrounding monasteries and castles to expand from small marketplaces into towns and cities, centres of trade and industry. As the risk of Muslim or pagan invasion subsided, commerce flourished, both on land and sea, and money changed hands faster and in greater quantities. With advances in navigation and shipbuilding, new mercantile societies began to assert themselves with greater confidence, demanding recognition and independence from their overlords.

Improved communications enabled by a greater freedom from foreign invasion permitted the papacy to insist upon and regulate a higher moral standard from its clergy while all secular attempts to steer Church policy were firmly resisted. Universities flourished and multiplied as demand grew for literate clerks and clerics, leading to a growing intellectual culture that avidly re-engaged with the classical works from ancient Greece and Rome. Great international monastic and **mendicant orders** spread across Christendom, led by spiritual pioneers who wished to follow the example of Christ through prayer and service to the poor and sick. Deeply felt reverence combined with Europe's growing financial and creative muscle to provoke the building of great monasteries, churches and cathedrals; symbols of devotion expressed through the best work medieval man had to offer.

Mendicant orders: Religious orders (i.e. the Franciscans and Dominicans) of friars who, unlike other traditional monastic institutions, did not live in a monastery but travelled from place to place. They spent their lives preaching and providing pastoral care whilst sustaining themselves by begging.

A strong sense of Catholic Christian purpose emerged as the countries of Christendom worked together to push back its borders through missionary work and crusade. This growing sense of identity, however, alienated marginal groups, such as Jews and heretics, leading to hostility and persecution.

Kings and princes drew upon the growing literate classes to provide themselves with administrative systems that were better suited to the collection of tax and the enforcement of royal will, while simultaneously attempting to suppress ambitious towns and powerful nobles. Although all rulers emphasised their adherence to the Catholic faith there was an ongoing rivalry between temporal rulers and leading churchmen. In every kingdom, churchmen possessed considerable military and political strength in addition to their ability to steer the spiritual lives of their congregations. This power, largely independent of royal control, posed a potential threat to the authority of regional rulers, provoking conflict in the many areas where their interests overlapped.

The huge international networks created by orders, such as the Teutonic Knights, Hospitallers and Templars, were situated at the heart of these economic, political and social upheavals. Smaller orders generally had little influence away from their respective frontiers and therefore this section will focus on the role of the major orders away from the battlefront. The fundamental challenge for the orders' representatives in these regions was to farm and extend their commanderies in an effort to raise resources for each order's military and charitable functions. To this end, they were required to work with local nobles, encouraging them to: offer recruits; donate alms; and take part in crusading operations. They also needed to ensure that their commanderies survived and, if possible, prospered in a changing environment.

POLITICS, REGIONAL CONCERNS AND LOCAL ELITES (PATRONS 4)

Medieval Europe was the scene of many wars during the twelfth and thirteenth centuries. The kings of England and France often took the field against each other as did the rulers of Iberia, the princes of Germany and the Italian cities to name but a few. Moreover, the ongoing struggle for authority between secular rulers and the Church continually broke into conflict. For the military orders just about any warfare between Christians in Western Christendom posed a problem, because it could disturb the communications networks on which they relied. The Italian wars of the 1240s and 1250s, for example, fought between the pope and the emperor, endangered their supply routes across northern Italy and it may well be imagined that slow-moving convoys of goods en route to the Mediterranean ports would have been easy prey for marauders. Raiding expeditions or passing armies could also cause damage to a commandery's agricultural infrastructure, while warfare could occupy the time and funds of families who might otherwise be persuaded to travel on crusade. By contrast, in times of peace, the steady improvement of maritime and overland communications permitted commanderies in regions as distant as Scotland and Scandinavia to play a meaningful role in the supply of resources to frontline work in the Baltic, the Holy Land and Iberia. Each of these establishments was a vital component in the wider order and it was the responsibility of each commander to ensure the prosperity of the estates in his care. With these considerations in mind it is hardly surprising that, as we have seen, military orders personnel were among the leading peacemakers of their time. This commitment to mediation was institutionalised in 1261 when Pope Urban IV endorsed the military order of the Blessed Virgin Mary, which was intended specifically to prevent civil disruption and violence. Shortly afterwards, it was deployed in Bologna to end the factional fighting that had sprung up there. This order did not subsequently grow significantly in power, remaining only small scale, but its mere existence stands as a testament to contemporary belief that the military orders were well suited to work of this kind.

Commanderies varied in composition between regions, but generally they were managed from a central complex. At Cressing-Witham in Essex there still stand two great barns and a well from the original Templar commandery established in 1137. These barns would have been used to store their crops and tithe income. Archaeological and documentary evidence have demonstrated that there was in addition a chapel, a cemetery, a dovecote, a windmill, a watermill and a main hall (Andrews, 1993). By the early fourteenth century it controlled around 2010 acres of land which were used to manage arable crops (including wheat, barley, beans and oats), livestock (including, cows, pigs, geese, but primarily sheep) and woodland. In other areas of England and Europe, commanderies might draw upon other sources of revenue including: shops, mines, tithes, salt-pans, markets, mills, toll-bridges, houses, docks and property. Like many religious orders, military orders were also famous for reclaiming marginal land and in 1201 Peter II of Aragon established the military order of St George of Alfama specifically to settle the uncultivated region of Alfama. In England the Templars founded new towns including Baldock and Witham. These urban developments could be profitably exploited through the holding of markets (and the rental of market stalls), tolls and the sale of plots of land.

In most cases successful development required the support of local nobles, churchmen and the management of regional disputes; a microcosm in many ways of the orders' involvement in international politics. Often regional establishments rose to prominence through the patronage of a leading family who might then encourage their neighbours and followers to

imitate their example. Offering support to religious institutions was a fundamental aspect of noble life and reflected an individual's piety and status. To
take one example, Templar holdings in the county of Champagne developed
swiftly during the twelfth century. The order's first master, Hugh of Payns,
was a vassal of Count Hugh of Champagne (1093–1125) and the count
himself became a Templar in 1125. His descendants and their followers then
continued to grant land, rights and riches to the order over subsequent
decades and the order purchased further holdings itself. During this period
the military orders acquired thousands of such sponsors and many became
closely affiliated to the orders. They were known by the titles such as *confrater*
or *donatus* and their support frequently took the form of ongoing financial
aid. In return they received certain rights, which could include burial in the
order's grounds and prayers for their soul and those of their family after
death (Schenk, 2008: 79–103). Families that were already connected with
the military orders were also ripe recruiting grounds for new brethren and
affiliates and the sources include many instances where a recruit might enter
the order at a ceremony attended – or even led – by an uncle or cousin
(Schenk, 2008: 155–161). Such long-term relationships between order and
family, multiplied thousands of times across Christendom, were the life-
blood of the military orders and were to the advantage of both parties.

Nevertheless, relations with such patrons could deteriorate and this
occurred with Templars and the counts of Champagne towards the end of
the twelfth century. Concern began to be expressed at the scale of their possessions and in 1191 they were prohibited from purchasing urban property
and castles. The Templars then changed tactics and acquired large areas of
forest which they began to cultivate, but this only provoked further complaints from those who depended on the woodland for their livelihoods. In
response, the counts decided to confiscate various properties and legal battles ensued. Eventually, in 1253 Countess Margaret felt compelled to prevent
them from acquiring, whether by purchase of donation, any further fiefs in
Champagne (Evergates, 2007: 55). The story of the Templars in Champagne
is reminiscent of the military orders' relationships in many areas, where their
growing power could provoke anxiety amongst the very people who had
sponsored their rise. This was not always the case and some orders sustained
links with families that lasted for centuries. Even so, for orders that relied on
goodwill, it would have taken diplomacy and sensitivity to manage a commandery's ongoing economic growth without being perceived as a threat.

Relations with clerics also required careful handling. Across Christendom
most monastic orders, like parish priests, were subordinate to the local
bishop. For the smaller military orders this was also true, but many of the
larger ones were exempted from the authority of all churchmen except
the pope. This was not necessarily a problem and some clerics developed a

strong rapport with their local commanderies, but on other occasions an order's independence could cause disagreement, particularly in areas where lines of jurisdiction were unclear. One particularly contentious matter concerned tithes (the tax levied by the Church of one-tenth of an individual's produce). Technically, exempt orders did not have to pay this tax, but it was an issue with many grey areas – i.e. if an exempt order acquired land which had formerly paid tithes, should it continue to pay these taxes or should the order's exemption extend to cover this land? This problem caused trouble in almost every region and sometimes disputes could drag on for decades. This was certainly the case with the order of Calatrava and the archbishops of Toledo during the late twelfth and early thirteenth century. Other issues tended to revolve upon orders acquiring church buildings and cemeteries and then using their exemptions to deny the local bishop any influence over the revenues and personnel therein. It may have been with such concerns in mind that the bishop of Lübeck in *c.*1224 endeavoured to prevent the Teutonic Knights from gaining any property within his city. In short, commanderies may have been set up to provide support for a distant frontier, but they did not exist in isolation and they had to manage their relations with local elites carefully while shaping their own conduct in such a way that they did not suffer adversely from regional conflicts.

CRUSADERS AND PILGRIMS

In the kingdom of Jerusalem during the spring of 1252 the Master of the Hospitallers received a complaint from Jean of Joinville, seneschal of Champagne, while King Louis IX's crusading army was encamped outside Caesarea. According to his report a troop of French knights had been hunting a gazelle when they were set upon by a group of Hospitallers who had forced them to give up the chase. A small enough incident perhaps, but the Hospitaller master was furious. He assured Joinville that the perpetrators would be arrested and he chose to humiliate the brothers responsible by forcing them to eat their meals on the floor, sitting on their mantles. Shortly afterwards, Joinville and the other French knights told the Hospitaller master that they were satisfied, but the master said that he had no intention of ending the punishment and it was only when Joinville threatened to join the knights by eating his own meals on the floor that the master relented. The Hospitaller master's vigorous reaction on this matter is not surprising. As he pointed out to Joinville, the abuse of pilgrims was in direct contradiction to his order's work, which centred on their care and sustenance.

Pilgrims and crusaders were important to the military orders on all frontiers. Like many later orders, the Hospitallers had been founded to provide visitors to Jerusalem with medical assistance and accommodation. The Templars were also established to protect pilgrims as they visited religious sites in the Holy Land. Both orders later took responsibility for the maintenance and defence of pilgrim sites including, Mount Tabor (the place of the Transfiguration), Jabal Quruntul (believed to have been the place where Christ was tempted by the devil) and Cana (the place where Jesus turned water into wine). In addition to their spiritual commitment to such charitable services, more secular-minded brothers would also have been aware that pilgrims were vital for the ongoing prosperity and protection of the Latin East. Whether they arrived individually, in groups or as part of great crusading operations, pilgrims could render military assistance to the Latin East and all would spend money, boosting the economy. For the frequently undermanned and under-resourced defenders of the Latin East this was a vital source of aid that the military orders fully understood. The orders of Iberia and the Baltic likewise recognised their reliance on crusaders and ensured that they were properly supported. When Duke Albert of Saxony arrived in Livonia in 1219, the Swordbrethren gave him a hero's welcome and organised banquets and festivities in which he was plied with wine, mead, beer and any food he might request.

When seeking to recruit crusaders, the large military orders could draw upon their networks of commanderies and representatives. Commanderies could disseminate news and appeals for help to every corner of Western Christendom. Establishments on major roads could then provide accommodation and refuge for emissaries and preachers tasked with gathering crusading forces. In some cases the orders used their own personnel to lead recruitment drives. An early example of this is the first Templar master, Hugh of Payns, who helped to create the crusading expedition which reached the east in 1129 (see Chapter 1). Likewise, in the 1220s, the Teutonic Order's master, Hermann von Salza, assisted Emperor Frederick II of Germany to raise crusading forces by travelling across Europe seeking recruits in person for his forthcoming crusade. At the same time, the order helped to build ships that would be suitable for employment in the Nile Delta (Frederick's initial target). Frequently the orders were also involved in the financial preparations for crusading. Following the battle of Hattin, the Templars and Hospitallers assisted Henry II of England to levy a special tax known as the 'Saladin Tithe' to raise money for his crusade (later carried out following his death by his son Richard I). The papacy also relied heavily on the orders for the collection and safe passage of Church taxes destined for the east. The orders' infrastructure and general trustworthiness as professed religious made them ideal for this purpose.

Having helped to raise such forces, the orders then offered crusaders ongoing assistance to make their campaigns as successful as possible. They generally contributed a contingent to supplement the available crusading forces; their officers frequently settled disputes between rival crusaders; whilst experienced brethren could offer local expertise and advice to crusading commanders confronted with the challenge of waging war in an alien environment. During Albert of Saxony's above-mentioned expedition to Livonia, he relied upon Volkwin, master of the Swordbrethren, both to organise the army and to decide upon strategy, reportedly commenting: 'all my knights and men-at-arms will follow your leadership right into Heaven' (tr. Smith and Urban, 2001: 13). Certainly, crusaders ignored the military orders' counsels at their peril. On 8 February 1250, during Louis IX's crusade against Egypt, the French army stood on the point of victory. The cavalry led by Robert of Artois had advanced alone and had taken the Egyptian host totally by surprise, overrunning their camp outside the town of Mansura. Reining in after their charge, the Templar master suggested that Robert should wait for the remainder of the French army to arrive before following up the attack. Robert, however, ignored his advice and led a charge directly into the town where he and his horsemen and the Templars were overwhelmed.

Upon reaching their destination, smaller bands of pilgrims often connected themselves to an order, which would provide them with accommodation, medical care, burial (for those seeking to end their days in the Holy Land), guides to visit the holy sites and, for warriors, the chance to fight within the order's squadrons. In many cases knights made a commitment to serve with an order for a specified period, often a year. According to one tale reported by the Teutonic Knights' official chronicler, a pilgrim knight having completed a year's service with the order in Prussia died during his homeward journey and was buried. Later, however, he miraculously emerged from his grave to report to his son that his work with the brethren had saved him from his former sins. The author's purpose in this tale was seemingly to demonstrate to his audience the considerable spiritual rewards that could be gained through supporting the order, presumably in the hope of attracting such assistance in the future. Likewise, in the Holy Land, this form of service was sufficiently popular for Templars to create guidelines in their rule to regulate the lifestyle practised by such warriors while living within their communities. The papacy encouraged this process, issuing indulgences both for knights and other pilgrims who wished to offer their support to an order [see **Doc. 6, p. 159**]. In 1238, Gregory IX permitted the Order of Alcántara to offer indulgences to the soldiers serving with them who died in battle against the Muslims. This was a mutually beneficial arrangement for all parties with pilgrims acquiring the promise of an indulgence while the order gained their unpaid assistance.

Financial help could also be offered. When Prince Edward of England (later Edward I) visited the Holy Land, the Hospitallers guaranteed loans raised by him totalling 5000 marks. The Templars also supplemented his finances. Not only did this give Edward the funds to remain in the east, but it was also possible for magnates in England to repay the loan to the Hospitaller authorities in London, who could then despatch the money with their next shipment of troops. Through such procedures, the Hospitaller network played an important role helping crusaders to overcome the financial challenges involved in travelling to the east. The orders' international frameworks could also help co-ordinate efforts to ransom Christians held captive by the Muslims. In 1272 Duke Henry of Mecklenburg attempted to visit Jerusalem in secret but was captured by the Muslims. Despairing of his return, his wife Anastasia contacted the Teutonic Order in Lübeck in 1287 (northern Germany) and deposited 2000 marks with them to be used for his ransom. This transaction was confirmed three days later and a request was sent on her behalf to the order's representatives in the Holy Land. In August 1289 the order's grand commander replied, reporting that he had investigated the matter but had not been successful. He attempted to return Henry's personal effects, but the Duke's son wished them to be given to the order. Receipts were then issued for the restoration of the original 2000 marks. Although the Teutonic Knights were unsuccessful on this occasion, Anastasia's ability to contact the order on the shores of the Baltic and for her wishes to then be carried out in the kingdom of Jerusalem in a fully documented series of transactions reveals the order's organisational sophistication. Henry was subsequently released in 1298 after 26 years in captivity.

The work of ransoming captives was important and many frontline religious orders were established solely to perform this function. Among the most famous of these was the Trinitarian order established by John of Matha in 1198, which operated in both Iberia and the Levant. This order drew much of its identity from the military orders, its members wearing a blue and red cross on their mantles and devoting one-third of income from all their houses across Europe to the payment of ransoms; a similar structure to responsions. Their establishment – like the first military orders in the twelfth century – reflects a further innovative adaptation of the monastic model to engage with a pressing need. Other ransom hospitals were also founded including the orders of Merced in Iberia – confirmed by the papacy in 1235 – and the hospital of the Holy Redeemer at Teruel in 1188 (run by the order of Mountjoy). The orders of Calatrava and Santiago also managed ransom hospitals.

Crusaders were often deeply impressed by the frontline work conducted by the military orders and many expressed their admiration through gifts. One such pilgrim was Sweder of Dingede who made grants to the Teutonic Knights in Lankarn and Schalkwijk (Holland) during the Fifth Crusade's siege of Damietta. Having returned home he continued to offer support and in 1231 he and his wife Beatrix took new crusading vows which were redeemed with cash payments to the order. In some cases relationships forged while on crusade could last for generations. When Margrave Dietrich of Meissen marched to aid the Teutonic Knights in Prussia in 1272 he was following a father who had campaigned there in 1234 and a grandfather who advocated the militarisation of the order in the Holy Land in 1198.

HERESY, MENDICANTS AND POLITICAL CRUSADING

The military orders, like the crusades, were primarily instruments of the papacy. A ruler might hope to bend an order or a crusading army to his wishes, but fundamentally, only the papacy could authorise the formation of either. During the twelfth century, both these weapons proved powerful tools in the hands of a capable pope and swiftly crusading operations expanded to embrace Iberia and the Baltic. Many military orders were established in these regions soon after crusading operations began and, as we have seen, several prospered. During the thirteenth century, however, as crusading continued to broaden in scope to encompass expeditions launched against the pope's political enemies and heretical groups, the military orders proved unable or unwilling to adapt to these new challenges.

For much of the century, the papacy was locked in conflict with Emperor Frederick II of Hohenstaufen and his descendants. This struggle was an overriding priority for the papacy for which it was willing even to sacrifice the interests of the Holy Land. As the conflict dragged on attempts were made to call upon the military orders to render support. Initially they were asked to act as mediators, but towards the end demands were made for money and troops. The latter two of these requests involved the orders diverting resources that could otherwise be used in defence of the east. Naturally they were hostile to the idea but in 1267 the Hospitallers grudgingly agreed to supply troops for the papacy and around this time the decision was taken to tax all the orders for long periods, including those with exemptions from taxation. This episode reflects the changing climate of the thirteenth century. Previously, the military orders had spearheaded the papacy's drive to defend Christendom's frontline, particularly the Latin East. In this effort their work had been central to papal policy. Now, however, with the advent of internal wars and crusades for which they were less appropriate, sustaining the orders on the frontiers was simply one priority among many.

A further serious threat to the Church emerged towards the end of the twelfth century from major heretical movements. Heresy had long been a problem, but this was a time in which improving communications allowed ideas to be disseminated at greater speed and to a wider audience. Heresy took different forms. During the eleventh century the Church had begun to demand an increasingly high level of moral conduct from its clergy. This was intended to strengthen the spiritual authority of the priesthood, but it also enabled dissent from the laity at times when they felt that this standard was not being met (Roach, 2005). Undercurrents of anti-clericalism grew and bands of laymen demanded a greater stake in their own spiritual life. In time they formed movements, most prominently the Waldensians. This group remained largely Catholic in doctrine but rejected the authority of priests. More serious was the development of Catharism, a heresy that fundamentally reinterpreted orthodox Christian teaching. This sprang up in many areas, particularly in Italy and southern France. Originally, it may have been an import from the Byzantine Empire where such ideas were rife; its transmission perhaps a side-effect of the growth of Mediterranean trade and crusading.

The struggle to suppress these heresies became a vital imperative for the papacy, which was alarmed at their rapid growth. The threat from the Cathars in southern France was particularly acute and in 1209, when initial attempts to root them out failed, a crusade was launched. Given that both the Templars and Hospitallers had extensive estates in this area it might be thought that they would have been active in their support of the crusade, but their help was rarely offered and never demanded. The orders were already over-stretched. Moreover, their local properties relied upon the co-operation and goodwill of local communities, some of whom were connected to heretics. Some attempts were made to found new military orders to face the Cathars. In 1221 the Militia of the Faith of Jesus Christ was established and appealed to the papacy, asking to be able to use the Templars' rule. Sometime later an institution was created known as the Order of Faith and Peace. Its purpose was to prevent violence, rather than specifically combating heresy and it followed the rule of the order of Santiago. Clearly, contemporaries could see applications for new orders in this context, but neither prospered. It might be that a military order was too blunt an instrument in the subtle work of detecting heretics in closed communities. Far more relevant tools for the eradication of heresy were the new orders of friars: the Franciscans and Dominicans. Unlike monks, the friars lived in the world, preaching and spreading the word of Jesus Christ. Working in the growing towns and with strong institutional links to the great universities, they better reflected Christendom's changing character, while their direct interaction with the populace, and therefore its dissenting influences, offered a more relevant response to the threat of heresy.

In time, the friars extended their evangelical activities to include the expansion of Christendom's frontiers. In doing so – just as the military orders and ransom hospitals had before them – they reflected a new attempt to deploy professed religious on the frontline. Dominican and Franciscan houses were established in the Baltic, Iberia and the Holy Land, aiming to win converts to Catholicism. For regions such as the Holy Land, where missionary activity had not formerly played a major role, the friars reinvigorated this dimension of Catholicism's confrontation with Islam. In the Baltic and Eastern Europe, on the other hand, missionary activity had been conducted for centuries and the incoming friars continued this work, albeit with a new energy. They also travelled widely across Asia with some brave individuals penetrating as far as Mongolia and the Far East. Their renewed emphasis on expansion by evangelism often stood in contrast to the military orders which rarely showed much enthusiasm for preaching. In the Holy Land and Iberia, they might employ Muslims or seek diplomatic links and friendships with Muslim rulers, but this was generally the extent of their engagement. There was some variation; the order of Santiago seems originally to have shown some initial interest in conversion, but the military orders did not train their personnel for this role and some even discouraged their Muslim subjects from converting because non-Christians paid higher taxes. In the Baltic, there were stronger links between orders and missionaries, but as we have seen by the mid-thirteenth century many feared that the Teutonic Order's ongoing campaigns damaged missionary activities.

The rise of the Mendicant orders and their deployment on the frontline alongside military orders and crusaders challenged contemporaries to combine the friars' attempts to win voluntary coverts with the conduct of war. Contemporary opinions on the compatibility of war and conversion varied. Some believed that they fully complemented one another. Writing in the 1270s, Humbert of Romans, former Dominican master general (1254–1263), outlined an argument voiced by many others that military conquest could create a more secure environment for preaching. He and others also advocated force as a means of compelling Muslim rulers to admit friars into their realms. Furthermore, the Franciscan and Dominican orders worked as preachers rallying crusaders for all frontiers while their friars accompanied campaigns (including those raised by the military orders). Some friars, however, were less certain. Writing in c.1266 Roger Bacon, a Franciscan, described the futility of the wars conducted by the military orders claiming that their endeavours only entrenched an enemy's resistance to either conquest or conversion. Similar views had been voiced previously, even in the twelfth century, when Walter Map had pointed out that where the apostles had successfully spread the word of God across much of the world in a short space of time, the Templars had failed even to hold their narrow frontier. Clearly, he considered that the word was mightier than that sword.

None of these evolutions – whether the rise of heresy, political crusading or the establishment of the friars – posed an overt threat to the idea of the military order. Even so, they created a new environment in which both the relevance of the military orders' vocation and their ability to react to the Church's emerging needs were less clear.

ATTITUDES TO THE MILITARY ORDERS IN THE HOLY LAND BEFORE 1291 (CONTEMPORARY ATTITUDES 3)

In *c.*1283, the Catalan missionary Ramon Lull wrote a romance entitled *Blanquerna*. This work outlined his philosophy on many matters through a fictional tale of a young man's rise from obscurity to the papal throne. In one scene, a messenger arrived at the papal court carrying a message from the 'Sultan of Babylon'. In his letter, the Sultan expressed his amazement at the devices used by the Church to spread Christianity. He argued that their efforts to win conquests by war better resemble the policies of Islam than the teaching of Jesus and his apostles, who converted many by preaching and martyrdom. He concluded by pointing out that their failure to achieve victory in the Latin East indicated that they did not have God's support. The pope, deeply moved by the Sultan's words, then summoned the masters of the Temple and the Hospital and demanded that they unite to form a new order entitled, 'the Order of Science and Chivalry'. This order was to establish schools and colleges where they could learn how to preach the Christian message and acquire the languages to communicate these arguments. Equipped with these skills he believed that this order would be able to prove itself both on the battlefield and in debate. At a later point a knight from the order of Science and Chivalry reached the Sultan where he indeed defeated the Sultan's men both in argument and combat.

This story is a product of Ramon's imagination, but it reveals his concerns surrounding the military orders' vocation (and indeed the wider Catholic engagement with Islam). Clearly he was aware that former policies had failed and a new approach was needed. His conviction that the orders should conduct evangelism alongside warfare reflects likewise the above-mentioned influence of both the Mendicant Orders and missionary activity on crusade strategy. The idea of unifying the military orders was similarly a proposal that was keenly discussed in European courts. This approach was propounded by many commentators, including several popes, who felt that by doing so the orders could consolidate their resources into a single administration and erase former rivalries. Eventually, calls for this solution reached such a pitch that in *c.*1306 the Templar master felt compelled to write to the pope to explain why it should not happen.

Ramon's overwhelming message was that the military orders needed to evolve and many other contemporaries took this view. One commonly voiced opinion was that they needed to become more efficient. Critics recognised that they were vastly wealthy but could not understand why they were unable to provide more effective protection for the Latin East. At the Second Council of Lyons in 1274 the dean of Lincoln argued that if the orders' resources were better managed then they could support the Holy Land on their own without constantly asking for aid. He was not alone in this belief and Document 7 [**p. 161**] records the monastic chronicler Matthew Paris' view that the Templars and the Hospitallers squandered their monies and actually sought to provoke conflict so that they could continue to tax pilgrims. Others complained that the orders expended their energies fighting among themselves. Protests of this nature were to continue for decades and were eventually used as an argument by those advocating the destruction of the Templars.

Alongside such calls for reform were cries of outrage from those who had learnt to fear the acquisitiveness of the local commanderies. As we have seen, the increasingly powerful orders frequently came into conflict with local families and in 1236 Pope Gregory IX warned the military orders of the many complaints he had received about their aggressive actions across Europe. Contemporary documents speak of debts, the infringement of other peoples' rights and disputes over property. Such actions would doubtlessly have been defended by the orders on the grounds that they were necessary to ensure the supply of resources to the east, but they also caused hostility and resentment.

Furthermore, in some quarters the brethren's moral conduct proved an ongoing source of criticism. During the Trial of the Templars, Albert I of Habsburg wrote to Philip IV of France that members of religious orders 'ought by the splendour of their life to be a mirror for others and an example' (tr. Barber, 1984: 27). He was absolutely right; the religious orders only survived because their patrons, supporters and well-wishers saw in their conduct a purity of life that they admired or wished to imitate. Writing in 1283 the Franciscan Salimbene of Adam lambasted the Order of the Blessed Virgin Mary precisely because it had – in his estimation – failed so completely at maintaining a high moral standard, becoming an object of public scorn. As we saw in Chapter 1, back in 1129 Prior Guigo of the Carthusian Order had expressed his fear that the Templars might be vulnerable to the vice of pride. His fears were well founded and many later commentators repeated this accusation.

Contemporaries in the thirteenth century had many reasons to distrust the military orders or at least to feel that they needed to adapt to new circumstances, but their complaints should not obscure the fact that in other areas the orders still enjoyed considerable support. Throughout the century, tens of thousands of pilgrims received assistance – whether in medical aid, military support, ransoming, hospitality, spiritual guidance, escorted visits to the holy places or transport, etc. – from the orders during their expeditions to Christendom's frontiers. They would then have carried their good reports back to their homes across Christendom, describing their experiences in conversation with families and friends. The many surviving donations received from grateful pilgrims reflect the continued goodwill their work inspired. Likewise, the papacy and the orders' long-standing supporters worked hard to inspire the populace with reports of their activities, while the sight of bands of knightly brethren en route for the east would have reminded all of their unceasing labours.

The surviving evidence from this period includes both eulogies and bitter denunciations, but these were the views of individuals among civilisations of millions. Gauging how representative their attitudes were of society as a whole is, as we have seen already, problematic, particularly because views will have varied enormously across regional and linguistic zones. In an attempt to measure trends in public support for the military orders, historians have conducted studies on the changing number of donations made to the commanderies of individual orders over time. The crucial finding of these investigations, including those by Gervers (1982) and Nicholson (1995), has been that during the later thirteenth century benefactions began to drop. Identifying this shift has been important for many reasons, not least because it provides vital financial context for studies, such as Bronstein's work on the Hospitallers (2005), which analyse the order's policies in the Holy Land during the thirteenth century. Accounting for this decline, however, is more complicated. One conclusion would be to connect this fall with the above-mentioned criticisms made of the orders, particularly those concerning their involvement in the repeated crusading defeats and the eventual fall of the Latin East. Certainly criticism must have played its part, but historians such as Nicholson (1995 and 2004) have pointed to a series of wider contextual factors that may have curbed patronage to the orders. As we have seen, during the thirteenth century, many crusades were launched within Europe, in which the orders played little part. New religious orders, particularly the Mendicants, were also attracting the attention – and therefore the donations – of many noble families. Charitable giving to monastic orders as a whole was also in decline across much of Christendom and many rulers were looking for ways to restrict benefactions to monastic orders with new legislation. Gervers (1982) and Bronstein (2005) likewise have stressed the impact of wider economic changes at this time, including rising inflation and the associated demand for more agricultural land. Overall, these different explanations challenge us to consider whether donations fell because the orders had brought themselves into disrepute or whether they were simply the victim of changing religious and economic circumstances over which they had little control. The Teutonic Knights were to some extent an exception to this trend and the flow of patronage into their coffers remained steady, bolstered presumably by their ongoing campaigns in Prussia and Livonia (Nicholson, 1995: 65), but the Templars and Hospitallers both suffered heavily.

Overall, by the late thirteenth century the military orders had both critics and advocates but the world around them was changing. As the century progressed, the friars and hybrid forms of crusading were demonstrating that they were both more adaptable and innovative instruments of papal policy while the military orders were proving both unsuccessful in their primary task of protecting the Holy Land and gradually unnecessary – for the Church at least – in the almost-complete Iberian *Reconquest*. They were far from obsolete but neither were they offering solutions to the new problems faced by the Church.

Further reading

Barber, M. (1984) 'The Social Context of the Templars', *Transactions of the Royal Historical Society*, 34, 27–46.

Bellomo, E. (2008) *The Templar Order in North-West Italy, 1142–c.1330*. Leiden: Brill, 2008.

Evergates, T. (2007) *The Aristocracy in the County of Champagne, 1100–1300*. Philadelphia, PA: University of Pennsylvania Press.

Forey, A.J. (1989) 'The Military Orders and Holy War against Christians in the Thirteenth Century', *The English Historical Review*, 104, 1–24.

Forey, A.J. (1993) 'Military Orders and Secular Warfare in the Twelfth and Thirteenth Centuries', *Viator*, 24, 79–100.

Forey, A.J. (2002) 'The Military Orders and the Conversion of Muslims in the Twelfth and Thirteenth Centuries', *Journal of Medieval History*, 28, 1–22.

Forey, A.J. (2008) '*Milites ad terminum* in the Military Orders during the Twelfth and Thirteenth centuries', in J. Upton Ward (ed.) *The Military Orders, Volume 4: On Land and by Sea*. Aldershot: Ashgate, 5–12.

Friedman, Y. (2002) *Encounter between Enemies: Captivity and Ransom in the Latin Kingdom of Jerusalem*. Leiden: Brill.

Gervers, M. (2002) 'The Commandery as an Economic Unit in England', in A. Luttrell and L. Pressouyre (eds) *La Commanderie, institution des ordres militaires dans l'Occident médiéval*. Paris: Comité Des Travaux Historiques Et Scientifiques, 245–260.

Kedar, B. (1984) *Crusade and Mission: European Approaches towards Muslims*. Princeton, NJ: University Press.

Lord, E. (2004) *The Knights Templar in Britain*. Harlow: Pearson.

Nicholson, H. (1995) *Templars, Hospitallers and Teutonic Knights: Images of the Military Orders, 1128–1291*. Leicester: Leicester University Press.

O'Callaghan, J.F. (1975) 'The Order of Calatrava and the Archbishops of Toledo', in *The Spanish Military Order of Calatrava and its Affiliates*. London, Variorum Reprints, 63–87.

Schenk, J. (2008) 'Forms of Lay Association with the Order of the Temple', *Journal of Medieval History*, 34, 79–103.

Selwood, D. (1999) *Knights of the Cloister: Templars and Hospitallers in Central-Southern Occitania, 1100–1300*. Woodbridge: Boydell and Brewer.

8

The Military Orders at the Time of the Trial of the Templars

THE EASTERN MEDITERRANEAN FOLLOWING THE FALL OF ACRE

In 1292 James of Molay became Templar master in a controversial election that was deeply riven by internal factions and overshadowed by the deteriorating political situation in the Eastern Mediterranean. By taking office he joined the remaining leaders of the Latin East in facing the bleak realities of this embattled theatre of war. According to a Hospitaller estimate the Mamluk Sultan could raise an army of 24,600 men – a force wildly in excess of the available Christian resources in the region (Irwin, 1994: 59). Without the support of a major crusade from Western Christendom a direct confrontation with the Mamluks would be unthinkable. Also, a long-term reconquest required settlers in huge numbers, but the former Latin population of the kingdom of Jerusalem was either in exile on Cyprus, in slavery or suffering in extreme poverty. The military orders still had forces available to supplement those from the surviving kingdoms of Armenia and Cyprus, but their supply networks were exhausted from years spent propping up the crumbling Latin East. In this environment, the only ways that a reconquest of Jerusalem could even be contemplated were either through co-operation with the Mongols, who still threatened the Mamluks' north-eastern frontiers, or with a far greater commitment from Western Christendom to lend aid to the east.

By this stage a general consensus had emerged within Christendom's decision-making circles that a new strategy was necessary for reconquest of the East. Such plans had been made before, during the later thirteenth century when it became apparent that the kingdom of Jerusalem could no longer compete with the Mamluk Empire. In 1272 Pope Gregory X had issued a general request for advice about a new policy for the revival of Christian fortunes in this area. Two years later at the Second Council of Lyons, many ideas were discussed but little was done. With the fall of Acre, however, the need for a new approach was particularly acute. Several proposals were put forward, advocating policies ranging from an increase in naval power to a greater emphasis on missionary activity, but many were shaped as much by the political interests of their authors as by the military realities in the Eastern Mediterranean. Again, the idea to unite the military orders was advanced, but this idea like many of the others was never put into practice. In 1306 Pope Clement V requested the presence of the Hospitaller and Templar masters to discuss the recovery of the Latin East. The Hospitaller master's plan was to launch a well-financed major new crusade to the east, preceded by a series of naval assaults on coastal positions and a general blockade of Muslim-held ports. James of Molay's (the Templar master) plan was broadly similar, emphasising the need for a large army and the prevention of supplies reaching Egypt from Europe. In reality, despite heroic new schemes imagining thousands of knights and mighty crusading armies, only a small number of contingents reached the east.

Meanwhile the military orders' Levantine squadrons did not stand idle. The kingdom of Armenia still held out and would continue to do so until its final collapse in 1375. The military orders devoted considerable resources to protecting Armenia's frontiers and garrisoning important fortresses. Indeed, many crusade strategists identified Armenia as a valuable base for the reconquest of the Levant. Meanwhile diplomatic links were encouraged with the Mongols by those who hoped for a co-ordinated pincer attack against the Mamluks. Several channels of communication with the Mongols were available and the Templars had contact with many missionaries, emissaries and merchants, who were penetrating into the interior of Asia Minor during the thirteenth century. In 1299 these plans seemed to be on the point of fruition. The Mongols had invaded and destroyed a Mamluk army in Syria. More importantly, they offered to return the Holy Land to the Christians in return for their assistance. The following year they took Damascus and drove south to Gaza, although they withdrew soon afterwards. The Christian forces utilised the resulting chaos to launch a series of raids along the Egyptian and Levantine coast and subsequently the military orders and Cypriots gathered at Tortosa in Syria, intending to join a second great Mongol incursion. Nevertheless, the intended unification of Mongol and Latin forces never took place – although some companies of knights assisted a subsequent Mongol offensive – and the Mamluks drove the Christians out of Tortosa to the offshore island of Ruad, which they later seized in 1302.

Based in Cyprus and with encouragement from the papacy, the military orders quickly adapted to their changed circumstances and began to build galley fleets with which to harry Muslim ports and shipping. The Hospitallers instituted a new official position, the **admiral**, and the Templars likewise

Admiral: The official in charge of naval activities in the Hospitaller order.

began to acquire warships. In 1306 Master Fulk of Villaret, formerly the first admiral of the Hospital, put these new forces to the test when he embarked upon a conquest of the isle of Rhodes. This was eventually completed with the assistance of crusading forces in 1310. Taking Rhodes was a shrewd move. It would add considerably to the Hospitallers' position and provide a much needed victory to send back to the continually disappointed advocates of Levantine crusading in Christendom. It would also give them territorial independence, an important consideration at a time when the military orders were dangerously implicated in rivalries over the Cypriot crown.

King Henry II of Cyprus had many opponents both foreign and domestic and, like so many monarchs, he had come to fear the military orders for their strength and political assertiveness. In 1306 he forbade them acquiring property on Cyprus and attempted to prevent the Hospitallers from building up their fleet. His power was also contested by his brother Amaury, who successfully seized power in 1307, although Henry managed to restore his position in 1310. Amaury himself received considerable support in his designs from the Templars, who also opposed Henry but in May 1308 his support from this quarter received an unexpected check when incredible news arrived from the west: the Templars had been arrested.

THE TRIAL OF THE TEMPLARS (PATRONS 5)

On 9 November 1307 Hugh of Pairaud, holding the position of Templar Visitor, put his hand on the gospels and confessed to an inquisitor that during his 44-year career in the order: he had denied Christ; he had spat on both an image of Christ and a crucifix; he had been involved in illicit kissing; he had worshipped a false idol; and he had authorised acts of sodomy. Moreover, despite some initial prevarication, he admitted that such acts were common within the order. His only defence was that while he had committed such grievous sins he had done so under compulsion and not with his whole heart. Hugh was not alone and out of the 138 depositions taken from other Templars between October and November 1307 only four did not confess or report serious crimes. For an order that was founded entirely on its commitment to serve God these statements could not have been more damning – but were they true?

These testimonies were extracted from the Templars following a general arrest of French Templars on Friday 13 October 1307 on the orders of King Philip IV. Since this time they had been tortured and brutalised by French agents and forced to sign confessions, admitting to these and many other crimes. Philip claimed that he was acting on the basis of reports he had received asserting the order's calumny, but in practice his evidence was slight. Whether Philip truly believed his own allegations is unclear, but he was certainly a man with many troubles. Over the past century the French crown had greatly strengthened its power, but recently a series of rather inconclusive conflicts with Flanders and England had demonstrated Philip's inability to finance his country's wars. As costs and debts had mounted he had tried to increase royal income by a huge variety of expedients. The clergy had been heavily taxed. He had seized property belonging to the Jews and in 1306 had expelled them from the kingdom. Italian bankers – major creditors to the crown – had also been arrested and the currency had been debased repeatedly, provoking general outrage. Everything had been tried, but nothing had worked. In this environment, no wealthy group or institution was safe and, although the Templars were struggling to finance their wars in the east, huge sums still passed through their hands and for several periods during Philip's reign they had acted as royal bankers and creditors. Templar wealth had been seized before when royal finances were at a low ebb and Prince Edward of England (later Edward I) had formerly broken into the Templar house in London and stolen huge quantities of valuables in 1263. Moreover, the order had not endeared itself to Philip in recent years and in 1302 some brothers had fought with the Flemings in their struggle against the French (Schotte, 2010: 45–56).

Nevertheless, unlike the Jews and bankers, the Templars were not without powerful defenders. As an institution of the Church, an attack upon them was an attack upon the papacy and when rulers had attempted large-scale confiscations of land from the military orders in the past – i.e. Frederick II's confiscations of Templar and Hospitaller property on Sicily or King Andrew's seizure of Teutonic Order territories in Hungary – they had immediately incurred the pontiff's wrath. The Trial of the Templars, however, took place in unusual circumstances. Over the past decade relations between Philip and the papacy had been tense, frequently flaring into conflict. Philip's taxation of the clergy; his attempts to dismiss a leading churchman; and the papacy's determination to stress its authority over a pious but distinctly independent-minded king led in 1303 to a vicious attempt to kidnap the pope in Anagni. By 1305 French influence over the papacy was considerable. The new pope Clement V was no puppet, but neither was he a free agent. French supporters dominated the College of Cardinals while Philip and his leading nobles had been a visible presence at Clement's coronation. Moreover, Clement never left France during his pontificate. The papacy's ability to defend the Templars was weakened further by the order's all too evident failure to prevent the collapse of the Holy Land. Although the brethren still had many supporters and recruitment remained buoyant, they *had* very visibly failed and, unlike the Hospitallers on Rhodes or the Teutonic Knights in the Baltic, had not found a new direction in these changed circumstances.

Thus when Clement received news of the Philip's arrests his response was cautious. Both he and the Templar leadership had known for some time that the king had been making accusations against the order and the brethren had apparently requested a papal enquiry so that they could clear their name, but neither had known of the arrests in advance. Clement's first reaction was to ask for more information and then he issued a carefully worded letter to Philip reproaching him for exceeding his authority by seizing churchmen. Clement's predicament was complex: on one hand, as the head of the Catholic world, he had a duty to act against so flagrant an assault upon the Church, but on the other hand, too direct a confrontation with the French crown might provoke a humiliating defeat that would strike a crippling blow to papal authority. His compromise was to institute a formal investigation into the Templars under his own management and to order the arrest of all Templars across Christendom. Ostensibly its purpose was to assess the Templars' guilt; in practice the real issues at stake were the king's desire for both increased authority and the Templars' wealth set against a weakened papacy's need to preserve its public credibility.

As a first stage, cardinals were sent to Paris to speak with the Templars and to find out if their confessions were genuine. Their findings were exactly what Philip did not want: James of Molay, Templar master, and Hugh of Pairaud among others revoked their confessions and graphically described the tortures that had been inflicted on them. With news of these revelations Clement decided that he had sufficient evidence to halt the proceedings against the order. This did not, however, shake Philip's resolve; he still held both the brothers and their lands in his custody and he immediately launched a covert propaganda offensive, blackening the order's name and undermining the authority of the Church. Leading churchmen, great nobles and representatives from many towns were consulted on this matter or summoned to denounce the order in an attempt to bring greater pressure upon Clement. Some were more willing to co-operate than others and the University of Paris politely but firmly refused to offer Philip the full legal mandate he required. Even so, by May 1308 he felt secure enough of his position to lead a huge entourage to confront the pope in person in Poitiers. What followed was a piece of diplomatic theatre in which Philip's agents attempted to force the pope into agreement while attempting to establish indisputable divine authority for their actions. Nevertheless, despite many thinly veiled threats, Clement would not budge (Barber, 2006).

Faced with this refusal, Philip then presented the pope with 72 hand-picked Templars, who were almost certainly among those who had either proved the most tractable under threats or torture or who had personal reasons for defaming the order. In the resulting papal examination many, but not all, confessed to a range of crimes. From the pope's perspective theirs was highly tainted evidence, but these witnesses did create an opportunity. If he had previously agreed to the demands of the French crown it would have been obvious that he had simply yielded to royal pressure. Now however, by at least overtly accepting these witnesses' statements, he could present himself as the supreme judge swayed by force of evidence. By taking this escape route he could hope to avoid the risk of an immediate and highly dangerous confrontation with the French king. His solution was to institute two years of investigations into the Templars to be held across Christendom and to be concluded with a Church council at Vienne (Barber, 2006).

After a year's further postponement, this council finally met at Vienne in 1311, but by then much had changed. During the intervening period, enquiries had been held across Christendom, but the response had been mixed at best. In Paris almost 600 Templars had assembled to defend the order, vigorously condemning the charges and asserting their innocence. Further Templars had renounced their former confessions, citing the tortures they had received, while growing attention was given to the deaths of many brothers from their inhumane treatment. As the momentum of the trial hovered in the balance Philip took matters into his own hands. Certainly if the order was found to be innocent then his own position would be threatened, not least because he had begun to exploit the Templar property to his own ends. Philip's response was first to disrupt the hearings and then on 12 May 1310 to have 54 Templars burnt to death outside Paris. All were executed still protesting their innocence. In later days more Templars were burnt. These brutal actions effectively destroyed the Templars' attempts at self-defence. Many were then coerced into making confessions and finally in May 1311 the papal commission in France ground to a halt. Across Europe, reactions were mixed. Edward II, king of England, was initially openly critical of the trial and later interviews with Templars elicited only a handful of admissions – under torture – that would corroborate any of Philip's claims. In Aragon, the Templars were in a better position to resist arrest and held out for long in their many fortresses. Nevertheless, in the investigations following their eventual surrender, scant evidence was found of wrongdoing. Further enquiries in Iberia, Sicily, Cyprus and Germany were similarly fruitless and it was only in parts of southern Italy where a handful of further confessions were made.

By the time of the Council of Vienne, however, the papacy was fully committed to the dissolution of the Templars and the evidence it had amassed was compiled in such a way as to give the impression of an overwhelming case against the order. Some Templars came to the council to offer a defence but they were simply thrown in jail. Many prelates complained about this, saying the order's members should have an opportunity to speak, but any discussion of such a hearing was quashed when on 22 March 1312 Philip descended upon Vienne with a force of troops. Two days later, under heavy pressure, the decision was finally taken to suppress formally the order of the Temple. Many were appalled at the conduct of the trial, but their outrage could not affect the outcome: the Templars were finished and, while some brethren were granted pensions, on 18 March 1314 James of Molay was burnt to death. Templar lands in all areas except Spain were given to the Hospitallers, although in France Philip was permitted to reclaim his 'expenses' from the former Templar properties (eventually set at 200,000 livres). In the event it was to be many years and many long legal battles before the crowned heads of Europe yielded these estates. In Iberia, the Templars' former lands were used to found new institutions including the Order of Montesa in Valencia in 1317 and the Order of Christ in Portugal in 1319. In Castile the order's lands were supposed to go to the Hospital, but were seized by various existing orders, including Calatrava and Santiago.

The Trial of the Templars is an ugly story of strong-arm tactics, torture and political intrigue, but one which underlines the structural vulnerabilities in the concept of the military order. The Templar master might sit at the high-table of politics and command huge resources but ultimately his was a fragile institution because while its riches and estates in Western Christendom were an asset, they were also a source of temptation for rulers who were fully aware of their wealth. As Philip's actions prove, these could be taken with little effort in most countries and only in the frontline regions of Iberia was any serious attempt made at resistance to the arrests. The trial also laid bare the vulnerability of an order with strong ties to both ecclesiastical and secular patrons. The struggle for authority between churchmen and lay rulers is a defining feature of the Middle Ages and at times of conflict, with close ties of dependency to both, the military orders could be caught directly in the middle. As we have seen, in 1229 the Teutonic Knights had been trapped in this way during the war between Gregory IX and Frederick II. In this case the brothers had a narrow escape with the establishment of peace in 1230. The Templars were not so lucky.

The trial leaves historians with a number of major questions of which the most significant revolves around the guilt or innocence of the Templars. This has been hotly contested in the past but for many decades now historians, including myself, have generally accepted the allegations to be fundamentally false. This conclusion is based on a number of premises of which the most important are as follows: first, a natural scepticism towards evidence given under torture; second, Philip's very obvious need for the order's money and his evident attempts to steer the trial to his own purposes; third, the absence of rumours (outside the French court) suggesting any prior suspicion concerning the allegedly widespread crimes for which the order was condemned; fourth, the conspicuous lack of evidence of guilt from virtually all regions outside France; and fifth, the doubt with which so many well-informed European rulers met the colourful but outlandish charges. In addition to this, I find myself agreeing with the many trial witnesses who argued that the Templars would hardly have shown such commitment to the Holy Land during the late thirteenth century if their order had really been riddled with such practices.

Nevertheless, several historians have argued that while the order may have been generally innocent, there may have been areas where such practices may have crept in. Riley-Smith (2004, restated 2010) describes an order which, at the turn of the fourteenth century, was structurally on the point of collapse and makes the point that in this disorderly condition it may not have been possible to prevent sinful customs infiltrating distant establishments. Elements of Riley-Smith's conclusions have since been rebutted by Forey (2009), who challenged the belief that the order had fallen into such disarray by this stage. Likewise Nicholson (2010) has offered further criticisms, disputing the evidence used by Riley-Smith which relies on testimonies given under torture. More recently, D. Bryson (2010) has attempted to identify where such localised abuses might have taken place.

This issue of Templar guilt is perhaps the most famous controversy created by the trial, but it is not the only issue this event raises. Historians have long pondered questions including: Why did Philip arrest the Templars? Did he really believe his own allegations? Was Clement V a weak pope manipulated by a powerful king or did he simply act in the only way open to him given the dangers of his position? Formulating an answer to these or any of the other major questions surrounding the trial is a major problem for a historian given that the surviving sources (whether letters, legal documents, trial records, chronicles, etc.) are cumulatively a tissue of lies, misunderstandings, truths, half-truths, propaganda and evidence given under torture. Few can be accepted at face value and extracting the actual events that took place with any degree of accuracy from such tainted materials is a major challenge. It requires historians to understand in detail: the perspective of the authors involved, the context in which they wrote and the limits of their knowledge. The inherent difficulties in such a search are many and varied, but this in itself underlines the challenge of researching and writing history.

THE OTHER MILITARY ORDERS AT THE TIME OF THE TRIAL

While Western Christendom deliberated over the Trial of the Templars, the nature of crusading was shifting. Jerusalem had long been held up as the ultimate goal, but where in the late thirteenth century its recovery had at least been plausible, in the early fourteenth it was looking progressively unrealistic. By the 1310s both the Mamluk Empire and the Turkish emirates of Asia Minor had become extremely powerful and posed a serious threat, by land to Armenia and the Byzantine Empire, and increasingly by sea as Turkish war fleets began to prey on Christian shipping in the Aegean. The strategic situation in this theatre was changing and contemporaries were beginning to comprehend that defence rather than recovery was the priority. Opposing these forces were the remaining Christian outposts of the Eastern Mediterranean, such as Cyprus and Hospitaller Rhodes, but these required support from their allies to the west. This imperative was well understood in European courts and was much discussed, but little help materialised. In 1334 the first of many naval leagues was established in an effort to guard against Turkish raids launched from Asia Minor. The Hospitallers joined the resulting fleet which won a victory over the Turks at Adramyttium. However, the campaign – which had been prepared as the first stage in a wider crusading strategy – was not followed up. Over time, Western Christendom became increasingly preoccupied with its own controversies and the flow of warriors travelling to the Eastern Mediterranean dwindled. The remaining defenders in this region were by now firmly on the defensive.

With the suppression of the Templars, the Hospitallers were the sole remaining military order of any size in the region. The Teutonic Knights maintained a small presence but their emphasis was by now in Prussia and Livonia. Even so, Fulk of Villaret's conquest of Rhodes created new opportunities. The Hospitallers set about encouraging settlers to move to the isle, while their knights conquered surrounding islands and areas of the Anatolian coastline. The order's fleet was also becoming a formidable force and in 1312 defeated a Turkish squadron, while later raids were made on Turkish fortifications on the mainland. The order also offered sporadic support to Armenia. Through such actions the Hospitallers demonstrated to watching eyes in Western Christendom that they still had a role to play in the Mediterranean. This was important, both for the encouragement of their patrons and to give them credibility at a time when the Templars were under scrutiny. Even so this was a time of hardship for the order. The conquest of Rhodes proved extremely expensive and its attendant costs plunged the order deeply into debt. Naturally the order looked to its western estates for the monies to fund such ventures, but monarchs proved increasingly unwilling to permit the export of money to fund ventures beyond their borders.

During this period the administrative tools available to many rulers in Western Christendom were becoming progressively more sophisticated, permitting a far greater centralisation of power. As their control tightened, many kings sought to increase their influence over the military orders. This can be seen particularly with Philip IV of France. By the time of the Templar Trial the Hospitallers had already been restructured into 'tongues' (a system in which brethren were grouped according to their regional origin) with each area granted representation in the order's decision-making. Philip resented this system because the redistribution of power it involved reduced the level of influence formerly enjoyed by the order's French brethren (Burgtorf, 2008: 139). Proposals were also put forward by Philip's circle suggesting that the military orders should be combined and placed under the control of a member of his family. Furthermore, although Philip agreed in principle that the Templars' former properties should be transferred to the Hospital, he attempted to profit from the arrangement by making his support conditional on receiving financial concessions and authority over the order.

As has been shown in the above chapters the military orders were shaped to a large degree by their patrons. This was true throughout their history and during the fourteenth century particularly strenuous efforts were made by several major rulers to bind military orders closely to their interests. Several Spanish orders, which had always been closely associated with their Iberian overlords, were passing under royal sway. In time, the kings of Castile and Aragon became accustomed to conferring leading positions within orders, such as Alcántara and Calatrava, on royal favourites while the military orders' objectives began to become synonymous with those of their royal masters. The Trial of the Templars can likewise be seen as an attempt by a secular patron to dispose of an order as he saw fit.

Fortified in their Prussian and Livonian lands the Teutonic Knights were in a better position to preserve their independence, but even they faced severe challenges at this time. With the conclusion of the Second Prussian Rebellion in 1283, the order had an opportunity to recommit itself decisively to the defence of the Holy Land. Such a move was not impossible and as late as 1305 the Hospitallers included them in proposals for the reconquest of the Eastern Mediterranean. Nevertheless, the faction within the order advocating a continued concentration on the Baltic wars was in the ascendancy. Lithuania was still a major threat on the Teutonic Knights' Eastern marches and covetous eyes were being cast on Pomerellia (a highly strategic region held by Poland which lay between the Teutonic Knights' Prussian lands and its supporters in imperial territory). In 1308 the King of Poland appealed to the brethren for assistance after Pomerelia was attacked by the Duke of Brandenburg. The order responded swiftly to his appeal, conquering the region and then demanding payment from the Poles. The Poles then refused to pay, giving the order an excuse to claim the area for themselves. This was an ugly business for a religious order that was supposed to offer leadership for the expansion of Christendom. It was also a lesson in just how dangerous an order could become to its erstwhile benefactor. Even so, this episode did not attract nearly as much attention as the order's deeds in Livonia.

The problem was as old as the Livonian colony itself. Power was shared primarily between the archbishop of Riga and his supporters, the citizens of Riga and the Teutonic Order, formerly the Swordbrethren [see **Doc. 4, p. 156**]. Such power sharing was the cause of many disagreements and in 1297 these same divisions emerged again at a time when the territory was heavily embattled against the neighbouring Russians and Lithuanians. Disputes over relatively minor local issues stoked existing tensions to provoke a civil war in which the people of Riga, supported by the archbishop and the Lithuanians, confronted the order militarily, whilst sending vigorous denunciations of the order's actions to the pope. The papacy took this matter seriously and began a series of judicial hearings to address the matter. These, however, reached no clear resolution and long drawn out attempts at peacemaking failed. Eventually in 1310 (while the Templars themselves were standing trial) Pope Clement V launched a further investigation into the Teutonic Knights' conduct. Many accusations were made, including the by now familiar charge that they were obstructing the work of missionaries. At the same time complaints were arriving from Poland concerning the order's conduct in Pomerellia. In 1312 the archbishop of Riga with the approval of the papal commission excommunicated the order's Livonian branch for its actions. At this moment with the recent dissolution of the Templar order it must have seemed that the Teutonic Knights' future was likewise in jeopardy, just as the Swordbrethren's had been in the 1230s. In time, however, the Knights were able to negotiate their way to safety and many contemporaries spoke out in their favour, but even so this was only the beginning of a far longer conflict fought both in Livonia and in the papal law courts. These then were anxious days for the military orders when for one reason or another they found their actions or vocation called into question.

By the 1330s the surviving military orders inhabited a very different world to that of the thirteenth century. The Teutonic Knights' policies had attracted suspicion and eroded goodwill among their neighbours, but they *were* also a regional power, firmly in control of two highly developed states. Their authority had passed far beyond the censure of secular patrons, who in other areas of Christendom, particularly Spain, had brought other orders firmly under their authority. The Hospitallers had also achieved autonomy through the conquest of Rhodes but while this gave them a degree of independence they were also firmly engaged in manipulating their international networks to rally crusaders against the rising Turkish threat. In general, the remaining military orders were by now weathered institutions of the Catholic establishment. The idealistic enthusiasm that had greeted their first appearance in the twelfth century had now worn thin as contemporaries were confronted by the reality of their human limitations. Of course they still had their supporters and they still had vital roles to play, but the former sense of euphoria that had inspired the formation of so many orders had largely eroded.

For Christendom's monarchs the military orders had originally offered solutions at a time when they were heavily committed to the struggle against the Moors, Turks and Pagans. In the early twelfth century, this had been an overwhelming imperative on all fronts and the introduction of orders dedicated to this task had made perfect sense. By the fourteenth century, however, conflict with Islam in Iberia was no longer the priority it once had been and while monarchs could occasionally force or cajole reluctant military orders to provide troops for wars against their Christian neighbours **[Doc. 10, p. 164]** they only ever did so unwillingly. In the Latin East, of course, the war with Islam went on, but the rulers of Cyprus and Armenia were well aware of the potential threat that could be posed by an over-mighty military order. Here, as in many regions across Europe, institutions founded initially through goodwill or in response to a threat, had grown to challenge the noble houses which had sponsored them. Faced with these realities, rulers turned instead to secular knightly orders dedicated to royal power and with a membership drawn from lay knights rather than professed religious. In 1330, for example, King Alfonso XI of Castile-León founded the Order of the Band which populated its ranks with those secular knights who had fought nobly for their king. This institution like others of its kind – such as the Order of the Garter 1344 (England) and the Company of the Star 1352 (France) – conferred many advantages upon the crown (Boulton, 1987: 96–210). They valued and rewarded qualities of royal service in a way the military orders did not. Also, given that their members were secular knights with incomes of their own, they did not require the huge landed endowments necessary for the establishment of a military order. In addition, the new Iberian orders of Montesa and Christ were from the outset bound to the authority of the reigning king to a much greater degree than the older Iberian military orders had been. Similar patterns can be found across Christendom at this time. Europe was changing: royal power was rising and where formerly crowned heads had been prepared to accept the presence of quasi-autonomous military orders – and indeed quasi-autonomous nobles – within their realms, the growing sophistication of their administrations enabled them to undercut such pretensions of independence and centralise as much authority as possible on themselves.

Further reading

Barber, M. (2006) *The Trial of the Templars* (2nd edn). Cambridge: Cambridge University Press.

Boulton, D. (1987) *The Knights of the Crown: The Monarchical Orders of Knighthood in Later Medieval Europe, 1325–1520.* Woodbridge: Boydell and Brewer.

Burgtorf, J., Crawford, P. and Nicholson, H. (2010) *The Debate on the Trial of the Templars (1307–1314).* Aldershot: Ashgate.

Edbury, P. (1991) *The Kingdom of Cyprus and the Crusades, 1191–1374.* Cambridge: Cambridge University Press.

Forey, A.J. (1994) 'Towards a Profile of the Templars in the Early Fourteenth Century', in M. Barber (ed.) *The Military Orders: Fighting for the Faith and Caring for the Sick.* Aldershot: Ashgate, 196–204.

Forey, A.J. (2001) *The Fall of the Templars in the Crown of Aragon.* Aldershot: Ashgate.

Forey, A.J. (2009) 'Notes on Templar Personnel and Government at the Turn of the Thirteenth and Fourteenth Centuries', *Journal of Medieval History*, 35, 150–170.

Housley, N. (1986) The Avignon Papacy and the Crusades, 1305–1378. Oxford: Oxford University Press.

Housley, N. (1992) *The Later Crusades: From Lyons to Alcazar, 1274–1580.* Oxford: Oxford University Press.

Leopold, A. (2000) *How to Recover the Holy Land: The Crusade Proposals of the Late Thirteenth and Early Fourteenth Centuries.* Aldershot: Ashgate.

Luttrell, A. (2007) 'The Hospitallers and the Papacy, 1305–1314', in *Studies on the Hospitallers after 1306.* Aldershot: Ashgate, article V, 595–622.

Menache, S. (1998) 'The Hospitallers during Clement V's Pontificate: The Spoiled Sons of the Papacy', in H. Nicholson (ed.) *The Military Orders, Volume 2: Welfare and Warfare.* Aldershot: Ashgate, 153–162.

Menache, S. (2003) *Clement V,* Cambridge Studies in Medieval Life and Thought: Fourth Series. Cambridge: Cambridge University Press.

Nicholson, H.J. (2009) *The Knights Templar on Trial: The Trial of the Templars in the British Isles, 1308–1311.* Stroud: The History Press.

Nicholson, H.J. (2010) 'The Changing Face of the Templars: Current Trends in Historiography', *History Compass*, 8/7, 653–667.

Riley-Smith, J. (2004) 'Were the Templars Guilty?', in S. Ridyard (ed.) *The Medieval Crusade.* Woodbridge: Boydell and Brewer, 107–124.

Urban, W. (1981) *The Livonian Crusade.* Washington, DC: University Press of America.

Part 2

DOCUMENTS

Document 1   BERNARD OF CLAIRVAUX'S TREATISE FOR THE TEMPLARS ENTITLED *IN PRAISE OF THE NEW KNIGHTHOOD* (1130s)

Prologue

To Hugh, knight of Christ and master of the Knights of Christ, Bernard, Abbot of Clairvaux in name only: Fight the Good Fight.

On three separate occasions, unless I am mistaken, my dearest Hugh, you have entreated me to write a sermon of encouragement for you and your fellow knights, and to brandish my pen against the tyranny of the enemy, since I am not permitted to brandish the lance. You state that it would be a great help to you if I encouraged with words those I cannot encourage with arms. Indeed, I put this off for some time, not because your request seemed worthless but in case a hasty, unconsidered assent should be a source of reproach in that with my lack of experience I presume to do what someone better than me could do better, and possibly do a very necessary thing in unsatisfactory fashion. However, seeing that my longish wait did not bring a solution, I finally have done what I can so that my willingness should not be put in doubt more than my inability. The reader will judge if I have carried out my remit satisfactorily. Although someone may not find this acceptable or sufficient, this does not concern me; to the best of my abilities I have not failed you in your request.

I Sermon of Exhortation to the Knights of the Temple

A new sort of knighthood is said to have sprung up in those lands and that region once visited in the living flesh by the One who was born on High;[1] He drove out from there by the might of His hand the princes of darkness,[2] and now by the hand of his brave warriors He will scatter and destroy their captains, the sons of the infidels.[3] He will redeem His people and raise the horn of Salvation for us in the house of his son David.[4] A new sort of knighthood, I say, unknown to the world, is fighting indefatigably a double fight against flesh and blood as well as against the immaterial forces of evil in the skies.[5] Indeed, where resistance is offered to a physical enemy by physical force alone, I do not deem this surprising, nor think it rare. But, each time war is waged against vices or demons by the force of the mind, then I would not call this miraculous, even if it is laudable, since the world is seen to be full of monks. However, when both sorts of men gird their swords of power[6] and don their belts of nobility, who will not consider this to be most worthy of total admiration, in as much as it is clearly unusual. Truly the knight is without fear and totally without worries when he has clothed his body with the breastplate of iron and his mind with the breastplate of the faith.[7] Indeed, endowed with both sorts of arms he fears neither demon nor man. Nor does he fear death, for he wishes to die. Why should he fear, whether living or dying, since for him life is Christ and death is reward?[8] He takes his stance for Christ willingly and faithfully but prefers to die and be with Christ,[9] for this is better. So, knights, go forth untroubled, and with fearless mind drive the enemies of the cross of Christ before you,[10] certain in the knowledge that neither death nor life can separate you from the love of God that is in Christ Jesus,[11] as you say to yourself in every dangerous situation: 'Whether we live or die, we belong to the Lord.'[12] How glorious is the return of the victors in battle! How blessed is the death of the martyrs in battle! Rejoice, brave champion, if you live and conquer in the Lord; but exalt and glory all the more if you die and are joined to the Lord. Life brings its rewards and victory its glory, but a holy death is rightly considered preferable to both. 'Blessed are they who die in the Lord',[13] but how much more blessed are they who die for the Lord?

Indeed, whether one dies in bed or in war, the death of his saints will doubtlessly be precious in the sight of the Lord.[14] However, the more precious is death in war, the more glorious it is. O life without cares when one's conscience is clear! O, I say, life is without cares when death is awaited without fear, even desired with sweetness and received with devotion! O knighthood truly holy and safe, totally free from that double danger that frequently puts at risk the sort of man for whom Christ is not the reason for his fighting. Each time you go into battle, you who fight a worldly enemy, there is the fear that when you kill your enemy physically, you kill yourself spiritually, or else that when you are killed by him you die physically and spiritually. It is the emotion of the heart not the outcome of the war that determines death or victory for the Christian. If the combatant's cause was good, the outcome of the fight cannot be bad, just as the end will not be judged good if the cause is not good, resulting from a good intention. If it should happen that you yourself are killed in your desire to kill another, you will die a murderer. If you have the upper hand, and in your desire to overcome or to avenge you happen to kill a man, you will live a murderer. Being a murderer is no advantage to a living or a dead man, to a victor or a loser. Cursed is the victory you achieve over a man if you succumb to vice, and under the influence of anger or pride, you exult over the man you have defeated. There exists the man who kills, not in his eagerness to avenge, nor in his passion for victory, but solely as a means of escape. But I would not call even this victory a good one, since death of the body is a lesser evil than death of the soul. It is not because the body is killed that the soul dies; but 'the soul that has sinned will die'.[15]

II Concerning the Secular Knighthood
What therefore is the end or result of this secular *malitia*, I do not say *militia*, if the killer sins mortally and the killed dies eternally? Indeed, to cite the

words of the apostle: 'He who ploughs ought to plough in hope and he who threshes does so in the hope of receiving the fruits.'[16] O knights, what is this error so stupendous, what is this madness so unacceptable, to fight at such great cost and effort, with no rewards other than those of death or crime? You cover your horses in silks and put over your coats of mail I know not what sort of cloth hangings; you paint your spears, shields and saddles; you decorate your bridles and spurs with gold, silver and jewels, and you hurry to your deaths with such great pomp, with shameful madness and shameless rashness. Are these military insignia or are they women's baubles? Perhaps the enemy's blade will respect the gold, will spare the jewels, will be unable to pierce the silk cloths? Finally, as you yourselves have learnt from experience on numerous occasions, there are three things essential to any warrior; a knight should be energetic, strong and vigilant in protecting himself, free in his movements and ready to strike; you, on the other hand, wear your hair like a woman so that it obstructs your eyes, your long, flowing robes hamper your steps, and your tender, delicate hands are hidden in voluminous enveloping sleeves. Over and beyond these points, if the cause for which such a dangerous service is undertaken is really quite frivolous and lacks seriousness, then this has the effect of bringing fear to a soldier's conscience. The only things that cause conflicts and start wars are feelings of irrational anger, the pursuit of vain glory,[17] or the desire for some piece of land. It is certainly not safe to kill or be killed for such causes.

III The New Knighthood

However, the knights of Christ fight the battles of their Lord in all peace of mind, in no way fearing to sin in killing the enemy or to die at his hands, since indeed death, whether inflicted or suffered, is not tainted by crime but is marked by a large degree of glory. In one case it is acquired for Christ while in the other it is Christ who is acquired, Christ who willingly accepts the death of his enemy in revenge and even more willingly offers Himself to the knight in consolation. Thus, I say, the knight of Christ kills in safety and dies in greater safety. He obtains an advantage for himself when he dies, and for Christ when he kills. He beareth not the sword in vain: for he is the minister of God[18] to bring revenge upon they that do evil, and praise for they that do good.[19] Obviously, when he kills an evil-doer, he does not commit a homicide, but rather, as one might say, a malicide, and clearly is considered the avenger of Christ against those that do evil[20] and a defender of Christians. When, however, he is killed, it is recognised that he has gone to Heaven, not to his death. The death that he inflicts is reward for Christ, the death he suffers is reward for himself.[21] In the death of an infidel the Christian glories because Christ is glorified; in the death of a Christian, the generosity of the King is revealed when the knight is led off to his reward. 'Therefore the righteous will rejoice over him when he seeth the vengeance.'[22] The man will say of him: 'Verily there is a reward for the righteous; verily he is a God that judgeth them in the earth.'[23] Even infidels need not be killed if there were some other way of preventing their attacks and onslaughts on the faithful. For the moment however, it is better that they be killed, than to let the rod of the sinners govern the fate of the righteous, in case the righteous put their hands to evil use.[24]

How is this? If striking with a sword is for a Christian a totally forbidden act, why therefore did the herald of Christ tell the soldiers to be content with their wages?[25] Why did he not tell them to refrain from all military service? If however, as is the case, it is open to all men, as long as they have been divinely called to this, and have not made profession of a higher calling, I ask you, by whose strong hands if not by theirs shall Sion, the city of our strength,[26] be held for the protection of us all? When they have expelled the transgressors of the holy law, the righteous people shall enter the city in safety and guard the truth.[27] Let the nations that seek war be surely scattered[28] and those that attack us be cut down;[29] let all evil-doers be driven from the city of the Lord,[30] they who strive to remove the priceless treasures of the Christian people that have been placed in Jerusalem, who strive to defile the holy places,[31] to hold as their inheritance the sanctuary of the Lord.[32] Let both swords of the faithful[33] be drawn against the necks of their enemies to destroy all arrogance that raises its head in opposition to the knowledge of God[34] that is the Christian faith, lest the Gentiles say: 'Where is their God?'[35]

After their expulsion He will return into the house that is His inheritance. In the gospel He spoke in anger of it: 'Your house shall be left to you desolate',[36] and through His prophet he complained: 'I have forsaken my house, I left my inheritance.'[37] He will fulfil that prophecy: 'For the Lord has redeemed his people and has delivered them,[38] and they shall come and shall give praise in Mount Sion and they shall rejoice in the good things of the Lord.'[39] Rejoice, Jerusalem,[40] and know now the time of your visitation![41] 'Break forth into joy and give praise together, ye waste places of Jerusalem, for the Lord hath comforted his people: he hath redeemed Jerusalem. The Lord hath prepared his holy arm in the eyes of all the nations.'[42] You had fallen, o maiden Israel and there was none to lift you up.[43] Rise up now, shake off your dust, maiden, captive daughter of Sion.[44] Rise up, I say, and stand on high, and observe the joy that comes to you from your God.[45] 'Thou shalt no more be termed "forsaken" neither shall thy land any more be termed "desolate"; for the Lord hath delighted in thee, and thy land shall inhabited.'[46] 'Lift up thine eyes round about and behold: all these are gathered together and have come to thee.'[47] This is the help sent to you by the Holy One.[48] Through them right now is completely fulfilled that ancient promise to you: 'I will make thee an everlasting excellency, a joy of many generations, and thou shalt suck the milk of the Gentiles: and thou shalt be nourished by the breast of kings.'[49] Also 'Just as a mother consoles her children, so will I comfort you, and you shall be comforted in Jerusalem.'[50] Do you not see how this new knighthood is frequently sanctioned by the testimony of the ancients, and that 'as we have heard, so we see in the city of the Lord of virtues'.[51] As long as the literal interpretation does not prejudice the spiritual meaning from which we hope in eternity, we borrow from the words of the prophets whatever is applicable to the present time, in case our beliefs should disappear because of what we see, and the poverty of reality diminish the riches of our hopes; the testimony of today would be the loss of tomorrow. Moreover, the temporal glory of the earthly city does not subtract from the heavenly advantages, it adds to them, if we accept without hesitation that this city is a figure of our Mother who is in Heaven.[52]

IV The Life of the Knights of the Temple

But now as a model to imitate or as a cause of shame for our soldiers who are plainly fighting for the devil and not for God, let me give a brief account of the existence and behaviour of the knights of Christ, how they live in peace and war, to show clearly the differences that separate God's knights from secular knights. First and foremost, whether in war or peace, discipline is always observed. There is no condemnation whatsoever of obedience, since, as the bible testifies, the son who has not been disciplined will perish,[53] and 'rebellion is as the sin of witchcraft, and stubbornness is as iniquity and idolatry'.[54] Their comings and goings are decided by their leader,[55] their clothes are those that he has distributed, and no garment or even food is accepted from another source. Further, all excess is avoided in food and clothing; only the strictly necessary is considered. They live together in cheerful, sober fashion without their wives and children. So that they respect the perfection of the gospels, they possess no personal property but inhabit one house in a single way of life in their concern to maintain a common spirit without dissent.[56] You might say that this numerous band has a single heart, a single soul.[57] Thus each one strives to obey the leader rather than follow his own wishes. At no time does idleness cause them to sit around or curiosity to wander around, but when they are not on military action – a rare occurrence – so that they earn their bread,[58] they repair the cuts in their armour and clothing, or make good old materials, or do some tidying up. Otherwise they do whatever the Master wants done or is necessary for the community. Social rank does not count for them; it is the better man, not the nobler, who is respected.[59] Individual precedence is not fixed, so that each carries the burdens of another at one time or another to fulfil the law of Christ.[60] If they are caught speaking in an insolent way, or doing something unnecessary, or laughing excessively, or grumbling under their breath, or whispering, none of this goes unpunished. They hate chess and dice, abhor hunting, and get no pleasure from the common and stupid practice of hawking. They reject and abominate actors, magicians, storytellers, lewd songs and plays as being vanities and pure madness. They cut their hair knowing that according to the apostle it is shameful for a man to have long hair.[61] Never well-groomed, rarely clean, their hair shaggy and neglected, filthy, dusty, their skin burnt by their breastplates and the sun.

When war is announced they arm themselves within with faith and without with iron, not gold, so that they strike fear into the enemy by their arms and do not provoke his greed by their gold. They choose their horses for their strength and speed, not their colour or their trappings. Their thoughts are on the battle and victory, not display and glory. Their aim is to instil fear, not admiration. Then they are not rumbustious or headstrong, as though carried away by a lack of seriousness, but they assemble and form their battle formation thoughtfully, carefully and with foresight, as we read concerning the fathers of Israel.[62] Like true Israelites[63] they go to war as peacemakers,[64] but when the battle actually starts they finally put aside their former gentleness as if they were saying: Do not I hate them, O Lord, that hate thee? And am I not grieved with those that rise up against thee?[65] They charge their adversaries as though they consider enemies to be sheep, not fearing a bit the savagery of the barbarians or the size of their army, even if they themselves are a mere handful in number. Indeed they are aware that their hope of victory comes from the strength of the Lord of hosts,[66] not from any confidence in their own forces.[67] In the words of Maccabaeus they believe it is very easy for Him to shut up many in the hands of a few: and there is no difference in the sight of God of Heaven between liberating with many or few men. For victory in war is not in the multitude of the army, but strength cometh from Heaven.[68] They have experienced this on very many occasions, with the result that often one man has as it were pursued a thousand enemy, and two men have routed ten thousand.[69] In short, in some wonderful, unique way they are seen to be meeker than lambs and fiercer than lions, so that I am almost in doubt as to whether they ought to be called knights or monks. Unless, of course I were to call them by both names, which would be more exact, as they are known to have the gentleness of a monk and the bravery of a knight. What can be said about this fact other than that it was done by the Lord and is a wonder in our eyes?[70] God has chosen such men for Himself, from the ends of the earth He has gathered his servants among the bravest of the Israelites, who, sword in hand, faithfully watch over and guard the sepulchre, the bed of the true Solomon. All of them are skilled in the art of warfare.[71]

V The Temple

The knights live in an egalitarian fashion in a temple in Jerusalem that is not the equal of Solomon's ancient and renowned temple as a building, but is not endowed with less glory. While all the magnificence of Solomon's temple lay in corruptible materials, gold and silver,[72] dressed stone and various woods,[73] all the beauty and pleasing charm of the decoration of this one lies in the religious piety of its inhabitants and their most orderly way of life. Solomon's was a sight to be beheld because of its multiplicity of colours; this one is to be revered for the multiplicity of its virtues and holy deeds. Sanctity befits the house of God[74] as He is pleased by beautiful morals and not by polished marble. He prefers pure minds to golden walls. The facade of this temple is also decorated, but by arms not by jewels; its walls are covered with hanging shields, not with ancient golden crowns.[75]

Instead of candelabra, incense burners and spice jars the house is protected on all sides by bridles, saddles and lances. Clearly, all of these things demonstrate beyond doubt that the zeal of these knights for the same house of God is as fervent as that shown by a former leader of knights, when he was angered to the point of violence and entered the temple, with a weapon in his most holy hand. They weapon was not an iron sword but a rope whip and with it he drove out the merchants, scattered the coins of the money-changers, overturned the stalls of the dove-sellers.[76] He did this because he considered it the utmost disgrace for a house of prayer to be polluted by this sort of merchant. His devoted army has been moved to anger just as their King had been, judging it much more disgraceful and far more unbearable for the holy places to be polluted by infidels[77] than to be infested with merchants. After expelling all the filthy infidels and tyrannical madmen from this and the other holy places, his knights have taken up residence with horses and arms in the holy house and are carrying out honourable and useful tasks day and night. They are zealous and sincere in the diligent services in honour of the temple of God, with continuous devotion making offerings of a truly peaceful nature – brotherly love, devout obedience and voluntary poverty – not the flesh of animals as was practised by the ancients.[78]

These things are done in Jerusalem and the whole world is aroused. The islands hear and people from afar take notice.[79] From East and West they burst forth like a torrent of nations in glorious flood,[80] a river in spate bringing joy to the city of God.[81] What seems to be most gratifying and is certainly a most useful event is that in such a huge host of men who converge there, only a very few are not criminals, sinners, kidnappers, evil-doers, murderers, perjurers and adulterers.[82] Everyone agrees that their departure brings about a sort of twofold benefit and a twofold feeling of joy, since they not only make their own people happy by leaving, but by their arrival also those whom they hurry to help. They thus bring relief to both sets of people, those whom they no longer harass but especially those whom they protect. So Egypt is happy to see them go[83] at the same time as Mount Sion is no less happy to have their protection, and the daughters of Judah rejoice.[84] The former rightly revels in being liberated from their hands,[85] the latter rightly in being liberated by their hands. The former willingly loses its most cruel devastators, the latter joyfully gains its most faithful defenders. Thus the latter experiences a most sweet consolation while the former experiences an equally salubrious desolation. Thus Christ operates, thus he knows how to take revenge on his enemies,[86] so that the more powerfully he triumphs over them the more gloriously he triumphs, and not only over them, but also through them. This is both pleasing and useful in that those whom he had to put up with as opponents for a long time are now beginning to be his champions. He who turned his one time persecutor Saul into his preacher Paul,[87] is now making knights of his enemies. Wherefore I am not surprised if, as the Saviour testifies, that heavenly court rejoices more over one sinner who repents than over several righteous men who do not have need of repentance,[88] as long as the conversion of the sinner and the evil-doer is seen to bring as much definite good as his former life brought harm.

Hail, therefore, holy city, sanctified as His temple the Most High,[89] who will save so great a nation in you and through you. Hail, city of the Great King[90] out of which new and happy wonders have come in virtually all times since the creation for the benefit of the world. Hail, mistress of the nations, leader of the provinces,[91] property of the patriarchs, mother of the prophets and apostles, cradle of the faith, glory of the Christian people, city that God has always allowed to be stormed so that you might give brave men the chance to show their bravery and earn salvation. Hail, promised land, that formerly flowed with milk and honey solely for your inhabitants,[92] now you offer to the whole world the life-sustaining food that is the means of salvation. You are a good land, I say, the best land, that received in your most fertile womb a heavenly seed[93] from the treasure-chest of the Father's heart and brought forth such a great crop of martyrs from that heavenly seed. Moreover, out of all the rest of the nations of the faithful your fertile earth has produced over all the world crop-yields thirty, sixty and a hundredfold.[94] Having happily banqueted on and most satisfyingly partaken of the great quantity of your sweetness, those who have seen you proclaim everywhere the memory of your abundant sweetness,[95] and they talk of the magnificence of your glory[96] to those who have not seen you, even to the ends of the earth.[97] They relate the miracles that are performed in you. 'Glorious things are spoken of thee, O city of God.'[98] But now from your numerous delights let me single out one or two to the praise and glory of your name.

1. Luke 1:78.
2. Ephesians 6:12; Isaiah 10:13.
3. Ephesians 2:2.
4. Luke 1:68–9.
5. Ephesians 6:12.
6. Luke 22:38.
7. 1 Thessalonians 5:8.
8. Philippians 1:21.
9. Philippians 1:23.
10. Philippians 3:18.
11. Romans 8:38–9.
12. Romans 14:8.
13. Revelations 14:13.
14. Psalms 116:15.
15. Ezekiel 18:4.
16. 1 Corinthians 9:10.
17. Galatians 5:26.
18. Romans 13:4.
19. 1 Peter 2:24.
20. Romans 13:4.
21. Philippians 1:21.
22. Psalms 58:10.
23. Psalms 58:11.
24. Psalms 125:3.
25. Luke 3:14, i.e. John the Baptist.
26. Isaiah 26:1.
27. Isaiah 26:2.
28. Psalms 68:30.
29. Galatians 5:12.
30. Psalms 101:8.
31. Leviticus 19:8.
32. Psalms 83:13.
33. Luke 22:38. See above, note 14.

34. 2 Corinthians 10:5.
35. Psalms 115:2.
36. Matthew 23:38.
37. Jeremiah 12:7.
38. Psalms 77:15.
39. Jeremiah 31:12.
40. Isaiah 66:10.
41. Luke 19:44.
42. Isaiah 52:9–10.
43. Amos 5:2.
44. Isaiah 52:2.
45. Baruch 4:36.
46. Isaiah 62:4.
47. Isaiah 49:18.
48. Psalms 20:2.
49. Isaiah 60:15–16.
50. Isaiah 66:13.
51. Psalms 48:8.
52. Galatians 4:26.
53. Ecclesiasticus 22:3.
54. 1 Samuel 15:23.
55. Luke 7:8.
56. Ephesians 4:3.
57. Acts 4:32.
58. 2 Thessalonians 3:8.
59. Romans 2:11.
60. Galatians 6:2.
61. 1 Corinthians 11:14.
62. 2 Maccabees 12:20.
63. John 1:47.
64. Matthew 5:9.
65. Psalms 139:21.
66. Psalms 46:7, 11.
67. Daniel 8:24.

68. Maccabees 3:19.
69. Deuteronomy 32:30.
70. Psalms 118:23.
71. Song of Solomon 3:7–8.
72. 1 Peter 1:18.
73. 1 Kings 6.
74. Psalms 93:5.
75. 1 Maccabees 4:57.
76. Matthew 21:12–13; John 2:14–16.
77. Ezekiel 22:26.
78. 1 Kings 8:23.
79. Isaiah 49:1.
80. Isaiah 66:12.
81. Psalms 46:4.
82. 1 Timothy 1:9–10.
83. Psalms 105:38.
84. Psalms 48:11.
85. Luke 1:74.
86. Nahum 1:2.
87. Acts 9:1–22.
88. Luke 15:7.
89. Psalms 46:4–5.
90. Psalms 48:2.
91. Lamentations 1:1.
92. Exodus 3:8.
93. Luke 8:15.
94. Matthew 13:23.
95. Psalms 145:7.
96. Psalms 145:5.
97. Isaiah 49:6.
98. Psalms 87:3.

Source: Bernard of Clairvaux, 'Liber ad milites Templi de laude novae militiae', in J. Leclercq and H.M. Rochais (eds) (1963) *Sancti Bernardi Opera* (vol. 3). Rome: Editiones Cistercienses, 213–39. Translation from M. Barber and K. Bate (2002) *The Templars*. Manchester: Manchester University Press, 215–227.

THE FOUNDATION OF THE ORDER OF CALATRAVA **Document 2**

This extract outlines the foundation of the order of Calatrava in 1158. It forms part of the chronicle Historia de Rebus Hispanie, *written in the 1240s by Roderigo Jiménez de Rada, archbishop of Toledo from 1209–1247.*

Once these things were accomplished, King Sancho came to Toledo and a rumour spread that the Arabs were coming with a great army to Calatrava. However, the brothers of the Order of the Knights Templar, who held the citadel of Calatrava, fearing that they could not withstand the attack of the Arabs, approached King Sancho, entreating him to take back both the citadel and the town of Calatrava, because they did not have the resources for resisting the Arabs, and not one of the nobles had been found to be willing to face the risk of the defence. However, at that time there was in the royal city a man of religion, Raymond, abbot of Fitero, and with him, a certain monk who was called Diego Velasquez, a noble man once active in military service, originating from the lands of La Bureba and raised with King Sancho from his youth, who, seeing that the king was concerned about the danger at Calatrava, persuaded the abbot to request Calatrava from the king; and, although the abbot had from the beginning shown himself obdurate, he finally assented to the beseeching monk, formerly a knight, and, approaching the king, he requested Calatrava. And, although some considered it foolish, yet, as it pleased the Lord, the king assented and the abbot and the monk together came without delay to archbishop John, who was then in charge of the church in Toledo; and he, hearing of their holy purpose, gave thanks to God and immediately gave help of his own means and caused it to be preached publicly that all those going to the help of Calatrava would obtain pardon of all their sins. And such great excitement arose in the city that there was scarcely anyone who either did not go in person or generously bestow horses or arms or monies in support. And King Sancho, without delay, gave to the abbot and St. Mary of Fitero the town and fortress of Calatrava in perpetuity. And the abbot came, together with the monk Diego Velasquez, under the Lord's guidance, to Calatrava and it came about, with the will of the Most High ordaining, that the army of the Hagarenes (The Muslim army), about which the rumour had spread, did not advance. And then many, whom devotion inspired, with their clothing adapted as military mobility required, received their rule and without delay began to engage in slaughter and battle against the Arabs and, with the Lord aiding, the work prospered in the hands of the monks. Then, having returned to the monastery, the abbot, coming to Calatrava, brought with him cattle and flocks and other movable goods in which Fitero at that time abounded and also a mass of warriors, for whom he provided pay and provisions, excepting the weak and sick, whom he left behind in the care of the monastery; and, as I have heard from those men who had seen it, he brought with him almost twenty thousand sheep. And he was the first abbot in Fitero, but he died and was buried in the town which is called Ciruelos, near Toledo, where God, as it is reported, worked miracles through him. However, Diego Velasquez, whom I too remember having seen myself, lived for a long time afterwards and died in the monastery of San Pedro de Gumiel and was buried there; may he rest in peace.

Source: Roderigo Jiménez de Rada, *Historia de Rebús Hispanie sive Historia Gothica*. Juan Fernández Valverde (ed.) (1987) Corpus Christianorum: Continuatio Mediaeualis LXXII. Turnholt: Brepols, 234–236.

Document 3   PRINCE BOHEMOND III OF ANTIOCH OFFERS PROPERTIES TO THE ORDER OF SANTIAGO IN RETURN FOR THEIR ASSISTANCE (SEPTEMBER 1180)

By the 1180s the Latin East was closely assailed on many fronts and its rulers strove continuously to seek military assistance from overseas. This document reflects Prince Bohemond III of Antioch's attempts to convince the Spanish order of Santiago to send warriors to defend his principality. The suggestion has been made that the castle was no longer in Christian hands at the time of this concession.

In the name of the Father and the Son and the Holy Ghost. Amen. Since I, Bohemund, by divine favour Prince of Antioch, son of Prince Raymond of good memory, have come to know that only that which is done in fear and love of God leads to the salvation of the soul, I have purposed in my heart to distribute to those serving as knights for Christ a necessary share from the lands and possessions belonging to the honour of Antioch so that through this share I, aided by their prayers, may obtain eternal reward from God; therefore, let it be known to the community of the Faithful that, when we were in the palace at Antioch, with both the barons and the rest of our men residing with us, we, by the advice and wish of our most pious lord father Patriarch Aimery, donated and granted to Pedro Fernandez, venerable master of the order of St. James of the Sword, and the holy convent of the same religious order the castle of Vetule[1] with its appurtenances apart from what William Bucellus kept for himself therefrom when he restored the castle to our hands, and with the exception of four villages which the Templars hold, namely, Bessil, Carnehalia, Neni and Nementa[2] and excluding Ifala and two areas of wasteland belonging to the Templars.

   Moreover, we have bestowed on them the castle of the Gerrenes with its appurtenances, with the exception of those villages which we have allowed to be held by the Old Man of the Assideans;[3] likewise, we have bestowed on them Gerras with its appurtenances, Baldenia with its appurtenances, Buckebis[4] with its appurtenances, and Gipsum with its appurtenances, excepting the villagers of Montana Revelata[5] who wished to stay on the plain and to come to us or to our men.

If, indeed, any of our barons wish to make a grant of their alms to them, they will be able, with our permission, to bestow on them a money fief worth 100 bezants; others of 1050 bezants, 500 and under 25.

We have bestowed the whole of this on Pedro, venerable master of the aforementioned order of St. James of the Sword, and on the holy monastery of the same religious order, to be held and possessed, in perpetual right, for the salvation of our soul and for the souls of our kinsmen, on condition that, if they come within one year from the current month of September with so great a force of their brother knights that they are able, with God's support, to conquer for themselves the land granted by us, they may hold it in fief and hereditary succession in perpetual right; and that, if they do not come within the prearranged term, it will be our decision either to keep that land for ourselves or to bestow it on whomever it pleases us.

Furthermore, so that this our grant may have valid substance, we have arranged for confirmation of our personal seal to be furnished by the undersigned witnesses by their stamp.

The witnesses of this document are our lord Aimery, patriarch of the Holy See of Antioch; Rainald of Margat; Guiscard of Insula; Hugh of Logiis; Roger of Sourdeval; Baldwin, the Constable; Oliver, the Chamberlain; Gervase, the Steward; Roger of Corbeil, duke of Antioch; and Guiscard of Nazareth.

This deed is done by the hand of John, our chancellor and archdeacon of the Holy See of Antioch, in the year of the incarnation of the Word 1180, the 17th of our reign, 13th indiction.

1. Mayer has identified the castle of Vetule as Qal'at Beni Israil near Jabala.
2. Mayer has identified these villages as: Bissin, Qarn Hiliye, Ninet and Ninnenté.
3. This is a reference to the leader of the Assassins, often called 'Old Man of the Mountains'.
4. Mayer has identified *Buckebis* as *Burg Abū Qubais*.
5. The *Jebel el Ansariye* (a mountain range inland from the port of Latakia and running parallel to the coast).

Source: J.L. Martin (ed.) (1974) *Origines de la Orden militar de Santiago (1170–1195)*. Barcelona, Consejo Superior de Investigaciones Cientificas, 296 (doc. 112). H.E. Mayer (ed.) (1993) *Varia Antiochena: Studien zum Kreuzfahrerfürstentum Antiochia im 12. und frühen 13. Jahrhundert*, Monumenta Germaniae Historica: Studien und Texte Band VI. Hannover, 114–117.

Document 4   POPE INNOCENT III CONFIRMS THE TREATY BETWEEN THE
SWORDBRETHREN AND THE BISHOP OF RIGA

Innocent, Bishop, servant of the servants of God, to our beloved brother,
Albert, bishop of Riga, greetings and apostolic blessing.

When the dispute between you and the brothers of the Order of the Knights
of Christ regarding the division of the lands which, by the grace of the Holy
Spirit, were recently converted to the worship of the Christian faith, was
brought under our judgement, you, with our mediation, finally reached this
agreement, namely that the brothers themselves may hold one third part of
these same lands, that is Lettigalia and Livonia, from the bishop of Riga,
providing him with no temporal [military] service therefrom except what
they direct in perpetuity for the defence of the Church and of the province
against the pagans; whoever is their Master at any time will, indeed, always
promise obedience to the bishop of Riga, but the brothers or clerics who
will minister to them in spiritual matters will pay to him neither tithes, nor
first-fruits, nor offerings, nor episcopal tax. However, the colonists of the
aforesaid allotment of land will render tithes to their churches from the part
of the produce belonging to them, of which one fourth part will be paid to
that bishop, unless this same bishop, for a necessary and rational reason,
voluntarily has it remitted. Moreover, the brothers themselves and their successors will have the right to present to the bishop of Riga for the aforesaid
churches, when posts are vacant, suitable persons, whom he will not delay
to invest with the care of souls. Furthermore, when you and any of your successors have visitations conducted, they will offer you sustenance in their
house, together with twenty horses, once in each year; in their parishes,
however, they will undertake to make provision for you twice in each year.
For the lands which the said brothers will, with the help of God, acquire
hereafter outside Livonia or Lettigallia, they will not, in fact, answer at all to
the bishop of Riga, nor will he trouble them concerning these lands in any
way; but they will arrange matters, in whatever manner is reasonable, with
those bishops created there or they will comply with what the Apostolic See
should decree in this regard. Also, while observing the rule of the brothers
of the Knights of the Temple, they will bear a different symbol on their
habits to show that they are in no way subject to them. The aforesaid brothers
will also have a free burial place for the use of the brothers and their religious
community as well as those who may choose to be buried among them,
without prejudice to the canonical tax of those churches from which the
corpses of the dead are received. Thus, we, assenting to this same arrangement, ratify it by apostolic authority and reinforce it by the endorsement of
the present document. And so let it not be permitted for any man to infringe
this deed of our ratification or to oppose it by imprudent act. If anyone pre-
sumes, however, to attempt this, let him know that he will incur the wrath
of Almighty God and of the blessed apostles Peter and Paul.

Given at the Lateran, on the thirteenth day before the Kalends of November in the thirteenth year of our pontificate.

Source: Migne, J.P. (ed.) (1855) *Patrologiae cursus completus, Series Latina* (vol. 216). Paris, cols. 326–327. Bunge, F. (ed.) (1967) *Liv, est- und-kurländisches urkundenbuch* (vol. 1). Aalen, pp. 23–34.

HERMANN VON SALZA'S LETTER TO POPE GREGORY IX CONCERNING HIS ACTIONS ON CRUSADE (LATE MARCH 1229)

Document 5

At this time Hermann, master of the Teutonic Order, was on crusade with Frederick II, who had been excommunicated by Pope Gregory IX before his arrival in the east. This letter reflects Hermann's efforts to account for his continued presence in the crusader army even though Gregory had previously ordered all the military orders to offer Frederick no assistance.

Brother Hermann of the Hospital of St. Mary of the House of the Teutons in Jerusalem, your humble servant, with due and devoted respect. It will already have come to your attention that the lord emperor, along with the whole Christian army, came to Jerusalem on the day of the Sabbath (17 March) and there, the following Sunday, wore the crown in honour of the Eternal King. He was then counselled by many to have the divine office celebrated there, since he had liberated that land, on account of which he had been bound by the chains of excommunication, from the hands of the Saracens. We, in truth, as one who values the honour of the Church and the Empire and intends the exaltation of both, opposed the aforementioned advice for we saw it was not expedient either for the Church or for him [the emperor]. Thus, assenting to our counsel in this respect, he did not hear divine service but took the crown directly from the altar without consecration and wore it on the throne, as is customary. Also that day, in the presence of the archbishops of Palermo and Capua and many other magnates and also rich men and poor men, he spoke clearly before all the words reported below and he enjoined us to relate his words to them in Latin and German.

Accordingly, firstly he stated how he had taken the cross at Aachen and how he had often requested and obtained from the Church a time limit and deferment for crossing over the sea [to the Holy Land] and he explained how difficult affairs had often hindered his purpose and journey. Moreover, he blamed the lord pope and the Church in many things before all those present, for he [the pope] had obliged him strictly to cross the sea and subsequently had denounced him, because he had not otherwise been able to avoid blasphemy and infamy in the sight of men, and subsequently had written to the lands overseas in hostility to him (the emperor) because it had been said that he had not crossed over the sea but had gone to other regions to gather an army against the Church, and because, if the lord pope had known of his intention he would have written in his favour, not against him, and he (the emperor) believed that the troubles which had been brought forth for him by certain people in the lands overseas, and which injured the whole Christian people, were displeasing to the lord pope. He also explained in this way that he had proposed a long time before to the whole Christian army that, to settle the discord which had developed between the Church and himself, he was willing to do those things which seemed to serve the honour of God and the Church as well as the Empire and to stand so firm for the creation of concord that it would be clearly obvious on his part that it [discord] would in no way remain. Also, if any troubles should be caused by him or his followers for the Church in any a manner, then he would wish to destroy them so that the enemies of the cross of Christ and other false Christians who rejoice in the disruption of peace and concord would be confounded, and [he explained] that he does not wish either to praise himself or to seek to have exaltation and favour divinely conferred upon him but, as much as God exalts him, to that extent he wishes to humble himself before the Most High and, on that account, before his appointed representative on earth. On his behalf we related these things and also others of a similar nature which would be too long to tell. Moreover, such was the joy on his entry into Jerusalem and at the time when the words which we set out above were being recounted to all the Christians and the inhabitants of the city that it could hardly be explained in speech. Once these events had taken place, the archbishop of Caesarea arrived on the following Monday, sent by the lord patriarch, and he placed the Church of the Holy Sepulchre and all the holy places under interdict, as a result of which the whole army was greatly disturbed and angry at the Church because he did not even show any clear reason why this had been done. Thereupon even the lord emperor, who was troubled [by these events], sent for the archbishop of Caesarea, who, however, did not attend, and for all the prelates, and he complained publicly in the presence of these men that the holy places which for so long had been under the power of the Saracens and were now liberated by divine aid had been placed under interdict by the patriarch and thus given back to the captivity of their former misery by the banning of the divine office. Also, he asserted that, if he himself or any of his followers had offended the patriarch in any way, he was willing to commit himself fully to their judgement and will. Thus, having arranged conscientiously for the rebuilding of the city, he set off back towards Jaffa on that day. We later learnt, however, that the lord patriarch placed Jerusalem and the holy places under interdict because the Saracens would have custody over the Temple of the Lord and the Temple of Solomon and because their rite is proclaimed and practised by them there. It should be brought to your attention that the Saracens do not occupy the

Temple itself except that a few of their priests, weaponless old men, are in the building itself to offer prayers and to purify it. The emperor's men, however, guard and fortify the exterior gates so that neither entrance nor exit is accessible to the Saracens themselves or others except insofar as it is pleasing to the emperor's men. We saw and heard these things and, in truth, it was thus stated in our presence. Moreover, the Christians also receive the offerings which are given in the Temple of the Lord to the rock where Jesus Christ was offered up.[1] Also, it is said of old that, before the loss of the Holy Land, the Saracens observed their rites in almost all the cities of the Christians and cried these out in their proclamations [calls to prayer], just as Christians in Damascus and in other Saracen lands preserve their rites. Truly, we write of these things to you not because it may please the lord emperor because in fact he would not willingly have done differently if he had been able, but, as God recognised, he could not in any other way establish peace and truces. All the above, therefore, we have written to you so that, if by chance it should be written to you otherwise by another, you might know the truth – it is as we have written – and might not trust every person. In addition, since we know that you prize peace and concord between Church and emperor and you labour conscientiously to achieve this, we could attentively advise you in this regard if it should be necessary. Finally, Brother S., the bearer of the present document, will make known all reports to you more fully.

1. This is a reference to Jesus' presentation in the Temple shortly after his birth (see Luke 2: 22–24).

Source: J.L.A. Huillard-Bréholles (ed.) (1852) *Historia Diplomatica Friderici Secundi* (vol. 3). Paris, 99–102.

POPE GREGORY IX ENCOURAGES THE FAITHFUL TO SUPPORT THE   **Document 6**
TEUTONIC KNIGHTS IN THEIR CONSTRUCTION OF MONTFORT
(10 JULY 1230)

In the years directly before this letter the Teutonic Knights had been acquiring substantial landholdings to the north of Acre. The largest of their purchases, funded by the duke of Austria, was made in 1220 and consisted of an estate centred on the small castle of Castrum Regis. The Teutonic Knights began work on a second and larger castle (Montfort) in 1226 and received support from crusading forces during the following year. Constructing castles, however, was extremely costly and this document reflects the papacy's desire to assist the order in this venture. It also helps to explain the significance of such fortresses and shows how the Church could use indulgences to help gather support.

Gregory, bishop, servant of the servants of God to all the faithful of Christ whom these letters reach, greeting and apostolic blessing. Our beloved sons, the brothers of the Hospital of St. Mary of the Teutons in Jerusalem, new Maccabees at a time of grace, renouncing secular desires and surrendering their possessions, have followed the Lord, taking up his cross. They are the very ones who are striving to free the Eastern Church from the filth of the pagans and to expel the enemies of the Christian name; they do not fear to lay down their souls for their brothers and they seek to defend from the attacks of the pagans those pilgrims setting out to the holy places, both going and returning. Indeed, just as our beloved son Hermann, master of the Hospital itself, being in our presence, proposed to laudably pursue so holy and devoted an undertaking in the land which the noble man the duke of Austria bought for the aforesaid brothers as a mark of devotion, they began to build the castle of Montfort, situated on the pagan frontier near the territory of Acre, from which immense benefit is known to result for the Christians in those lands since, like a kind of bridle restraining the Saracens from their habitual assaults, it gives to the faithful assured freedom on every side; however, on account of the continuous multitude of expenses which hang over them, through providing support for the Holy Land and particularly for the relief of the poor and for the needs of the sick, their own resources are not sufficient for them to finish and maintain the aforesaid castle but, so that it may be completely strong and administered with a powerful hand, the aid of the faithful is important for them, especially since it is far from the sea, for which reason it cannot be provided with necessary assistance by sea like the other cities and fortresses of the kingdom of Jerusalem; we advise and encourage you all in the Lord, commanding that, for the remission of your sins, you give pleasing support of devotion for this undertaking to these same brothers or their envoys when they approach you, so that through your help the aforesaid castle can be finished and maintained and, by these and other good deeds which you will have done at the Lord's inspiring, you may be able to attain the joys of eternal happiness. Moreover, we, trusting in the mercy of almighty God and, by His authority, of the blessed apostles Peter and Paul, remit annually a seventh part of imposed penance to all who in this matter help the aforementioned brothers and provide services for them from the goods conferred on them by God; the present communication to be valid for at least a ten-year period hereafter. Given at the Lateran on the sixth day before the ides of July in the fourth year of our pontificate.

Source: E. Strelke (ed.) (1975) *Tabulae Ordinis Theutonici*. Toronto: University of Toronto Press, 56–57.

MATTHEW PARIS DESCRIBES THE PUBLIC REACTION TO AN APPEAL FOR   **Document 7**
HELP SENT BY THE TEMPLARS IN JULY 1244

*By the mid late thirteenth century many commentators across Christendom
began to voice concerns that the military orders were not maximising their
resources in the struggle for the Holy Land. This passage, written by Matthew
Paris, a monk at the Benedictine at St Albans Abbey, underlines the scepticism
he felt upon receiving an appeal for help sent by the Templars in the Latin
East.*

When, however, these matters reached the attention of many Christians,
they scarcely put any faith in their [the Templars'] writings or words, first on
account of the age-old infamy both of the Templars and of the Hospitallers,
inasmuch as it is said that they regularly provoke discord between Christians
and Saracens in order that, with the conflict prolonged, they can collect
the money of pilgrims arriving from all parts; secondly, on account of their
mutual discord; and thirdly, on account of the fact that they plotted the
seizure of the emperor. Moreover, the Templars have nine thousand manors
in Christendom and the Hospitallers in fact have nineteen thousand,
along with benefits and various revenues arising from confraternities and
preaching fees and accruing from their privileges. Therefore, any one manor
can without difficulty procure, in support of the Holy Land, one knight,
equipped well and without any deficiency, and also with all things fully
pertaining to a knight; hence the Christians, reflecting on these matters,
assert that they [the Templars] always cloak their treachery and that their
wolfish perfidy is concealed under sheep's clothing. For, if there had been
no animosity with treachery, such a great number of resolute Western
knights would have forcefully broken through the defences of all the Eastern
peoples.

Source: Matthew Paris (1880) *Chronica Majora* (vol. 4), Rolls Series, L.H.R. Luard
(ed.), London, 291.

EBERHARD OF SAYN, VISITOR OF THE TEUTONIC KNIGHTS, OUTLINES THE   **Document 8**
ARRANGEMENTS FOR THE ORGANISATION OF THE ORDER IN PRUSSIA AND
ITS RESPONSIBILITIES TO MASTER AND CHAPTER IN THE HOLY LAND

Brother Eberhard of Sayn, acting for the master of the Hospital of St. Mary
of the Teutons in Jerusalem, to all the brothers of that same Order in Prussia
whom the present document reaches, greetings and brotherly love in the
Lord. We do not wish you to be unaware, brothers, that, although we were

empowered by mandate of the general master and the overseas chapter to conduct a visitation in your land, we, wishing to await the presence of Brother Otto, our envoy, who, for the business of your lands, was sent to the lands across the sea, have not bound you by any special mandate. We have learned from his report that, with the consent of our oft-mentioned master and the chapter, you will comply with those points which are itemised below and which he has also left to our discretion to be defined.

Consequently, we authorise you to have a conventual seal with which you are able to ratify the privileges of the vassals of the house in Prussia and the annual rents due from other men. The inscription of this seal will be the following: 'The seal of the brothers of the House of the Teutons in Prussia'. This same seal is to retain its validity for as long as it may please the general master and the overseas chapter. For this seal, such safekeeping is to be undertaken as is stated in the Statutes.

Also, we instruct you to hold every year, on the Feast of the Exaltation of the Holy Cross, a General Chapter in Elbing, deciding matters there. Also, we wish that same house to maintain the strength of a convent and to be the head of the other houses in Prussia, in such a way, however, that, when important matters to be discussed arise, at least eight individual brothers from Balga and the same number from Christburg are to be summoned to attend.

Item: as our master, Brother Henry of Hohenlohe, of happy memory had prohibited any goods from being granted in fief to any persons in the land of Kulm, we wish this to be complied with within Wysla, Drivancia and Ozza, unless it is done by special licence of the general master and the overseas chapter.

Item: we instruct that commanders of towns and provinces be appointed and dismissed with the consultation of the convent.

Item: we strictly prohibit brother officials from giving money to their superiors in secret, but require them to do so with a written record and the attestation of the brothers who are among them.

Item: no provincial preceptor may send out visitors without the convent's consent.

Item: brothers returning to their house may not complain about their apparel and scrip to their superiors.

Item: we wish commanders who are dismissed to report upon the goods of the house to their successors with the written record and the attestation of the brothers.

Item: brothers who, in chapter, speak reasonably in accordance with the rule and the statutes may not be unfittingly reproved by their superiors.

Item: all brother officials are to render accounts as set out in the rule.

Item: any brother making an appeal reasonably in accordance with the rule and the statutes is to be heard.

Item: no commander having under him two or more brothers is to appoint a cellarer unless he is a brother.

Item: no one may be received [immediately] as a full member of the Order unless he forgoes his novitiate and promises obedience to the general master and the overseas chapter and to others deputising on their behalf elsewhere.

Item: every Sunday, in chapter, one article of the rule and one article of the statutes and of the laws are to be recited in the presence of the brothers.

Item: brothers may not be punished except as is stated in the laws of the Order.

Item: no preceptor may have the power to establish new statutes except with the consent of the convent and the ratification of the general master and the overseas chapter.

Item: the preceptor may not leave the land of Prussia for distant regions except with the consent of the convent.

Item: every year, letters are to be sent to the lands across the sea and, in the second or third year, a high-ranking brother of the community of the convent is to be sent in person.

Item: all brother clerics and other brothers are to be bound under the statutes of the Holy Land as the authorities require.

Item: no one brother may be dismissed in any court when he can be corrected.

Item: may we advise in all possible ways that arms not be entrusted to brother officials because they are employed to greater advantage when remaining in the houses [i.e. the order's outposts] unless, with the consent of the preceptor and marshal and prudent brothers, they are granted to the better archers.

Item: because you are beset by enemies on both sides and since not every person is to be trusted, it seems to us to be appropriate and very useful that the brothers bear swords in towns; but we leave this clause to the discretion of the preceptor and marshal and brothers.

By mandate of the general master and the General Overseas Chapter, we have set out these points in writing for reasons of expediency and we wish them to be complied with.

Source: M. Biskup and I. Janosz-Biskupowa (eds) (2002) *Visitationen im Deutschen Orden im Mittelalter: Teil I: 1236–1449*, Quellen und Studien zur Geschichte des Deutschen Ordens L. Marburg: N.G. Elwert, 3–5 (doc. 2).

Document 9   KING ALFONSO III OF ARAGON PERMITS THE TEMPLARS TO EXPORT SIX
HORSES TO THE LATIN EAST (25 APRIL 1286)

*By 1286 it had been many years since Aragon had lost its landward frontier
with Islam. Nevertheless, the needs of the Latin East remained acute. In this
environment, greater demands were placed on the Aragonese Templars to send
aid to the east. This document, concerning the export of a handful of horses,
reflects just one of the many shipments of supplies sent from across Europe to
support the east.*

To all officials and others etc. May you know that we, by special favour, have
granted to our venerable and beloved brother Berenguer of Cardona of
the order of the knights Templar that he can export from our land and bring
into the lands overseas six horses for the defence of the Holy Land. Therefore
we command you, with regard to the aforesaid horses [which are] to be taken
away from our land and to be brought into the said regions, to create no
hindrance or opposition, by reason of any prohibition made to the contrary,
to him or, in his stead, to the bearer of the present communication; indeed,
we wish the present communication to be upheld within the borders of our
kingdom. Given, at Huesca, seven days before the kalends of May.

Source: A. Forey (ed.) (1973) *The Templars in the Corona de Aragón.* London: Oxford
University Press, 402 (doc. 30).

Document 10   KING JAMES II OF ARAGON DEMANDS THAT THE TEMPLARS HELP TO
DEFEND HIS KINGDOM AGAINST CASTILE (17 AUGUST 1300)

*The military orders were generally resistant to the idea of fighting in wars
against fellow Christians; however, there were times when rulers demanded
military support. In this document King James II outlines his reasons for
requiring Templar support against a Castilian attack while indicating that
he would take action against the order if it failed to respond to this request.*

James [of Aragon] etc. To the religious man acting for the Master of the Order
of the Knights Templar in Aragon. Greetings etc. Since it has come to our
notice that Ferdinand, son of the former Lord Sancho of Castile, advancing
with his men, an armed force of cavalry and infantry, towards these lands,
proposes by so rash an undertaking to invade our kingdom of Aragon, with
the result that he has already almost reached the borders of the kingdom
of Castile, we, intending to resist him manfully and powerfully, have com-
manded nobles, retainers, knights and others of the said kingdom to be
prepared. In a case of this kind, you are bound to help us in the defence of

our kingdom, thus we require you and call upon you and firmly and expressly command that, immediately on receipt of the present communication, you, with the knights and men, which the said Order has in the kingdom of Aragon, make yourself ready with horses, weapons and your other equipment so that, as soon as you are required by us or it becomes known to you otherwise, by summons or through other means, that our aforesaid enemy has advanced against these lands, you come in person, without any delay, to us in person wherever we are and awaiting no other order from us. You should know that, if you do otherwise, we shall proceed, in accordance with justice, against you and the goods of the said Order just as against those who so heartlessly refuse to fight for their country. Given, at Zaragoza, sixteen days before the kalends of September A.D. 1300.

Source: A. Forey (ed.) (1973) *The Templars in the Corona de Aragón*. London: Oxford University Press, 412 (doc. 41).

Sources for the military orders

Statutes

There are many primary sources in translation for the military orders. Among the most important are editions of the statutes which defined the orders' governance and daily life. Currently, these are available for the Templars, Hospitallers, Teutonic Knights and the order of Santiago.

Barber, M. and Bate, K. (tr.) 'The Latin Rule of 1129', in *The Templars*. Manchester: Manchester University Press, 31–54.

Gallego Blanco, E. (tr.) (1971) *The Rule of the Spanish Military Order of St. James, 1170–1493*. Leiden: Brill.

King, E.J. (tr.) (1934) *The Rule, Statutes and Customs of the Hospitallers, 1099–1310*. London: Methuen.

Sterns, I. (1969) The Statutes of the Teutonic Knights: A Study of Religious Chivalry. Unpublished doctoral thesis, University of Pennsylvania. This can be ordered from the University of Pennsylvania, although parts have been published on www.the-orb.net

Upton-Ward, J. (tr.) (1992) *The Rule of the Templars*. Woodbridge: Boydell and Brewer. Parts have been published on www.the-orb.net

Upton-Ward, J. (tr.) (2003) *The Catalan Rule of the Templars*, Studies in the History of Medieval Religion XIX. Woodbridge: Boydell and Brewer.

Political/military roles on the frontier

For the political/military roles played by the military orders in each theatre of war, there are many accounts which include a few references to the orders' actions, but there are very few in which the history of an order is the main focus. Most medieval writers set out to write a history of a region or country and therefore they referred to the military orders only where they affected the course of events. William of Tyre, the great chronicler of the Latin East, is typical in this sense because while there are passages in his work devoted to the Templars and Hospitallers, these are only a handful of pages within a far larger work.

William of Tyre (1943) *A History of Deeds Done beyond the Sea* (2 vols), E.A. Babcock and A.C. Krey (tr.). New York: Columbia University Press.

In this way, conducting research into these aspects of the orders requires a researcher to locate as many sources as possible for their given region and then to hunt through the indices looking for references to the individual orders. When these references are compiled and contextualised then gradually it becomes possible to frame some idea of their policies. It would take far too long to list all the works which contain some references to the orders, but there are a number of collections of primary materials that can provide a good starting point. These include: Ashgate's *Crusade Texts in Translation* series, Oxford University Press's *Oxford Medieval Texts*, Columbia University Press's *Records of Western Civilisation* and some *Penguin Classics*. A full list of these works can be found on their respective web pages. It is also worth noting that because the affairs of the Holy Land were so important to contemporaries across Christendom, references to the events of that land can be found in chronicles and sources from very different regions; for example, many English chroniclers showed an acute interest in the Latin East.

An exception to this trend, however, is the Baltic. In this region there are some accounts which devote a large part of their attention to either the Swordbrethren or the Teutonic Knights. These are listed below:

Fischer, M. (tr.) (2010) *The Chronicle of Prussia by Nicolaus von Jeroschin: A History of the Teutonic Knights in Prussia, 1190–1331*, Crusade Texts in Translation XX. Ashgate: Aldershot.

Henry Lettus (2003) *The Chronicle of Henry of Livonia*, J.A. Brundage (tr.). New York: Columbia University Press.

Smith, J. and Urban W. (tr.) (2001) *The Livonian Rhymed Chronicle* (2nd edn). Chicago, IL: Lithuanian Research and Studies Center.

The first and last of the above chronicles were written by members of the orders, but here again they are in a minority. Few other narrative sources originated from within an order. The author of the *Deeds of the Cypriots* was closely affiliated to the Templar order. Some correspondence generated by brethren in the Latin East has also survived and been translated.

Barber, M. and Bate, K. (tr.) (2010) *Letters from the East, Crusaders, Pilgrims and Settlers in the 12th–13th Centuries*, Crusade Texts in Translation XVIII. Aldershot: Ashgate.

Crawford, P. (tr.) (2003) *The 'Templar of Tyre': Part III of the 'Deeds of the Cypriots'*, Crusade Texts in Translation VI. Aldershot: Ashgate.

From the Islamic perspective, many writers were interested in the military orders and their histories contain some illuminating passages concerning Muslim attitudes towards them. A small sample of these is shown here:

Ibn al-Athīr (2006–2008) *The Chronicle of Ibn al-Athīr for the Crusading Period from al-Kāmil fī'l-ta'rīkh* (3 vols), D. S. Richards (tr.). Aldershot, Ashgate.

Usama ibn Munqidh (2008) *The Book of Contemplation and the Crusades*, P. Cobb (tr.). London: Penguin.

Landowning and legal documents

Of all the groups of sources available for the military orders in translation, legal documents are probably the least well represented. There are a few collections of source material which include some translated landowning documents and legal transactions. The most important of these is the compilation of materials produced by Barber and Bate which contains 300 pages of translated materials, including sections from chronicles, songs, the order's statutes and many legal documents.

Barber, M. and Bate, K. (eds and tr.) (2002) *The Templars*. Manchester: Manchester University Press.

Constable, O. (ed.) (1997) *Medieval Iberia: Readings from Christian, Muslim and Jewish Sources*. Philadelphia, PA: University of Pennsylvania Press.

Evergates, T. (ed. and tr.) (1993) *Feudal Society in Medieval France: Documents from the County of Champagne*. Philadelphia, PA: University of Pennsylvania Press.

Gervers, M. (ed.) (1982) *The Cartulary of the Knights of St. John of Jerusalem in England. Secunda Camera: Essex*. Oxford: Oxford University Press. The documents in this collection are in Latin but there is a summary of each in English.

Gervers, M. (ed.) (1996) *The Cartulary of the Knights of St John of Jerusalem in England, part 2. Prima Camera: Essex*. Oxford: Oxford University Press. The documents in this collection are in Latin but there is a summary of each in English.

General sources and the Trial of the Templars

There are also a number of collections of translated primary sources on crusading, often designed for teaching, which include materials for the military orders.

Allen, S.J. and Amt, E. (eds) (2003) *The Crusades: A Reader*. Peterborough, Ont: Broadview Press.

Housley, N. (ed. and tr.) (1996) *Documents on the Later Crusades, 1274–1580*. Basingstoke: Macmillan Press.

Riley-Smith, L. and Riley-Smith, J. (eds and tr.) (1981) *The Crusades: Idea and Reality, 1095–1274*. London: Edward Arnold.

In addition to the materials available in Barber and Bates' book there are some further sources in translation for the Trial of the Templars including:

Gilmour-Bryson, A. (tr.) (1998) *The Trial of the Templars in Cyprus: A Complete English Edition*, The Medieval Mediterranean XVII. Leiden: Brill.

Nicholson, H. (tr.) (2011) *The Proceedings against the Templars in the British Isles* (2 vols). Aldershot: Ashgate.

Attitudes towards the military orders

Throughout the twelfth and thirteenth centuries many contemporary writers voiced their opinions of the military orders. These included philosophers, travellers, key churchmen and academics. Many of their works are in translation, but there are too many to list here. A detailed survey of attitudes towards the military orders has been conducted by H. Nicholson – (1995) *Templars, Hospitallers and Teutonic Knights: Images of the Military Orders, 1128–1291*. Leicester University Press – and a good starting point would be to read her work; identify key thinkers; then try to locate a translation of their works. There are also many chansons and medieval romances which include references to the orders and a survey of these has been carried out by H. Nicholson – (2004) *Love, War and the Grail: Templars, Hospitallers and Teutonic Knights in Medieval Epic and Romance*. Leiden: Brill. In her bibliography, Nicholson provides a list of primary sources including those in translation.

Archaeology

In addition to the documentary sources for the military orders there are, of course, the many castles, towers and buildings they built across Europe and the Middle East. These places are well worth a visit, but your ability to understand and interpret them will be dramatically improved by reading the relevant works produced by archaeologists. There are a particularly strong range of materials in English for the Latin East and these include:

Boas, A. (2006) *Archaeology of the Military Orders*. London: Routledge.

Kennedy, H. (2001) *Crusader Castles*. Cambridge: Cambridge University Press.

Pringle, D. (1997) *Secular Buildings in the Crusader Kingdom of Jerusalem: An Archaeological Gazetteer*. Cambridge: Cambridge University Press.

Pringle, D. (1993–2009) *The Churches of the Crusader Kingdom of Jerusalem* (4 vols). Cambridge: Cambridge University Press.

References

Andrews, D. (ed.) (1993) *Cressing Temple: A Templar and Hospitaller Manor in Essex*. Chelmsford: Essex County Planning Department.

Barber, M. (1984) 'The Social Context of the Templars', *Transactions of the Royal Historical Society*, 34, 27–46.

Barber, M. (1994) *The New Knighthood: A History of the Order of the Temple*. Cambridge: Cambridge University Press.

Barber, M. (2006) *The Trial of the Templars* (2nd edn). Cambridge: Cambridge University Press.

Barber, M. and Bate, K. (eds and tr.) (2002) *The Templars*. Manchester: Manchester University Press.

Barber, M. and Bate, K. (tr.) (2010) *Letters from the East, Crusaders, Pilgrims and Settlers in the 12th–13th Centuries*, Crusade Texts in Translation XVIII. Aldershot: Ashgate.

Boulton, D. (1987) *The Knights of the Crown: The Monarchical Orders of Knighthood in Later Medieval Europe, 1325–1520*. Woodbridge: Boydell and Brewer.

Bronstein, J. (2005) *The Hospitallers and the Holy Land: Financing the Latin East, 1187–1274*. Woodbridge: Boydell and Brewer.

Bryson, D. (2010) 'Three "Traitors" of the Temple: Was their Truth the Whole Truth?', in J. Burgtorf, P. Crawford and H. Nicholson (eds), *The Debate on the Trial of the Templars (1307–1314)*. Aldershot: Ashgate, 97–104.

Burgtorf, J. (2001) 'Leadership Structures in the Orders of the Hospital and the Temple (Twelfth to Early Fourteenth Century): Select Aspects', in Z. Hunyadi and J. Laszlovszky (eds), *The Crusades and the Military Orders: Expanding the Frontiers of Medieval Latin Christianity*. Budapest: Central European University Press, 379–394.

Burgtorf, J. (2008) *The Central Convent of Hospitallers and Templars: History, Organization and Personnel (1099–1310)*. Leiden: Brill.

Davis, R.H.C. (1958) *A History of Medieval Europe: From Constantine to Saint Louis*. London: Longmans.

De la Torre, I. (2008) 'The London and Paris Temples: A Comparative Analysis of their Financial Services for the Kings during the Thirteenth Century', in J. Upton Ward (ed.), *The Military Orders, Volume 4: On Land and by Sea*. Aldershot: Ashgate, 121–128.

Delaville Le Roulx, J. (1904) *Les Hospitaliers en Terre Sainte et à Chypre, 1100–1310*. Paris.

Edgington, S. (2004) 'Administrative Regulations for the Hospital of St John in Jerusalem Dating from the 1180s', *Crusades*, 4, 21–37.

Estow, C. (1982) 'The Economic Development of the Order of Calatrava, 1158–1366', *Speculum*, 57, 267–291.

Evergates, T. (2007) *The Aristocracy in the County of Champagne, 1100–1300*. Philadelphia, PA: University of Pennsylvania Press.

Favreau-Lilie, M-L. (2000) 'Mission to the Heathen in Prussia and Livonia: The Attitudes of the Religious Military Orders toward Christianization', in G. Armstrong and I. Wood (eds), *Christianizing Peoples and Converting Individuals*, International Medieval Research VII. Turnhout: Brepols, 147–154.

Fischer, M. (tr.) (2010) *The Chronicle of Prussia by Nicolaus von Jeroschin: A History of the Teutonic Knights in Prussia, 1190–1331*, Crusade Texts in Translation XX. Ashgate: Aldershot.

Forey, A.J. (1973) *The Templars in the Corona de Aragón*. London: Oxford University Press.

Forey, A.J. (1984) 'The Militarisation of the Hospital of St John', *Studia Monastica*, 26, 75–89.

Forey, A.J. (1986) 'Recruitment to the Military Orders (Twelfth to Mid-Fourteenth Centuries)', *Viator*, 17, 139–171.

Forey, A.J. (1992) *The Military Orders: From the Twelfth to the Early Fourteenth Centuries*. Toronto: Toronto University Press.

Forey, A.J. (2002) 'Provision for the Aged in Templar Commanderies', in A. Luttrell and L. Pressouyre (eds), *La Commanderie, institution des ordres militaires dans l'Occident médiéval*. Paris: Comité Des Travaux Historiques Et Scientifiques, 175–185.

Forey, A.J. (2006) 'Women and the Military Orders in the Twelfth and Thirteenth Centuries', in H. Nicholson and A. Luttrell (eds), *Hospitaller Women in the Middle Ages*. Aldershot: Ashgate, 43–70.

Forey, A.J. (2009) 'Notes on Templar Personnel and Government at the Turn of the Thirteenth and Fourteenth Centuries', *Journal of Medieval History*, 35, 150–170.

García-Guijarro Ramos, L. (2006) 'The Aragonese Hospitaller Monastery of Sigena: Its Early Stages, 1188–c.1210', in H. Nicholson and A. Luttrell (eds), *Hospitaller Women in the Middle Ages*. Aldershot: Ashgate, 113–152.

Gervers, M. (1994) '*Pro defensione Terre Sancte*: The Development and Exploitation of the Hospitallers' Landed Estate in Essex', in M. Barber (ed.), *The Military Orders: Fighting for the Faith and Caring for the Sick.* Ashgate: Aldershot, 3–20.

Gervers, M. (ed.) (1982) *The Cartulary of the Knights of St. John of Jerusalem in England. Secunda Camera: Essex.* Oxford: Oxford University Press.

Hiestand, R. (1980) 'Die Anfänge der Johanniter', in J. Fleckenstein and M. Hellman, *Die Geistlichen Ritterordern Eurpoas.* Sigmaringen, 31–80.

Irwin, R. (1994) 'How Many Miles to Babylon? The *Devise des Chemins de Babiloine* Redated', in M. Barber (ed.), *The Military Orders: Fighting for the Faith and Caring for the Sick.* Ashgate: Aldershot, 57–63.

King, E. (1931) *The Hospitallers in the Holy Land.* Methuen: London.

Lay, S. (2009) *The Reconquest Kings of Portugal: Political Cultural Reorientation on the Medieval Frontier.* Basingstoke: Palgrave Macmillan.

Lomax, D. (1958) 'The Order of Santiago and the Kings of León', in *Hispania: Revista epsañola de Historia*, 18, 3–37.

Mitchell, P. (2004) *Medicine in the Crusades: Warfare, Wounds and the Medieval Surgeon.* Cambridge: Cambridge University Press.

Mitchell, P., Huntley, J. and Stern, E. (2008) 'Bioarchaeological Analysis of the Latrine Soil from the Thirteenth-Century Hospital of St John at Acre, Israel', in V. Mallia-Milanes (ed.), *The Military Orders, Volume 3: History and Heritage.* Aldershot: Ashgate, 213–224.

Militzer, K. (1998) 'The Role of Hospitals in the Teutonic Order', in H. Nicholson (ed.), *The Military Orders, Volume 2: Welfare and Warfare.* Aldershot: Ashgate, 51–59.

Nicholson, H. (1995) *Templars, Hospitallers and Teutonic Knights: Images of the Military Orders, 1128–1291.* Leicester: Leicester University Press.

Nicholson, H. (2001) *The Knights Hospitaller.* Woodbridge: Boydell and Brewer.

Nicholson, H. (2004) *The Knights Templar.* Stroud: Sutton Publishing Ltd.

Nicholson, H. (2006) 'Margaret de Lacy and the Hospital of Saint John at Aconbury, Herefordshire', in H. Nicholson and A. Luttrell (eds), *Hospitaller Women in the Middle Ages.* Aldershot: Ashgate.

Nicholson, H. (2010) 'The Changing Face of the Templars: Current Trends in Historiography', *History Compass*, 8/7, 653–667.

O'Callaghan, J.F. (1969) '*Hermanndades* between the Military Orders of Calatrava and Santiago during the Castilian Reconquest, 1158–1252', *Speculum*, 44, 609–618.

O'Callaghan, J.F. (1986) 'The Order of Calatrava: Years of Crisis and Survival, 1158–1212', in V. Goss and C. Verzár (eds), *The Meeting of Two Worlds: Cultural Exchange between East and West during the Period of the Crusades.* Kalamazoo, MI: Medieval Institute Publications, 419–430.

Prutz, H. (1908) *Die geistlichen Ritterordern: Ihre Stellung zur kirchlichen, politischen, gesellschaftlichen und wirtschaftlichen Entwicklung des Mittlelalters.* Berlin.

Ramon Muntaner (2006) *The Catalan Expedition to the East: From the Chronicle of Ramon Muntaner*. R.D. Hughes (tr.). Woodbridge: Tamesis.

Riley-Smith, J. (1973) *The Feudal Nobility and the Kingdom of Jerusalem*. London: Macmillan.

Riley-Smith, J. (1997) *The First Crusades, 1095–1131*. Cambridge: Cambridge University Press.

Riley-Smith, J. (2004) 'Were the Templars Guilty?', in S. Ridyard (ed.), *The Medieval Crusade*. Woodbridge: Boydell and Brewer, 107–124.

Riley-Smith, J. (2007) 'The Military Orders and the East, 1149–1291', in N. Housley (ed.), *Knighthoods of Christ, Essays on the History of the Crusades and the Knights Templar presented to Malcolm Barber*. Aldershot: Ashgate, 137–149.

Riley-Smith, J. (2010) *Templars and Hospitallers as Professed Religious in the Holy Land*. Paris: University of Notre Dame Press.

Roach, A. (2005) *The Devil's World: Heresy and Society, 1100–1300*. Pearson: Harlow.

Salvadó, S. (2010) 'Icons, Crosses and Liturgical Objects of Templar Chapels in the Crown of Aragon', in J. Burgtorf, P. Crawford and H. Nicholson (eds), *The Debate on the Trial of the Templars (1307–1314)*. Aldershot: Ashgate, 183–198.

Schenk, J. (2008) 'Aspects of Non-Noble Family Involvement in the Order of the Temple', in J. Upton Ward (ed.), *The Military Orders, Volume 4: On Land and by Sea*. Aldershot: Ashgate, 155–161.

Schenk, J. (2008) 'Forms of Lay Association with the Order of the Temple', *Journal of Medieval History*, 34, 79–103.

Schotte, B. (2010) 'Fighting the King of France: Templars and Hospitallers in the Flemish Rebellion of 1302', in J. Burgtorf, P. Crawford and H. Nicholson (eds), *The Debate on the Trial of the Templars (1307–1314)*. Aldershot: Ashgate, 45–56.

Selwood, D. (1999) *Knights of the Cloister: Templars and Hospitallers in Central-Southern Occitania, 1100–1300*. Woodbridge: Boydell and Brewer.

Slack, C. (2001) *Crusade Charters, 1138–1270*. Tempe, AZ: Arizona Center for Medieval and Renaissance Studies.

Smith, J. and Urban W. (tr.) (2001) *The Livonian Rhymed Chronicle* (2nd edn). Chicago, IL: Lithuanian Research and Studies Center.

Stathakopoulos, D. (2006) 'Discovering a Military Order of the Crusades: The Hospital of St Sampson of Constantinople', *Viator*, 37, 255–273.

Stern, E. (2008) 'The Hospitaller Order in Acre and Manueth: The Ceramic Evidence', in V. Mallia-Milanes (ed.), *The Military Orders, Volume 3: History and Heritage*. Aldershot: Ashgate, 203–211.

Sterns, I. (1969) The Statutes of the Teutonic Knights: A Study of Religious Chivalry. Unpublished doctoral thesis, University of Pennsylvania.

Tibble, S. (1989) *Monarchy and Lordships in the Latin Kingdom of Jerusalem, 1099–1291*. Oxford: Clarendon.

Upton-Ward, J. (tr.) (1992) *The Rule of the Templars*. Woodbridge: Boydell and Brewer.

Walter Map (1983) *De nugis curialium*, M. James, C. Brooke and R. Mynors (eds and tr.). Oxford: Oxford University Press.

Wilkinson, J., Hill, J. and Ryan, W. (1988) *Jerusalem Pilgrimage: 1099–1185*. London: Hakluyt Society.

William of Tyre (1943) *A History of Deeds Done beyond the Sea* (2 vols), E.A. Babcock and A.C. Krey (tr.). New York: Columbia University Press.

Index